FILM IN ENGLISH TEACHING

Film in English Teaching

Edited by ROY KNIGHT

HUTCHINSON EDUCATIONAL
IN ASSOCIATION WITH THE EDUCATIONAL ADVISORY SERVICE
OF THE BRITISH FILM INSTITUTE

HUTCHINSON EDUCATIONAL LTD
3 Fitzroy Square, London W1

London Melbourne Sydney Auckland
Wellington Johannesburg Cape Town
and agencies throughout the world

First published November 1972

*This book has been set in Times type, printed in Great Britain
on smooth wove paper by Anchor Press, and
bound by Wm. Brendon, both of Tiptree, Essex*

ISBN 0 09 113510 9 (cased)
      0 09 113511 7 (paper)

Contents

How to use this book

Film in English Teaching, as the title suggests, is designed to introduce teachers of English to the regular use of film in their courses. The chapters (other than the first which is a general introduction) outline the work and ideas of five teachers at various age-levels of education, but nowhere should the work described be seen as confined to a particular age-group. Thus Truffaut's short film *Les Mistons* is referred to by three contributors, in secondary, further and higher education, but only in the first instance (Chapter 3) is the film discussed in any detail; and in Chapter 2 John Bennett gives an account of his use in a primary school of *A Short Vision*, which many teachers would find equally appropriate to studies in secondary and further education. As with a poem by Lawrence or Tennyson which may find its relevant place in an infants' lesson or an English Honours degree course or anywhere in between, so many films will prove equally valuable at various age-levels and with groups of varying ability, the method and approach being adapted by the teacher from his own knowledge of the material and his own understanding of the class.

The summaries which head the chapters and are given briefly in the *Contents* (p. 5) indicate the major approaches discussed in each chapter, and though there is correlation, we have attempted to avoid duplication. Philip Smith in Chapter 3 offers a detailed treatment of one particular Western film, while Jane Corbett in Chapter 5 discusses more generally the value and purpose of studying a genre, such as the Western.

Each contributor has attempted to deal with four aspects of his work: to provide some idea of its context (school organisation, the range of ability of the pupils or students, the environment of the institution); to outline a range of courses offered and how film finds a place within the syllabuses; to give a detailed account of several specific lessons indicating how they were structured and, in most cases, giving examples of the oral or written work contained in or arising from the lessons; and to offer some sort of personal *credo*, some account of what the use of film has contributed to his teaching and how it has developed. In some cases the use of film has been a deliberate device to achieve a breakthrough, to make a contact which could not effectively be established by more conventional methods of English teaching; in others, the use of film has been largely incidental – almost accidental, and only later has its value been systematically related to a teaching aim. It is significant that these varied points of entry into the use of film in English have, in general, led to the same conclusions about its value and effectiveness.

If the chapters are personal and often subjective accounts of ideas and methods, the Appendix material which forms a large part of the volume provides more objective information about practical problems, specific courses, sources of further help and advice, lists of books and periodicals. The volume concludes with a checklist of films mentioned, which provides both a source of further teaching material and a record of directors and distributors.

Since the contributions come from individual teachers (and writers), no consistency of style will be found in the chapters. Some may evoke sympathetic response, some may infuriate or challenge: this is perhaps the function of the book – to stimulate, to provoke thought and analysis of both method and content in English teaching, above all to describe and thus share experience rather than to prescribe and thus stultify experience. Where there is repetition it is on the common ground of the basic aims of English teaching, and the special contribution which film has made in a variety of institutions and for very different teachers in achieving these aims. In this sense, the book is no longer an account of experiment but a record of achievement which can provide the confident basis for the extension of this work into many more schools and colleges.

Acknowledgements

The Editor acknowledges not only the patient help of the contributors in seeing their accounts through many drafts and revisions but also the continuing advice and assistance of the Education Department of the British Film Institute who commissioned the work, and in particular Peter Wollen, Christopher Williams, Jim Hillier, who have shared the burdens of administration, editing and compilation of appendices and index; the time and consideration given by many teachers and lecturers whom he visited to discuss the ideas and form of the book, some of whose courses appear in Appendix D; Gerald Collier, Principal of Bede College, Durham, and David Williams and Daniel Millar, colleagues in the Film Department there, who provided both encouragement and support for the study-leave that enabled the work to be undertaken; and John Stevens of Hutchinson Educational whose wise comments and constant interest have helped to shape the book; and finally to the various editors of *Screen Education* and *Screen*, and to the officers and members of the Society for Education in Film and Television over two decades – to their persistence and devotion to the causes of film and teaching this book is gratefully dedicated.

1

Introduction – why film?

Concepts in English teaching, related to film
teaching – film grammar – history of film –
influence of Leavis – Hollywood social-realism –
thematic approach – integrated studies –
creativity and film-making – communications –
semiology – '*Half Our Future*' – aims of English
teaching – film and book compared – oral and
written work – feelings and experience – formal
qualities

Roy Knight, Principal, Whitelands College, Putney
(previously Principal Lecturer in Film, Bede
College, Durham)

Since to some – perhaps many – teachers reading this book the idea of
using film in teaching, other than in a traditional 'visual aids' context,
may be unfamiliar, and the idea of actually teaching film even stranger,
it might be helpful to begin with a brief survey of some of the ideas
which have directed and changed the film-teaching movement. And
since we are here concerned essentially with film in the teaching of
English, it is both illuminating and relevant to make comparisons with
the development of English teaching, which has, I shall suggest, under-
gone similar changes of emphasis.

Although there may be disagreement about the *sequence* of changes
at various age-levels or even in various geographical areas, and indeed
the introduction of a new approach tends to be added to rather than
supersede earlier approaches to the teaching of a subject, I would argue
that at various times in the past, the present or the near future, English
teaching can be seen to manifest one or more of the following concepts,
which I hope later to relate to similar concepts in film teaching:

a grammar – the analysis and possible synthesis of the structural
   elements of the English language

b composition – the practice of oral and written skills in exercises of a
fairly limited range prescribed by the teacher ('My pets', 'A day at
the seaside', 'How to mend a puncture', etc.)

c history of literature – reading, and possibly learning examples of,
the best novels, plays, poems, essays; handing down the tradition of
a received culture through the '100 Best Books'

d comprehension – the discussion of texts or passages from texts,
aimed largely at achieving a basic understanding of their content, at
times merely the factual content but later its intellectual, moral or
spiritual values

e creativity – 'free' composition in prose or verse, arising perhaps
from a stimulus provided by the teacher but not necessarily limited
by the teacher's demand to 'write about X'

f communication – English skills in both language and literature seen
as part of a communications process; concern with mass media
(newspapers and magazines) and with technical uses of language,
possibly extended now to include some consideration of linguistics
and/or semantics

g integrated studies – English seen as one aspect of humanities,
general studies, liberal studies, or an integrated subject

Thus, A. G. Razzell could propose in a recent paper on teaching in the
middle school (8–13) that:

> A case could be made out for the abolition of English as a subject
> from the timetable. . . . We best learn English by using it, and the
> teaching of English might well form an integrated part of the every-
> day life in the middle years of schooling.[1]

Let me immediately make clear that in listing, however crudely, a
variety of concepts in English teaching (or in film teaching) I am concerned essentially with description rather than prescription. In any
given lessons or syllabus many approaches will be combined, and no
one approach will necessarily be dominant. Nevertheless, it would be
possible to find at given moments in the past, or possibly in geographical
areas in the present (if we included English teaching in Africa, for
instance), modes of teaching exclusively devoted to or significantly
dominated by one of these approaches. Few English syllabuses until
fairly recently would have included the areas of creativity or communication as main-springs of the study; and the dominance of 'comprehension' passages to the virtual exclusion of studying full-length texts
in the classroom is not universally a thing of the past.

The teaching of film has run parallel with – sometimes behind, sometimes ahead of – the main streams of English teaching. I have been quite unable to date the origins of film-teaching, and I strongly suspect that these may, in some isolated instances, go back fifty years; but we might conceivably date the formal origins twenty years ago when, in 1950, the Society of Film Teachers was established, becoming in the autumn of 1959 the Society for Education in Film and Television (S.E.F.T.).

The dominant concern of film teachers in the earlier years of the subject was undoubtedly *film grammar*. Children were systematically taught the language and grammar of the film; or perhaps one should more accurately say, they were taught *a* language and grammar of *some* films: how to recognise a long shot (subordinate adverbial clause of place?), the difference between frame, shot and sequence (word, phrase and sentence?), the nature of transitions such as the cut, fade or dissolve (marks of punctuation?). I am not suggesting that direct equivalence with verbal grammar was invariably attempted, but merely that pupils were expected to be able to recognise and analyse the function of a 'long shot' or a 'dissolve', and subsequently to incorporate these into film-making exercises in a way similar to English teaching in which pupils were expected to be able to recognise various parts of speech, phrases, clauses and punctuation devices and then apply this knowledge to restricted exercises set to test their knowledge. Thus a teacher describes a lesson with a class of primary school children – this is Lesson 6 in a scheme of twelve lessons with 9–10-year-olds, their first introduction to film:

LESSON 6 Camera positions – I
Film: *TELLING A STORY IN PICTURES*
Four stills each illustrating one of the four basic camera set-ups: *Long Shot, Mid Shot, Close-up* and *Big Close-up*. Refer back to previous lesson and explain how a film camera is used to pick out important detail. Illustrate this with the four stills. The appropriate abbreviations (L.S.; M.S.; C.U. and B.C.U.) are written on the blackboard. Project the film. *Version 2* is again analysed. The class is asked to identify each shot, and the abbreviations are added to the scripts copied during the previous lesson.[2]

At no stage during the year is part or all of a professionally made feature or documentary film shown to the children, who in later terms script and shoot their own films (or a class film); but 'At all stages links with films showing locally and with current TV programmes should be introduced at every opportunity, for very little can be achieved if the work in the classroom is carried out in isolation and divorced from reality'. I am confident that with this particular teacher at that time with those children in that context, work of the kind described was both valuable and exciting; but it is interesting to contrast such an approach to film-making in the primary school with John Bennett's description of work about twelve years later (see next chapter), bearing in mind the changes that have taken place in professional film-making during this period.

There are a number of reasons for this early concentration upon the grammatical approach to film. The early Russian theorists such as Eisenstein and Pudovkin had been very much concerned with the language of film, and particularly the effects of editing and montage: was film similar to a verbal language or closer to a picture language, or perhaps to an ideographic language like Japanese? how did film convey concepts of time, place, relationship? In fact their search for a film aesthetic (whether in making films, lecturing to students, or writing about films) ranged very widely and with much complexity, but unfortunately some of their exploratory analogies became entrenched as precepts and formed the basis of an over-simplified and often irrelevant 'film grammar'. The grammatical approach also commended itself because it was seen to lead (even where it did not) towards film-making, and it seemed a sound educational principle that the theoretical should lead to the practical, though increasingly teachers have come to believe that the practical is more likely to lead effectively to the theoretical.

Furthermore, because the major classroom approach was through film grammar, the early materials for film-teaching were compiled to support such an approach – materials selected from rather 'academic' directors long trained to work by the rule-book, such as David Lean, Carol Reed and Anthony Asquith. And, then, *because* such material was available, and other material was not, courses of necessity had to be based on a grammatical approach. Thus A. W. Hodgkinson, examining the position film-teaching had reached in 1958, affirms:

Until recently, the emphasis has been on formal qualities – perhaps understandably, since it is more easy to illustrate these aspects than to discuss questions of content.[3]

As can be seen from the lesson described above, the grammatical approach could most easily be extended into the area of film-making, corresponding to *composition* in the English lesson. This might mean taking an incident from a novel or play or poem and writing (and perhaps later filming) the script according to the rules that have been instilled. The article from which I have already quoted ends with an example of a finished script:

THE VILLAGE BLACKSMITH by H. W. Longfellow

Film script by Eileen (aged 11)

1. L.S. The village smith standing under a chestnut tree.
2. M.S. (camera moves down to show his hands) The blacksmith's hands rubbing together.
3. M.S. (camera moves up to show his muscles) The blacksmith's large muscles.
4. L.S. The blacksmith moves slowly away from the tree. He walks towards the camera so that everyone can see his face with sweat pouring down it.
5. L.S. The blacksmith turns round and goes to the smithy door. He stops, has a look round and goes inside.
6. C.U. (inside the workshop) The blacksmith's hammer beating slowly down on a piece of iron.
7. M.S. The camera tilts up and guides us round the workshop until it reaches the window so that people can see the sun rising gradually to tell people that he starts work early in the morning.
   fade out   *fade in*
8. L.S. A crowd of children coming home from school look in on the blacksmith.
9. M.S. The flaming forge in the workshop.
10. C.U. A child's face smiling. The camera pans to show some more children with smiling faces glowing in the light of the forge.
    fade out   *fade in*
11. L.S. The blacksmith sitting among friends in the church.
12. M.S. The blacksmith's daughter singing in the church choir.
13. C.U. The blacksmith's face showing a very pleasing look.
14. M.S. The blacksmith thinking hard about his wife, wishing that she was still alive.
    fade out   *fade in*

15. M.S. The blacksmith under the chestnut tree still thinking. He
    wipes a tear from his eye.

fade out

The immediate response to a piece of work such as this is to regard it
as a remarkably accomplished achievement, revealing a thorough
understanding of the basic language of film: there are the detailed shots,
the subtle camera movements of tilting and panning, the transitions by
fading in and out marking a time sequence, etc., etc. But the secondary
response is to ask questions about it. Was it ever filmed? In fact, could
it be filmed within the resources of a primary school? And if it could be,
and were, would it in fact as a film reveal what was in the script?
('The blacksmith thinking hard about his wife, wishing that she was
still alive.') Can you in fact pan in close-up to show 'more children
with smiling faces glowing in the light of the flaming forge'? Can we
run the shot long enough to reveal that the sun is *rising*, seen through
the forge window? These questions may sound mean and petty, but
they are questions about the nature of film, about the grammar and
structure of film which is the very aspect of film which has been
systematically taught: and if the answer is that 'You cannot expect
eleven-year-old children to understand . . .', then why are we teaching
this subject in this way?

And one is also prompted to ask questions about Eileen. Did she
choose *The Village Blacksmith* as the subject of her film, or was she
asked to produce the film-script from the given poem? Might she,
perhaps, have preferred to film Johnny swinging his satchel at Billy's
head? And might she have produced a better script for this? And even
have been able to film it? The same sorts of question might well be
asked about any number of composition lessons in English, and are
not asked often enough. It would be pointless to elaborate examples of
this approach, either in film-teaching or in English: the point is that
the approach is common to both subjects, proceeds on the same
educational basis, and suffers from the same objections.

An alternative approach, relatively early in the development of film-
teaching, and one often linked with the approaches already described
was through the history of film (analogous to the *history of literature* in
English). And such an approach was largely motivated, I think, by
three factors.

Firstly, many of the teachers attempting this work had themselves
been excited by film and learnt its strengths largely in the film societies

which flourished so vigorously just before and just after the Second World War. Here had been seen the great works of the silent cinema – of Eisenstein and Pudovkin, the German Expressionist films of Pabst, Murnau and Leni, works by Griffiths, René Clair and Dreyer. These were undoubted masterworks which most children would never see outside a classroom; and clearly it was part of an education process to transmit these aspects of a cultural heritage. Secondly (as with film grammar) the relevant teaching material was easily available from archive sources, and the British Film Institute not only had 16 mm prints of most of these 'classics', but also historical compilations, extracts, programme and teaching notes, ready packaged. Here were film anthologies comparable with the literary anthologies: a veritable 'Golden Treasury' of film. And thirdly, silent films provided classical examples of silent film-making, and if the children went on to make films, these would be silent, and probably 'classical' too.

It would be quite wrong to suggest that all History of Cinema courses came to an abrupt halt with *The Singing Fool* and *Blackmail:* but more recent films available only from commercial distribution libraries were costly materials beyond the reach of most film teachers, except perhaps where a school film society flourished. And I suspect that in the teaching of film, as in some teaching of literature, there were slight puritan undertones, a feeling that the work must not be too enjoyable or it might savour of entertainment rather than education. What if the headmaster walked down the corridor and heard children laughing, perhaps at a Laurel and Hardy two-reeler? 'Mr X, I rather thought you were paid to *teach* these children something useful.' One would like to caricature the attitude, but alas it then rang only too true. There can be few English literature courses which now plod relentlessly and chronologically from Chaucer to (perhaps) Tennyson, or which bounce about the landmarks of Eng. Lit., and similarly few film courses now would adopt an exhaustive and systematic historical view of the cinema, which is not to say that all influences of history are ignored.

Up to this point, film-teaching may be seen as attempting to establish its respectability, to achieve a sort of parity of esteem with other subjects in the curriculum, to win its inscribed place on the timetable; film must be seen to have its own grammar, its own history, and to lead to the practice of acquired skills and understanding. Two major factors inhibited developments along these lines: one was the time/cost factor, and the other the supply of suitably qualified and equipped teachers. While it was possible to introduce the odd film lesson – perhaps a couple of periods per week with one or two forms – and to provide on this basis a supply of film material, whether films for viewing or film-stock for practical work, to extend the subject to the time needed for a really effective course (whether in film history or in practical film work) and to extend this course to all forms in a school over a period of two or three years, was a quite impossible objective in most schools. Even if time and money were forthcoming, where would the teachers come from? At this time, round about 1960–1, no university offered a course in film study – at least, not within the university curriculum, though some students might spend more time in the cinemas than the lecture theatres – and no training college offered it as a main subject of study, though several did run optional courses for groups of students or included some study of film within English, drama or education courses. There was therefore a very active period of stocktaking by all the organisations and individuals concerned with the teaching of film, leading to new lines of approach which must now be considered.

A great variety of factors motivated this reassessment and reorienta-tion. Perhaps the strangest was the incorporation into media studies and film teaching of many of the ideas derived from Dr F. R. Leavis, which had already made a profound impact upon the teaching of English in schools. I use the word 'strange' because there is a direct tension, in fact a conflict, between the ideas and methods of what, for want of a better term, might be called Leavisian criticism and the subject areas in which they might operate.

In the first chapter of '*The Great Tradition*' (1948), writing about the novel, Leavis makes a distinction between writers who have 'various kinds of interest to offer' and those whose contributions belong 'to the realm of significant creative achievement: and as a recall to a due sense of the differences, it is well to start by distinguishing the few really great – the major novelists who count in the same way as the major poets, *in the sense that they not only change the possibilities of the art for practitioners and readers, but that they are significant in terms of that human awareness they promote; awareness of the possibilities of life*' (my italics).[5] Later, discussing Jane Austen, the implications of quality are further elaborated: the writers most worthy of systematic attention will not only add to and illuminate the tradition already existing and provide an impetus to those following after ('change the possibilities of the art') and promote a new 'awareness of the possibilities of life', they will also manifest a unity of form and content, of style with purpose, achieved by a controlling distance. Thus Jane Austen's 'interest in "composition"' is not something to be put over against her interest in life; nor does she offer an 'aesthetic' value that is separable from moral significance. Her art proceeds from 'a preoccupation with certain problems that life compels on her as personal ones' but 'she is intelligent and serious enough to be able to impersonalise her moral tensions as she strives, in her art, to become more fully conscious of them, and to learn what, in the interests of life, she ought to do with them'. The critical arguments are subtle and complex, and to reduce them crudely to phrases such as 'a serious moral concern' as the criterion of excellence is to do a grave injustice to the critic; but it is nevertheless this area of critical concern – 'awareness of the possibilities of life', the relationship between the form of art and its 'moral significance' – that begins to be absorbed as a dominant element in the study of film.

But it is in this very process that a critical tension is set up, for if we move back to consider an earlier work by F. R. Leavis, in collaboration with Denys Thompson, *'Culture and Environment'* (1933), we begin to discover that in their view criteria such as are mentioned in the previous paragraph cannot, almost by definition, operate in a popular medium such as film. We are invited early in the book to concede that:

An education that conceives seriously its function in the modern world will, then, train awareness (a) of the general process of civilisation, and (b) of the immediate environment, physical and intellectual – the ways in which it tends to affect taste, habit, preconception, attitude to life and quality of living. For we are committed to more consciousness; that way, if any, lies salvation.[6]

This seems a clear enough invitation to examine film (and other media) which affect 'the general process of civilisation' and which form a dominant part of 'the immediate environment, physical and intellectual'. But when we later look for help in approaching so complex and so formative an influence as film, we find that its purpose and values have already been predefined.

Most popular uses of leisure come under the head of distractions . . . that is, they find compensation in Substitute-Living.

This form of compensation, then, is the very reverse of recreation, in that it tends not to strengthen and refresh the addict for living, but to increase his unfitness by habituating him to weak evasions, to the refusal to face reality at all.[7]

And in approaching the cinema (or radio, or now I imagine, television) we are referred to Mrs Q. D. Leavis's work on *'Fiction and the Reading Public':* 'The following hints, too, should be taken':

> The cinema, one notices, provides the same satisfaction (i.e. 'fantasy-spinning'). . . . True, the cinema has several advantages over the novel: the public have not to make the effort on translating words into images – that is done for them. . . . Moreover, attending the cinema, like listening to the gramophone or wireless, is a passive and social amusement, whereas, since reading aloud in the family circle is no longer practised, fiction is a solitary pleasure, and the public today prefers communal to private pastimes. Indeed, it is only the exceptional character that can tolerate solitude and silence, distressing to modern nerves. The British Broadcasting Corporation reports that in 1930 every other home had a wireless set, which in practice means not that a nation of music-lovers has sprung up, but that in any town two out of every three houses one passes in the evening are reading and talking with the support of a loudspeaker.[8]

I make no apology for quoting this passage at length because it significantly pinpoints the conflict that faces the teacher who would wish to show interest in and to give critical attention to almost any medium (film, television, radio, the gramophone) which provides the major 'cultural' environment of his pupils. *'Fiction and the Reading Public'* is, in my opinion, one of the most brilliant critical works of this century when focussing attention on material which Mrs Leavis has examined. But her wild assumptions and almost hysterical gestures towards material that she does not choose to examine reveal serious deficiencies of both attitude and method. The heavy irony of 'the cinema has several advantages over the novel: the public have not to make the effort of translating words into images – that is done for them' is revealed as utterly meaningless if for 'cinema' we substitute 'the paintings of Rembrandt or Giotto' or 'the stained glass and stone carvings of a mediaeval cathedral' – are these to be similarly dismissed because the public is saved the effort of translating words into images ? 'Listening to the gramophone or wireless is a passive and social amusement', and so, virtually, is attending a concert or recital: and one therefore wonders, if such experiences are to be virtually dismissed, how often Mrs Leavis has sung in a choral society, played in a chamber group or orchestra? But, even then, this would be suspect, since there is an implied virtue in the 'solitary pleasure' of reading, set against communal pleasures – and therefore, one must suppose, that the theatrical experiences of Greece and the Middle Ages and Shakespearian England also come under suspicion, since these were passive and social and communal and largely visual! It would be pointless to pursue this line of attack upon an attitude so unconsidered and so untenable if such attitudes did not persist even within the liveliest of debates about English teaching; and it might even be argued by those dedicated to film that in 1933 film masterpieces, even films demanding serious critical attention, were few and far between, and those that did exist were little known in the areas of British commercial film distribution.

But Denys Thompson's attitudes persist in his editorship of 'The Use of English', which most English teachers must regard as one of the most valuable periodicals for the exchange of ideas and expertise, and a constant source of exciting, sometimes inspired, writing; but almost invariably any reference to film or other mass media sparks off, even now, a tone of writing and a series of basic assumptions little different from those of Mrs Leavis more than thirty years ago. Thus David Holbrook, reviewing 'The Popular Arts' (1964) by Stuart Hall and Paddy Whannel, can persistently misread and misrepresent both its intentions and its methods:

> Heavily endowed with an excited assumption – that a new mass taste is emerging, from the emancipated 'tastes' of 'the people', liberated from the old 'paternalism' of middle-class culture, and so forth . . . they struggle for merits in the world of deliberate devaluation.[9]

Whereas the treatment of sex in the ballad (or in the poetry written by children he teaches) is for Holbrook 'the delicate preoccupation of folksong with relationship', 'sex (is) written into modern pop numbers merely to gain commercial zing'; and his conclusion is that since 'Pop is a plague, not a development at all', then 'there is little point in discriminating between pop and pop'. By now, then, we are virtually refused the right to discriminate between forms which have 'various kinds of interest to offer' and those which belong 'to the realm of significant creative achievement'. And all this is the more confusing

since over and over again Leavis or Thompson or Holbrook are willing
to assert a rich working-class vitality in selective examples of artistic
experience while refusing to examine other manifestations which are
dismissed in terms such as 'the offensive meaninglessness, the reduction
of life, the demonstrative sex cults, of the raucous mob'. It is strange,
and I think sad, that here the advocates of a serious critical concern
for art and literature find a common platform, and a common language,
with certain pressure groups such as the Clean-up TV Campaign, and
Mrs Mary Whitehouse's National Viewers and Listeners Council. The
tone is very similar: 'infected', 'spreading psychic spinelessness',
'deliberate exploitation', 'pursuit of the bitch-goddess', 'raucous mob',
'propaganda of doubt, dirt and disbelief', or:

> A group of wily, dedicated people, firmly entrenched inside the
> B.B.C., are plotting to denigrate the morals of the nation . . . they
> intend to sap away our beliefs, ridicule our moral standards and
> decry everything that the Union Jack stands for.[10]

This leads us directly to consider another factor which assisted in
the reorientation of film-teaching: the need to embrace a study of some
television forms, as well as film. In 1960 the Independent Television
companies had been effectively in operation for five years and the
B.B.C. for thirteen. The Pilkington Committee had been set up and
was receiving evidence (it reported two years later). And in the autumn
of 1959, after several years of pressure, the Society of Film Teachers had
transformed itself into the Society for Education in Film and Television.
Notions of 'film grammar' or 'history of film' had little connection with
a study of television. And the main areas of interest in television tended
to be more those of content than of form: issues of violence and sometimes of sex, the degradation of personality in some of the quiz-shows
which then formed a major factor in the TV diet, a vast and powerful
output of documentary programmes examining the human condition
in social, political or economic terms. Such television material invited
moral or sociological consideration as much as or more than formal
or structural analysis.

Another factor in rethinking an approach to film teaching was the
very subject-matter of film (and particularly Hollywood film) itself.
The 1950s had seen a further extension in Hollywood of social-realist
films, ostensibly concerned with 'real-life' problems of the city and the
community. The form had emerged in the late 1940s with films such as

Kazan's *Boomerang* (1946) and *Gentleman's Agreement* (1947) and Dmytryck's *Crossfire* (1947) concerned with social issues in American society, followed by Losey's fantasy *The Boy with Green Hair* (1948), Rossen's *All the Kings Men*, Wise's *The Set-Up*, and Mark Robson's *The Champion*, Brown's *Intruder in the Dust*, Kazan's *Pinky* and Robson's *Home of the Brave* (all 1949). These explored issues of political and commercial corruption, race and class privilege. In 1949 Stanley Kramer Productions was established as a company, destined to produce in the 1950s such films as Zinnemann's *The Men* (paraplegics), Benedek's *Death of a Salesman* (the selling rat-race), Benedek's *The Wild One* (teenage motor-cycle gangs), Dmytryck's *The Sniper* (psychological pressures) and *The Caine Mutiny* (war neurosis). Writers such as Paddy Chayevsky emerged from television to support a new low-budget realist cinema, with films such as Delbert Mann's *Marty* (1955) and *Bachelor Party* (1957), Brook's *Blackboard Jungle* (1955) or Martin Ritt's *A Man is Ten Feet Tall* (1956). Marlon Brando developed beyond the young anti-hero of *The Men* and *The Wild One*, to be replaced by James Dean during his brief screen career in films such as *Rebel Without a Cause* (Nicholas Ray: 1955), *East of Eden* (Kazan: 1955) and *Giant* (George Stevens: 1956). This list could be extended, but it is already abundantly clear that whatever the motives – some, the commercial exploitation of new stars; some, a defiance of or a compromise with the investigation of 'the alleged subversive influence in motion pictures' by the House of Representatives Committee for Un-American Activities (J. Parnell Thomas) in 1947 or the Senate Committee's further investigations in the 1950s under Senator McCarthy – whatever the motives Hollywood was developing and revealing a conscience, a social awareness; and the most effective way of evaluating these films, as documents rather than as works of art, was to consider their conscience and their subject-matter set against the society they were examining. This meant, in effect, incorporating film-study (and literature and television) into a *thematic approach*, which for convenience may be related partly to a critical method deriving from Leavis in its attempts to discern social relevance and moral significance, and partly to *comprehension* studies in English where passages are considered primarily for their content, information and ideas rather than for their formal or aesthetic qualities. This must not be read as stating that Dr Leavis advocates either a thematic approach or the value of comprehension exercises: he undoubtedly would abhor both; but I have endeavoured to trace some of the influences which, from scattered and distinctive origins, strangely cohere in initiating a new approach to the study of film.

The attraction of this approach is recorded in a number of books published (or written) in the early 1960s. 'The Popular Arts' by Stuart Hall and Paddy Whannel (1964) in its early chapters approaches its vast subject matter largely through formal considerations (minority art and folk art, comedy and music hall, blues and jazz, the Western and the Musical, etc., etc.); but in examining these ideas in the context of the school curriculum there is a heavy emphasis upon themes and topics (Society and the Hero, Young People, War, etc.). And a little later, in 1966, A. P. Higgins, writing about his work teaching television in two secondary schools, although himself approaching the topic largely through forms (Quiz, Comedy, Topical and Documentary programmes, Drama), adds a final chapter on 'A Thematic Approach', stating:

A glance through the discussions recorded in this book shows very clearly that the television lesson frequently touches on themes and topics of great importance to anyone concerned with education. Parents and children, youth, age, social class, race, politicians, war, policemen, crime, violence, health and disease, housing, fashion, have all entered into lessons held over a period of a few months. Other themes such as work and leisure, falling in love, marriage, animals, scientists, lawyers, teachers, etc. do not appear in the discussions recorded here, but they are frequently discussed in the television lesson. The kind of lesson described in this book starts from a particular programme or type of programme, and goes on to consider the themes it raises. A complementary method, which might well be used for some of the time, is to reverse the order: to choose a theme and trace it through a number of different programmes.[11]

Examples of course based on a thematic approach have been widely documented, for example in 'Talking about the Cinema' by Jim Kitses, which describes courses on themes such as Young People, War, The City, Love, Work, and Leisure, work done at the Kingsway College of Further Education and further described in Chapter 5 of this book. The thematic approach clearly invites, even if it does not positively demand, some movement towards integrated studies (the last of my original list of concepts of English teaching).

If a theme is to be explored, it will sometimes be difficult to confine, and wrong to do so, the exploration to a particular medium. We may just look at films dealing with, say, Young People; but our study of such films may well be enhanced by a consideration of books, magazines, advertisements, television programmes, fashions, music, etc., which are directed at or which exploit the talents of young people. And this will then require some sort of synthesis *in teaching* of such subjects as literature, music, art, history, current affairs, perhaps religious education: this may be achieved informally either by interdepartmental collaboration, or by the variety of interest and experience of one teacher within a particular subject-discipline; or it may be achieved formally by a restructuring of departments and timetable under a heading such as liberal or social or general studies. Thus an integrated studies approach does not necessarily demand either a departmental structure or a timetable recognising that 'studies' are 'integrated': the approach is rather a manifestation of an attitude of mind, a way of looking at knowledge and the educational process. If that attitude of mind is present, and if this approach is seen to be beneficial, then later the organisation may change to facilitate and extend it; but if reorganisation precedes thought, conviction and agreement, it may only produce a departmental and time-table structure which labels as 'general studies' what is in effect a series of subject-teachers giving lessons in sequence or in parallel within a given time-slot.

There remain two further concepts or approaches to the teaching of English or of film: the areas of 'creativity' and 'communication'. The use of expression such as 'creative writing' implies, almost certainly with good reason, that the bulk of writing demanded from children in schools is *not* creative, and not recreative, and thus the distinction between 'writing compositions' and 'writing creatively' is a valid one in some instances. Similarly, writing and filming scripts, if this follows some of the more stereotyped film-making projects which have already been described, may not express any sort of individual or group creative impulse. Perhaps in recognition of this, the British Film Institute devoted a Whitsun conference in 1965 to the topic of film-making, publishing papers from this conference the following year as '*Film-making in schools and colleges*'. This revealed that at many levels in education, film-making had developed into a much freer, more experimental, more 'creative' process.

The causes of these changes were largely technical, and in turn related to finance. Much more extensive use was made of 8 mm equipment and stock, and relatively cheap systems of sound-striping 8 mm film had replaced the earlier system of running a separate tape-track more or less in synchronisation with the projected film – never wholly satisfactory since tape stretched with repeated use while film did not. Cheaper, lighter, more easily portable tape-recorders, including battery-operated tape-recorders, had come on to the market, and more were in use in schools: the earlier tape-recorders available to schools could not even be lifted by many junior-school children, let alone carried around.

But the most significant change, though related to the technical and financial aspects of film-making, was really a change of attitude: there was a much greater willingness to let children learn by their mistakes (less costly in 8 mm than 16 mm). Where time was given to preparation it was much more likely to be practical preparation – choosing locations, rehearsing actors, trying out dummy set-ups and dry-runs, taking test shots – than painstaking analysis and scripting in the classroom. Films or short 'exercises' on film were often more personal, and much less the result of collaboration and compromise whereby what gets filmed is more likely to be what nobody can object to rather than what somebody really wants! Another contributory cause to this liberation movement was undoubtedly a growing interest in film among art-teachers, and in art colleges (or art departments of schools and colleges). This helped to shift the emphasis from the written script (which could almost be judged as a piece of literature, and even marked for expression and spelling as an English exercise) to ideas in the head communicated through film.

It would be quite wrong to suggest that school films in the period (say) 1955–62 were 'bad', and that those of the following period were 'good' – indeed, because of the very extension of this activity it is really a presupposition that there will be more 'bad' films produced, 'bad' here meaning films which do not fully reveal their creator's aspirations, films spoilt by technical flaws: but one cannot help repeating the epigram 'If a thing's worth doing, it's worth doing badly', which must support almost any beginnings in a creative field whether playing the piano, writing poetry, throwing a discus, or making a film. For children particularly, little sense of achievement is derived from having assisted someone else to achieve perfection: they want to achieve their own perfection, and this demands tolerance of imperfection during the learning process.

The final concept to be considered ('final' only in sequence of consideration here, and not in the sense of chronological development, or in the sense of ultimate attainment) is that of 'communication'. The key document here is perhaps Raymond Williams's book *'Communications'* which was first published in 1962 as a Penguin Special in the series 'Britain in the Sixties'. He himself acknowledges that part of its incentive was the conference organised by the National Union of Teachers in October 1960, Popular Culture and Personal Responsibility – another major contribution to the revaluation and reorientation of mass-media studies and film-teaching already referred to. We have seen how at various times in the teaching of both film and English emphasis has shifted between grammatical and formal analysis, a historical approach, an examination of content, subject-matter and tone, or the concept of practical more-or-less creative activity. The other area to be explored was clearly the 'means and method', the medium itself, and literature or film or television examined as means of communication.

The standpoint of Raymond Williams is almost diametrically opposed to that stated in *'Culture and Environment'*, though he is careful to point out that 'the great merit of earlier work in this field, of the phase associated with *'Scrutiny'*, was its remarkable and still growing influence in education'; but his major assertion is:

The deepest danger, now, is the external division (pushed by the media, ratified by education) between those arts which are thought of as serious, academic, and old and those which are experienced as lively, personal and new. To underwrite this division harms the traditional work and misses the chance of creating real standards in the new. In this respect, such new forms as jazz and the cinema are crucial. Yet for one school performance and discussion of a good contemporary film there seem to be hundreds of visits to films of the 'classics' – versions of Dickens and Shakespeare made respectable by that fact, yet often inferior, as cinema, to new work.[12]

Some film-teaching in the past has even tended to foster rather than break down the 'external division' that Williams describes, by creating a special selection of study films, recognised and respectable classics worthy of educational use, while rejecting or avoiding classroom discussion of the films that children actually see for pleasure. For this reason it must be implicit that any work in English (or any other subject) that seeks to exploit film whether for information or for experience will encourage the regular viewing and discussion whenever appropriate of films currently showing or recently shown in the commercial cinema and on television. For reasons of cost, the films hired for classroom use are likely to be at least four or five years old and probably older, and it is therefore important that the teacher himself regularly watches films on television and continues to visit the cinema in order that comparisons can be made with material more familiar to his pupils. This not only makes film study more 'real', but also extends the material relevant to discussion at little or no cost to the teacher.

However, any approach based upon 'communication' prevents the creation or application of any 'external division', since attention must first be focussed on the medium and the way that (in McLuhan's definition) it 'shapes and controls the scale and form of human association and action'; and furthermore, if we follow through McLuhan's concept that 'the "content" of any medium is always another medium', then the controlling factors in our approach will always be directed to purpose, means, form, social context, institution, etc., before the need arises to tackle subject-matter or moral significance. This does not mean that such areas will be ignored: moral issues arise in any area of 'association and action' – it only means that we ask first 'What is this? (this novel or film or poem or record) How does it work? For whom and on whom does it work?' before asking the more complex question 'Is it "good" or "bad"?', a question which has both aesthetic and moral overtones.

The most recent development in English teaching and, similarly, in film-teaching, has been to examine within the general theory of communication specific aspects which can be analysed using the methodology of modern linguistics, semantics or semiology. Professor Randolph Quirk, originally working in Durham and later in London, has proposed in the 1964 Report of the Secondary Examinations Council, a possible A-level English language syllabus which would include considerations of both the grammatical and lexical resources of language, tracing paradigmatic and syntagmatic relations of classes, systems and structures, and examining the transmission systems of language, both written and oral; and at the present time some of the newer secondary school textbooks in this country and in America are including sections with a linguistic rather than a grammatical basis for the analysis of English language.

On this basis, 'grammar' is near to achieving a new respectability; and critics such as Peter Wollen, writing about film, have led us back to the early Russian writers in a new attempt to establish a formal aesthetic of the cinema:

> There are two reasons why semiology (the study of the sign-system of any art) is a vital area of study for the aesthetics of film. Firstly, any criticism necessarily depends upon knowing what a text means, being able to read it. Unless we understand the code or mode of expression which permits meaning to exist in the cinema, we are condemned to massive imprecision and nebulosity in film criticism, an unfounded reliance on intuition and momentary impressions. Secondly, it is becoming increasingly evident that any definition of art must be made as part of a theory of semiology. Forty years ago the Russian Formalist critics insisted that the task of literary critics was to study not literature but 'literariness'. This still holds good. The whole drift of modern thought about the arts has been to submerge them in general theories of communication, whether psychological or sociological, to treat works of art like any other text or message and to deny them any specific aesthetic qualities by which they can be distinguished, except of the most banal kind, like primacy of the expressive over the instrumental or simply institutionalisation as art.[13]

To this point, I have attempted to trace with a certain rough justice (which may at times appear as crude injustice) the various influences which have developed and changed notions of film-teaching, and to relate these to similar concepts which have at various times affected the teaching of English. Although this account is historical (but not strictly chronological) most of the approaches outlined will somewhere survive or will be revived to deal with specific problems of teaching in specific contexts. So far, we have considered approaches to the teaching of film: but the concern of this book, its basic thesis, is *the place of film in the teaching of English.* Clearly in most schools English has replaced 'the classics' as the subject area within which the values and attitudes of what might be called 'the cultural tradition' are transmitted. D. H. Lawrence and Hugh Trevor Roper are perhaps today commoner (and more relevant) areas of study than Catullus and Livy. But over the whole range of school pupils, in ability and age, the aims of English teaching will vary. We must therefore bear in mind the possibilities of using film with some pupils to stimulate a deeper response to language and literature; but there will be others for whom this response can hardly be awakened, let alone deepened, and in these cases many teachers have found that film study enables them to achieve the ends which they would wish otherwise to achieve through literature – to create some critical standards, to get children talking about artistic experience, to write with personal conviction about things which they consider important.

This potentiality of film was clearly recognised in the Report of the Central Advisory Council for Education (England) entitled 'Half Our Future' (often known from its chairman as the Newsom Report). Early in the report, the value of discussion in developing judgment and discrimination is recognised, and films and television are areas about which young people do have views which with a little encouragement and training can be voiced very coherently. And a later section of the report states the case for the introduction of film and television so cogently that I make no apology for quoting it at length:

Here we should wish to add a strong claim for the study of film and television in their own right, as powerful forces in our culture and significant sources of language and ideas. Although the study of these media has for some time been accepted in a small number of schools as an important part of the curriculum, in the majority of schools they are used only as visual aids for the presentation of material connected with other subjects. Again, making a film is frequently seen as an interesting and unusual practical activity especially for the less academically gifted child; film and television clubs may be organised after school hours for the showing of feature films or informal discussion of evening programmes: all these ways of using film and television are valuable and constructive, and their extension is commended elsewhere in this report. The most important and most general use of these media, however, as major means for the mass communication of cultural experiences, is not generally dealt with in schools any more than it is in colleges or universities. Little attention is paid to the degree to which film and television enter into and influence the lives of our pupils and to these media as legitimate means for the communication of personal experience alongside literature, music and painting.

The culture provided by all the mass media, but particularly by film and television, represents the most significant environmental

factor that teachers have to take into account. The important changes
that take place at the secondary stage are much influenced by the
world offered by the leisure industry which skilfully markets products
designed for young people's tastes. The media help to define aspirations and they offer roles and models. They not only supply needs
(and create them) but may influence attitudes and values. Little as
yet has been effectively undertaken in schools in the way of offering
some counter-balancing assistance. We need to train children to look
critically and discriminate between what is good and bad in what
they see. They must learn to realise that many makers of films and
of television programmes present false or distorted views of people,
relationships, and experience in general, besides producing much
trivial and worthless stuff made according to stock patterns.

By presenting examples of films selected for the integrity of their
treatment of human values, and the craftsmanship with which they
were made, alongside others of mixed or poor quality, we can not
only build up a way of evaluating but also lead the pupils to an
understanding of film as a unique and potentially valuable art form
in its own right as capable of communicating depth of experience
as any other art form. Just as we have traditionally thought it important to broaden children's response to and experience of literature
and music, so we must now offer a comparative education in the
important and powerful visual media, both because these media at
their best have much that is valuable to offer and simply because
communication in the twentieth century is becoming increasingly
visual. The making of films when allied to studies of this kind becomes
a much more potent educational instrument. One of the difficulties
in extending this work is the shortage of teachers equipped to tackle
it. While there is a supply, even if inadequate, of specialist and other
teachers with some training in literature, music, art and drama,
there are very few teachers equipped to deal with the art forms that
most closely touch the boys and girls of this report. We are glad to
note that some training colleges have begun to respond to this
challenge by offering courses in film both as major and minor
elements in a course.[14]

'*Half Our Future*' has in mind the possible development of film and
television study as major curriculum areas, but, as the report points
out, there are as yet few teachers equipped to undertake such courses:
the more immediate aim must be, therefore, to incorporate such material

into a subject such as English which has similar aims and objectives.

What are the aims of teaching English? It is not possible to argue these through from first principles: one can only, at this stage, appeal to a general agreement that at some time in the pattern of English teaching from the primary level to the levels of further, and in some cases higher, education, some attention must be paid to at least four areas; let me risk stating these in what I should regard as an order of priority:

> first – an awareness and enjoyment of the widest possible range of literature
>
> second – an ability to express ideas, to communicate both information and feeling as fluently and coherently as possible in both speech and writing
>
> third – an extension of personal experience into areas of critical and moral judgment
>
> fourth – an understanding of the formal qualities of art

This is a total pattern, and the attainment of these aims will be limited both by the abilities of the pupils and by the interests of the teacher. I do not expect that many primary school children can be brought to a full understanding of the qualities of a Henry James novel! Indeed, this is something of a test case for me personally because I have not been brought to a full understanding of the qualities of Henry James; but I am at least aware that I do not enjoy what clearly delights some other people, and I can attempt to formulate what I am missing, as well as to communicate my own delight in (say) metaphysical poetry which others find distasteful. I can begin to operate in all four areas as a result of the English teaching that I have received.

The key question is therefore: how can film enable the pupils or students to operate in these four areas more effectively? Let us consider each area in turn.

Awareness and enjoyment of literature depend upon the ability to read – this is axiomatic; and equally axiomatic is that film will not teach children to read. What it can do, and clearly does do, is to provide those who can read with an added incentive to do so. Recent evidence tends to be drawn from television, but is equally relevant to film study. At the turn of the century – before the emergence of either film or television as mass media – about six thousand books were published annually in this country. By the mid-twenties (that is, in the period dominated by the silent film) this figure had doubled; by the late thirties (that is, the period dominated by the sound film) it had almost trebled; by the mid-sixties (the period dominated by television) the figure had exceeded twenty-five thousand; and today the figure is more than thirty-two thousand titles published in the United Kingdom, of which more than two-thirds are first editions.

No one would claim that this is a directly causal relationship, but it does illustrate that the growth of the mass media has in no way brought about a diminution of the number of books published. Higher numbers in full-time and part-time education account for some of this rise; and new subject areas bring about sudden fluctuations – there have been significant increases recently in the number of titles related to engineering and politics as new sciences and technologies evolve.

But the relevant factor is not the books published but the books borrowed from public libraries or purchased from shops. Both these figures have risen in the past fifty years, and go on rising. Library loans have increased by fifty per cent in the past seven years, and are now in the region of six hundred million issues per year. Book purchases have almost doubled in value during the last ten years, and even when the figure is corrected to allow for rising costs, there has been a fifteen per cent increase in book purchases between 1956 and 1966, though this has recently steadied to a little less than ten per cent. Much of this increase is, of course, due to the 'paperback' revolution, but in the paperback area alone sales have increased fourfold in the decade 1955–65 (from twenty million to more than eighty million a year).

It is difficult to obtain accurate statistics for the average number of books read or owned: books borrowed from libraries are often read by the family, giving two or three readers against a single 'issue' of the book. But a recent professional survey, on a broad and balanced statistical sample, suggested that the number of books read per head of the total population exceeded fifteen books per year; that one-third of the sample owned more than fifty books, and one-eighth owned more than two hundred. In 'real' terms this probably means that something like two-thirds of the population does read books (and a hundred years ago this figure probably would not have been higher than ten per cent) and that nearly half the population of the country reads as much as one book per month.

The night after Chekhov's '*The Three Sisters*' had been performed on television I tried to purchase a copy of the Penguin edition of Chekhov's plays, currently in print. I visited half a dozen book shops in three places (a university town, a provincial city, and a conurbation centre) and failed to purchase a single copy: their stocks had been sold the morning after the television play. There is an immediate demand for and sale of any 'book of the film' or book exploiting the characters or subject-matter of a television series: these are direct and causal relationships.

Fears, therefore, that film and television would result in a catastrophic decline in reading and book-buying are quite unjustified, and the reverse is clearly the case. This alone should be an adequate incentive to the English teacher to test the use of film to increase reading, and to extend understanding of what is read by discussion of film. At the simplest level, this might be the use of the film of the set-book or play, and there is a very large selection of films suitable for this purpose apart from the best-known Shakespeare 'classics'. A more subtle, and often more useful, approach is to make use of a film similar in theme or subject-matter but not the direct adaptation. Thus, in dealing with 'Lord of the Flies', it might be better not to use Peter Brook's film version of the Golding story, but perhaps to use *Les Jeux Interdits* in which two children create *their* own world of make-believe and ritual; or Bryan Forbes's *Whistle Down the Wind*; or, at sixth-form level, even Buñuel's *Exterminating Angel* which examines the behaviour of an adult group cut off from all contact with the outside world, recording the gradual break-down of their civilisation. A Jacobean revenge tragedy with its firm structural conventions, boldly projected characterisation, and traditional imagery, might for interest be compared with a Western film on a similar revenge theme. Since the purpose of any critical examination must include illumination, and since real understanding can only be brought about by challenge to analyse structure, characters, form, language, imagery, a comparison with a totally new context – one perhaps too often taken for granted – may well provide just the fire needed to ignite interest.

If we move to a consideration of the next of the aims of English teaching – the fostering of an ability to express ideas fluently and coherently – film again offers interesting opportunities. One of the disadvantages of making contact with the finest examples of literature, whether poetry or prose, is that it tends to leave one speechless, and reluctant to write another word: how can I begin to write my own thoughts or feelings at a level comparable with the author I have just read? And one need not dwell on the utterly pointless horrors of asking a class which has just read a poem or story to 'now tell the story in your own words' – *WHY?* But if the original experience has been in another medium, and perhaps one which relies less heavily on verbal dexterity, then there's much less inhibition about talking or writing about that experience. Later chapters in this book offer some examples of poetry and prose written in response to film, examples which I think make their point more effectively than I could argue. What is perhaps most interesting about some of these examples is that while ostensibly they are exercises in free composition or 'creative writing' they do often provide a subtle critique of the film, making points of observation, comparison and judgment which would be rare in the more formal context of writing critically about literature.

Above all, one cannot write or speak without having felt, and sometimes the verbal complexity or remoteness of the 'great' novel or poem provides a barrier to feeling, and thus a barrier to thought and expression. The direct impact of film, sometimes regarded by literary critics as a major disadvantage just because it tends to bypass language, is here clearly an asset. Film can achieve the breakthrough to feeling (sometimes at the level of crude sentimentality, but often with subtle complexities which to most children would be beyond understanding from a purely verbal stimulus), and thus liberate the word, whether spoken or written.

This leads us immediately to the third purpose suggested as an inevitable part of English teaching – the extension of personal experience into areas of critical and moral judgment. This is the transition from enjoying literature to 'using' it: and though I certainly would not want to argue that artistic experience must be useful in the way that we might collect small-talk, or quotations that may come in handy as later debating points, we do by absorbing the experiences of literature increase our intellectual and emotional stock and apply such experience to other situations. I have in the past been accused of 'using' *Saturday Night and Sunday Morning* (whether Sillitoe's book or Karel Reisz's film does not really matter) or a film such as *On the Waterfront* 'as if they were visual aids to encourage discussion about abortion or trade unions': in fact, I have never used either of these films in this way, but I would not admit to a feeling of guilt if I had. It seems to me that *Saturday Night and Sunday Morning* does have something to communicate about relationships and situations leading to the need for an abortion, and *On the Waterfront* does imply certain attitudes to the practices of trade unions in the same way that '*Macbeth*' communicates ideas about ambition or *All Quiet on the Western Front* about war.

After experiencing these films or novels or plays, my stock of abortion-feelings or trade-union-feelings or war-feelings or ambition-feelings is altered, and subsequently both my thoughts and actions may be altered as a result. One of the purposes of studying and discussing and writing about literature or film or any art form will be (some would say, must be) to examine to what degree the experience is 'significant in terms of that human awareness they promote, awareness of the possibilities of life'. Film as much as any other medium can promote this awareness; and in the broadest context of English teaching, for reasons already stated, it may play a particularly valuable role in stimulating such an awareness directly from an experience of film, and subsequently from an experience of literature.

But perhaps the most interesting use of film in English teaching is its use to increase an understanding of the formal qualities of art. I have already touched upon this point earlier with reference to an understanding of subject-matter: we sometimes appreciate the novel or play or poem more when set against a comparable film. We may by examining the narrative method of a film be led to a greater understanding of the narrative method of the novel or the play or the epic just because these methods are different. Few will be unacquainted with that persistent examination rubric 'compare and contrast'; and often enough the contrasts are more important and revealing than the comparisons. Film as art exploits virtually all the modes which are also exploited by literature: irony and satire, metaphor and symbol, dream and vision, concatenation and parallelism, allusion and quotation. It exploits these modes through its specific and peculiar formal structures. By examining these modes of operation in film, attention may be focussed upon their comparable operation in literature.

In the chapters which follow, teachers and lecturers give personal accounts of some of the ways in which they have found film helpful in achieving what they conceive to be the purposes of English teaching. Such accounts cannot be exhaustive: there will be other applications not here described, others not yet attempted. In the next few years, as in the recent past, with the raising of the statutory leaving age to sixteen, with the reorganisation of schools, with further experiments in curriculum, most teachers will be examining what they do and thinking about what they might do. One hopes that in the area of English teaching the already tried and proven values of using film might be extended and developed: it is an extension and development which few teachers who have tried it have cause to regret.

CHAPTER 1 REFERENCES

1 RAZELL, A. G. Schools Council Working Paper: 'The Middle Years of School from 8 to 13'. H.M.S.O., 1969.

2 ALEXANDER, S. P. G. 'Twelve Minus: film teaching in the primary school'. *Screen Education* No. 7, March/April 1961, p. 11.

3 HODGKINSON, A. W. 'Are they real?' *Film Teacher* No. 14, September 1958, p. 9.

4 ALEXANDER, S. P. G. op. cit., p. 13.

5 LEAVIS, F. R. *The Great Tradition*. (1st Ed. Chatto & Windus, 1948.) Peregrine Paperback 1962, p. 10.

6 LEAVIS, F. R. and DENYS THOMPSON. *Culture and Environment*. Chatto & Windus (6th Impression) 1950, p. 4.

7 LEAVIS, F. R. and DENYS THOMPSON. op. cit., 99 ff.

8 LEAVIS, Q. D. *Fiction and the Reading Public*. Chatto & Windus.

9 HOLBROOK, DAVID. Review of *The Popular Arts*. *The Use of English*, 1964.

10 CLAXTON, E. (Vice-Chairman, Clean-up TV Campaign). Speech quoted in *Censorship* No. 8, Autumn 1966, p. 10.

11 HIGGINS, A. P. *Talking about Television*. British Film Institute, 1966, p. 65.

12 WILLIAMS, RAYMOND. *Communications*. Penguin, 1962 (Revised 1968), p. 131.

13 WOLLEN, PETER. *Signs and Meaning in the Cinema*. *Cinema One* No. 9. Secker and Warburg, 1969, p. 16.

14 CENTRAL ADVISORY COUNCIL FOR EDUCATION (England). *Half Our Future*. H.M.S.O., 1963, paras. 474–6.

2

A primary school

Integrated studies – short films and extracts –
film-making exercises – film as school record –
creativity

John Bennett, Headmaster, Crowlands Junior
School, Romford, Essex

Much of the work described in this chapter was accomplished before
my present appointment, in a post-war junior school on the northern
boundary of the London Borough of Havering. The school has a
three-form entry and a roll of about four hundred and fifty children
and thirteen full-time teachers. Children are not streamed according
to ability, but according to age. This means that in addition to the full
range of intellectual ability being present in each class of about thirty-
five children, there are also marked differences in the general emotional
and social development between, say, the youngest and oldest classes
in any year group. It is common practice throughout the school for
children to be working either individually or in small groups for most
of the day. Groups usually contain a wide range of ability for many
activities.

The subjects sometimes considered under the umbrella title of
'Humanities' are studied together at the school, and known as Integrated Studies, though the precise interpretation of this term is slightly
different in each class. Examples of thematic work in this field might
be a study of a period in history, a country, heating and cooling,
people at work. Studies usually last from two to six weeks and children
are taught in groups or individually. The end-product whereby the
study is presented as a whole may be an exhibition of work in the form
of a wall display or large books, a tape-recorded programme, a series
of lecturettes, etc. The whole process of learning involves extensive
discussion and written work by the children. The role of the teacher
following this approach is to execute the planning stage efficiently,

devise assignments which are educationally valuable, and provide conditions in which the work can be carried out. During the lessons he moves from group to group teaching and suggesting starting points for further study and ensuring that all children are working to capacity. It is against this background of an integrated approach to the Humanities that English is taught.

At this level the teacher is primarily concerned with the child's development of language through the spoken and written word and with providing the optimum conditions for the development of the skill of reading. To this end, children are given assignments which give practice in reading and comprehension and where the execution of these tasks is motivated by the interest of the child their efficacy is so much the greater. Written work is extensive and closely supervised by the teacher. The approach is not successful with all children and each teacher is encouraged to be as flexible as possible in order to achieve the best method and the right degree of direction for any child or group. Some English work such as recording, discussion, or oral presentation of reports arises within the Integrated Studies area. Other facets of the English work such as poetry and fiction reading, drama and imaginative writing are usually study topics or class lessons distinct from the integrated study. Film may find its place in both of these areas of English study.

Our facilities for using film are fairly good: one classroom and the hall can be blacked out, and in other classrooms a back-projection 'daylight' screen is used. Our equipment includes 16 mm and 8 mm projectors, an 8 mm camera, a tripod with pan-and-tilt head, an editor-viewer for 8 mm, and splicers for 8 mm and 16 mm. There is a good quality slide projector and a strip projector. For the recording of sound there are good-quality mains recorders and a portable machine. An overhead projector has recently been acquired.

Since the general movement in primary schools is away from narrowly defined subject-areas rigidly timetabled, it is unlikely that in most schools film will be a curriculum subject at primary level; but the freer structure of subjects and timetable in fact creates even greater opportunities for film material to be introduced into the classroom, and perhaps film will most commonly be associated with various aspects of English teaching. The aim of film-teaching at this stage might be summarised as follows: for the teacher to help children to develop their powers of judgment so that they may benefit from those films and television programmes both factual and imaginative which have the capacity to enrich their lives. If, as a by-product, the children become more selective in their viewing, so much the better; but the main objective at this level is to deepen enjoyment and to provide a stimulus for expression through oral and written work, painting and drama.

Much of the film material I have used has been from free-loan libraries, with occasional extracts or short films from commercial or educational distributors. Many teachers use such films (advertising or promotional material) essentially as visual aids, and thus their major concern will be with the factual contents: how steel is made, in *Listen to Steel*; or how teeth are cleaned, in *Why Bother?* But though the film teacher or the English teacher may begin with a consideration of the factual content, this will be only a starting point from which to develop other ideas.

Using the Unilever film *Twilight Forest*, for example, we might begin to consider the factual content that it presents, but go on to discuss how the film establishes the intensity and density of the forest growth. Alternatively, one might look more closely at the incident where the giant tree is felled to find out how the feeling of suspense is created in picture language and this might naturally lead on to dramatic interpretation.

Children can be helped to an appreciation, at their level, of the effectiveness of techniques in films like *Mirror of Holland*, a view of that country through the reflections in its waterways, or *Dream of Wild Horses* and *Araby*, both about wild horses. Although this type of film tends to hold interest for only a short period, the quality of the children's response in the form of artwork or writing shows the experience has a richness and intensity which is of value educationally. This example, written by a ten-year-old child after seeing *Araby*, is typical; in it the child has added her own fantasy material to that presented in the film.

A large herd of pure white horses and their foals is galloping along, their manes flowing in the wind, their beautiful tails long and white and flowing. Their black hooves blend with the colour of their strong heels. The small foals lag behind. They gallop along the cool waves where the sun is setting and into the cool, clear sea never to be seen again. Mermaids ride them with seaweed for their bridle.

It is for the class teacher to decide which parts of the film to show after first viewing the film himself. Aspects of the film *Araby* that might be studied are the patterns of movement of the horses, the effectiveness of the sound-track, or the uses of light and shade.

We do not, at this level, have formal film lessons with the object of studying film grammar, genres, or directors, yet there is a framework within which the study proceeds. I use the content of films as far as possible as a stimulus to further activity after the viewing; through discussion and other activities I encourage children to look more deeply into both the content and the way in which this is presented by the film.

A free yet fruitful source of well-chosen film extracts can be found in the weekly educational programme *Picture Box*, on Independent television. The same programme is shown twice each week; the teachers' booklet contains a wide variety of suggested activities and reference material for follow-up work. The programme is suitable for children of eight to ten years. Apart from special occasions – a film-show for the whole school or a rare educational visit to a cinema – the teacher's main sources of film material for the classroom are likely to be free-loan libraries, the visual-aids libraries of the Local Education authorities, and television programmes such as *Picture Box*.

Occasionally one is able to show extract material: when I showed the opening of *Great Expectations* it proved to be one of the most successful pieces of film I have used with fourth-year juniors. I introduced the extract by telling the story as far as the point where Pip meets Magwitch. I said nothing about the setting of the film but asked about this in the discussion which followed. After the first viewing the end of the extract was greeted with gasps of dismay and demands for the rest of the story. The children did not appear to be frightened by the convict but were obviously startled at his first appearance. They remembered his dialogue with Pip almost word-perfect. There were the usual questions showing that they were trying to understand the setting: Why were there hanging posts? Why was the convict wearing chains? Why was the convict talking about the other convict when it was the police who were after him? They asked a number of questions about Compeyson. Other topics covered in the discussion and introduced by the children were the brutal treatment of prisoners, the life story of Magwitch, and the marshes.

When the children become really immersed in the story they will extend the situation in their own imaginations beyond the film material. Just before the sudden appearance of Magwitch there is a moment of suspense; the wind sways the trees in the graveyard and Pip is alone. One child wrote: 'Suddenly I feel as if I am being watched . . .' Another child, accounting for the name Pip, attempted a copy of the way in which Joe Gargery spoke in the film: 'My name is Pip, which is the name as what my father was.' The following piece was typical of the written work produced by those who did not wish to join in the discussion:

I had a bunch of flowers to lay on her grave, and I was running quite fast along the road across the windy marshes, for every time I went to see my mother the hanging posts frightened me. I got there. When I found my mother's grave, I pulled out the old flowers and set the new ones down. I noticed the trees were rustling and the bushes moved. I became very frightened and I was just going to run home when I bumped into someone. I looked up and then I heard the rumble of his chains and I knew he was a convict. He had scars all over his face and hands. He shook me upside-down and found what he wanted – an apple to eat. He asked questions of all sorts. He sat me on an old gravestone and threatened me. He told me to get food for him. I said if he didn't lean me back so far I wouldn't be sick and would attend better and he put me up again. He said that if I didn't bring him food tomorrow he would tear out my heart and liver at night, so I swore to God I would. I ran along the road as fast as I could to my cottage.

Another film which produced lively discussion and interesting work was *A Short Vision*, a six-minute animated film which explores in artistic terms the horrors of nuclear war. The film has value in its powerful and immediate visual impact; but it does also raise the problem of whether one should show war films (or anti-war films, such as this one) in a primary school. It has been stated that this film is unsuitable for children under fourteen years of age, because in it the mother figure is destroyed. Before the screening I explained that this was not a happy film. In it, innocent people and animals died and were powerless to resist. The film did frighten a number of children. Most saw it as a war film but somehow more immediate than the kaleidoscope of newsreels and the more typical war dramas. Identification seems easier to achieve and more intense in response to animated films. One ten-year-old child wrote:

A good horror film, the beating music and sounds went well with the scene. The thing that looked like a flying saucer was Hate. Hate destroyed the world. The flame at the end of the film was the last flicker of life and that went out when it destroyed the moth.

Another wrote:

Everyone or everything that saw it was destroyed. First the people looked up and it seemed as if they were screaming. They put their hands over their eyes but their eyes fell out. They perished miserably.

In the film the wise men are destroyed; they looked at the object. But the innocent, those asleep, animals and children also fall victims to the terror. This statement in the film provokes a kind of discussion in which it is possible to see many children asking questions but not really wanting answers, and more children giving impossible and fantastic answers in an attempt to avoid a doctrine of futility; they see in part the message of the film and will not face it, and this is a perfectly natural reaction and to be expected; it is not for the teacher to try to impose an adult reaction by appeals to logic or reason. Many adults have a similar attitude towards the effects of smoking or their ability as car-drivers!

I have included the following extracts from discussion to show the kind of level at which appreciation of this film can take place. The children are talking about the flame.

Ken   No, it was just an emblem.
Chris   What do you mean, an emblem?
Ken   Just to show the dying of the world, the last bit of life on it. That was the last thing.
Teacher You mean it wasn't necessarily real?
Ken   No.

Or again, later in the discussion:

Teacher We have weapons, now, in real life which could do this.
Marion   And the people who sleep will be the people who don't like to fight – the children and the mothers – and they will die as well. And the animals would die, wouldn't they?
Teacher Yes.

John   Even though they didn't fight?
Angela   They didn't have enough time to act; it was too late.
Theresa   Perhaps that thing that came was Hate.
Teacher   Hate. I think that is a good description. It's something
          that we don't really understand but we know it exists. It
          causes things to happen.
Theresa   When it came it was too late, but what would have hap-
          pened if it wasn't too late?

During a discussion with another fourth-year class one child wrote
down as many words as she could which were used to describe parts of
the film.

Before the attack: wild-life forest, peaceful, quiet, dark, sleeping
                     city, rows of dimmed lights, hundreds of dimmed
                     street lights in patterns, no one stirred.
The Weird Object: dark, moving, changing shape, sinister, mysteri-
                     ous, peculiar, unusual, gloomy, frightening,
                     terrifying, threatening, dangerous, sly.
Destruction: terror, fear, burning, searing, ageing, changed to
                     skeletons, spine-chilling eyes, melted, forced
                     out, rotted slowly, heat burned their flesh away,
                     disintegrated, shrivelled up, poured out, blub-
                     bered out, flowed out, pouring blood, perished
                     to a skeleton.

We might contrast the thoughtful discussion or the rich vocabulary
arising from work on *A Short Vision*, with the more down-to-earth
realism (despite the pageantry) of the Agincourt extracts from Olivier's
Henry V. Kenneth afterwards describes the scene:

King Henry's men were preparing large wooden spikes to try and
hold off the oncoming French. The French trot towards Henry's
men. The camera moves along beside them as their trot changes to a
gallop. (*The famous tracking shot*) Henry signals his men to fire
their arrows. The arrows glide through the air like a flock of birds
at the French. Many men were struck and fell off their horses. More
arrows were fired as the English ran up to the French with swords
and battle-axes. Both sides lost lots of men either killed or injured.
Even the horses were being killed. . . .

Most teachers of English, whether using literature or film to stimulate discussion and writing, will balance material which is outside the children's experience with material having strong links with their age-range, locality or interests. The extract from Bryan Forbes's *Whistle Down the Wind* is one that I have used several times, and which has a very strong appeal to young children. I usually tell the story (sometimes leaving out the ending until after the first viewing) and explain where the extract fits into the plot. The story concerns the reactions of three children of different ages, living with their aunt and partly deprived of love and of adventure, when they discover a man in their barn whom they imagine to be the Messiah – he is, in fact, a murderer on the run.

I show the extract two or three times, and after the first viewing usually ask the children to look for specific points – to note what effect the music has, to think about the settings and the dialect. In the discussion it is important to let the children say what they have to say, and to allow discussion points to come from them rather than from the teacher. If there is a pause, I usually wait or ask a child a general question inviting an easy response, which usually starts the discussion going again. Where I have tape-recorded these discussions and listened to them later, I have found that most of the 'vital' teaching points that I wanted to introduce have arisen in the discussion anyway, and the children have dealt with them naturally at their level rather than in response to 'what teacher wants us to talk about'.

Perhaps one of the reasons why *Whistle Down the Wind* is so popular is because the story is told from the child's point of view; in the film the grown-ups are in a different world. A proportion of the class have usually seen the film before. The extract can be used as a starting point in a free drama period. In the following transcript from a piece of free drama by three nine-year-olds, based on the extract, it can clearly be seen how closely the children have copied the idiom of the film script without actually making use of any part of the film plot. The three children, Kathy (eldest), Anna and Charles are in bed. The elder child is trying to get the others off to sleep.

Kathy	Come along, Charles and Anna, go to bed now.
Anna	But I don't want to go to bed.
Kathy	Go on to bed.
Anna	I don't want to.
Kathy	If Auntie comes in and finds you not in bed you know what

	she'll do. She'll tell our Dad. Lie down.
Anna	No.
Kathy	Lie down.
Anna	Do I 'ave to lie down, Kathy?
Kathy	Yes.
Anna	Well, I'm not going to. Charles won't, so I won't.
Kathy	Lie down, Charles.
Charles	Oh, alright. You're just a silly cow.
Kathy	Don't use that language.
Charles	Ouch, I bumped my head.
Kathy	That's what you get for it. That's Jesus.
Charles	That's not Jesus – it's just a feller.
Kathy	Shut up.
Charles	Yer not going to tell Auntie, are yer?
Kathy	No. Alright then, lie down.
Anna	I won't tell her either, Kathy. Good night, Kathy.
Kathy	Good night, children.
Anna	Tell Charles to move up.
Kathy	Move up, Charles.
Charles	No I won't.
Kathy	Quiet, Auntie's coming now. Here she is. Hello, Auntie.
Auntie	Are they asleep? (pause)
Kathy	Yes, they're asleep, Auntie.
Charles	Has she gone, Kathy?
Kathy	Yes, Charles. I told you Auntie was coming. You didn't believe me, did you?
Charles	Our Anna's asleep.
Kathy	Yes, I know. She's a good girl. You're a bad boy. . . .

Summarising, then, the varied activities resulting from viewing films are designed to bring out children's responses at a level that is intelligible to their peers. At the simplest level, this may be the oral or written recapitulation of the subject-matter, but almost inevitably the work transcends this; discussion of the particular may open up more general areas of interest, in which the children test their own experiences against those recorded in the film, and these discussions in small groups may be in the presence of the teacher or without him. But beyond this 'talking over and around', the teacher will have planned the material with definite aims in view to extend the children's experience of what they have seen through drama, writing or art work, introducing individually or collectively other resources of the children, including their imagination. Thus film in the classroom will lead to work not only within specific English disciplines, but also to art and drama and practical film-making, and these latter areas of activity stimulate further exercise of English skills.

My work with children in practical film-making might be divided roughly into the following categories:

a Short exercises in standard or Super 8 mm movie film, or 35 mm transparencies, with or without sound on tape

b Exercises involving film or optical toys to show how single still pictures are made into movies

c Documentary film records of school activities, such as a class project, a school visit or journey abroad

d Viewing and discussion of photographs and home movies that the children or their parents have taken, and have brought to school.

Exercises in standard or Super 8 mm are as many and as varied as the children who do them. The children usually work either individually or in pairs at times when other children in the class are working on their own or in small groups; film is just another medium for recording experience or for imaginative expression, and film-making is just another activity going on. Money for this kind of exercise is very tight so for the sake of economy I try to find out what the children really want to do before they start shooting.

All the following forms of exercise may at some time be attempted by children in primary schools, and the list is not exhaustive: filming drama, re-creating an incident for the camera, looking closely at an object from various angles or in various degrees of lighting, making a 'story' film, arranging a series of still pictures to form a story, making 'scratch' films on blank stock and magnetic track, and editing exercises. Editing exercises may make use of pieces of film that have been edited out of professional films, and blank film may sometimes be obtained from the same sources.

Early attempts at animation through making scratch-films help children to see how movie films are made up from a series of stills. By drawing simple patterns or figures on magnetic track they learn to control the pace of movement. As sixteen drawings have to be made for each second of viewing it is essential to keep patterns simple. The needle-end of a pair of compasses makes a tolerable scriber and colour can be added with felt pens. This is an exercise in which the whole class can take part, the keener children producing more than one piece of work. For re-editing pieces of discarded professional film an animated viewer is really necessary if anything more than a rough job is required. 16 mm splicers which use Sellotape are very much quicker than those which depend on film cement.

An alternative suggestion that may be attempted involves the drawing of a series of pictures for projection on an overhead projector. It is possible to buy 50 ft. rolls of acetate for these machines. Children can make up a story or use a well-known one (e.g. the Nativity or the Norman Conquest) and on the acetate roll make a long frieze or picture scroll. Coloured drawings using 'miracle' pens or 'soft-chalk designers' can be completed by the children once the roll space has been allocated by the teacher. The finished article, frieze or 'tapestry' can be wound across the overhead projector, the audience seeing only a small part at any time. A sound accompaniment made in a drama or music lesson might be added 'live' or on tape. A further development of the work would be to make a movie film or a series of coloured slides of the projected images from the O.H.P.

An 8 mm animated film using puppets or cut-out drawings of figures with articulated limbs might be made. The scope for this kind of work is very wide and can also involve a large number of children in artwork once the basic storyline has been decided upon. This kind of exercise and more especially the work on the overhead projector is exploiting various senses of film form, for example, the panning shot, the sequence of incidents and the difference between long shot and close-up.

I have found that children are fascinated by the Praxinoscope and Zoetrope optical toys. These can be made in the classroom; a zoetrope measuring about twelve inches in diameter can be constructed from dark, coloured card and a wooden disc for a base. The children draw, or cut-out and stick-on, their patterns on rectangular pieces of thin card and fit them into the toys for viewing. A record-player turntable is quite successful for revolving the zoetrope; effects change appreciably at different speeds. Plenty of opportunities should be given for children to see each other's work. After one or two attempts the children are particularly creative in this activity and derive great enjoyment from viewing the work done. Much spontaneous discussion arises around the toys as to the effectiveness of each child's work and children are spurred on to alter and improve their drawings for greater effect. This is an exciting, creative and cheap manner in which to learn something of the language of moving pictures. Further information on the construction of optical toys can be found in A. Kinsley's *Animated Film-making* (Studio Vista).

It has been the school policy for some years to take some movie film of our school journeys, and in recent years children have taken an increasing part in the making of these films. *Valkenburg 69* was one such film in which two children shot a high proportion of the material. For this film, the children decided to take a series of shots in about five or six situations and try to express something of the mood of the children taking part in the journey, e.g. having a midday meal at a hotel (it was fortunate that the dining room was a kind of conservatory and there was ample daylight), climbing a mountain and looking down at the River Rhine at Königswinter, the chairlift at Valkenburg, enjoying continental cakes and pastries at a pavement café. The planning of shots arises as the children talk about how they hope the finished film will appear on the screen. Here is a typical piece of conversation as they toiled up the mountain above Königswinter:

Teacher   Let's stop here for a rest and wait for the others to catch up.
Michael   (peering down at the Rhine through his viewfinder) I think we could make something of this climb.
Pauline   We could take shots going up, then at the top.
Michael   Then go in (*zoom in*) on the ferry boat down there, because we're going on that when we go back aren't we?
Pauline   And if we take a big close-up of it when we get down again, that would get us down on the film, wouldn't it. I mean we would go in on it from the castle up there, then would come the close-up.
Michael   Yes, we'll do that then. Here would be a good place to start filming. I will get some shots of the others as they come up the road.
Pauline   Yes, then take a low-angle shot of the castle up there on top and that will be a good introduction to our shots from the top looking down at the river.

Whether or not there is a formal film script, I find this kind of conversation going on and feel that my role as teacher is to ask questions designed to help the children see more clearly what they are trying to do. Such questions might be of the kind: What will happen if . . . ? With that particular camera angle what will the camera actually see . . . ?

The final category is self-explanatory. Many children are prepared to bring photographs, slides or movie-films, from home. They talk about them in small interested groups. Obviously the flow of material would cease unless considerable tact was used by the teacher; no family wishes to be told how they should have taken their home movies!

It is generally accepted that children who can think in the abstract can make good progress in mathematics. Most work in 8 mm, particularly since as much editing as possible is done in the camera, involves the child in thinking in terms of what the film will look like on the screen. Questions such as how fast the action is going on in the film, and whether to pan or cut are constantly in their minds. Of course, if everything is scripted in the tradition of the 'group-made' film then many of these problems are solved at an early stage and conclusions are committed to paper. But if much of what used to be thrashed out by a written record of story-planning and scripting is now done orally and at the time of shooting then the teacher, at least, should have a fairly clear idea of what is going on and keep asking questions to stimulate some progression of thought and to encourage artistic self-discipline. If the teacher finds himself 'providing' the basic story, surreptitiously lining up shots, taking the 'difficult' ones himself and doing most of the editing and titling, then, for the children, the activity must surely be educationally indefensible. Perhaps the answer at primary level is not to be over-ambitious.

By comparison with many activities in the primary school, practical work in film may be considered a relatively expensive activity in terms of capital outlay, running costs, and time, though it is in fact no more expensive than any other specialised activity in craft, science or physical education. Almost all practical art activity – games, drama, pottery, textiles, etc. – involves costly equipment and a lavish investment of time. The only justification for any expenditure is the value of the experience educationally, and the quality of the children's work within such experience. In the process of performing the activity, devising a story, situation or incident to exploit, the children are engaged in group conversation involving a new register. The language of pictures is well known to them in that they see a great deal of film and television, but for the vast majority it is only a received language. Children hardly ever transmit a series of pictures as a method of communication. It is not sufficient for children merely to find out what will happen if a series of shots is presented in a particular way. As with art and the craft of writing, children gradually realise that expression in film is a compromise between what they think (i.e. what they want to say) and what the medium can contribute to the expression of that thought. The children soon learn that the camera has an eye but not a brain, and cannot by itself discriminate as they can. Personally, I do not subscribe to the view that it is the teacher's role to provide the materials and then hover in the background while the children get on with it. One would hardly give a sewing machine to a child who had no background of needlecraft and say, 'Be creative and express yourself!' The teacher has to provide a secure learning environment where children are willing to take part in the activity.

Initially the teacher can help individual children to hold the camera effectively. A short film consisting of material that has been edited out of previous work might be projected to show what happens when the camera is not held steadily or when the hosepiping, shaking and fast panning become more dominant as the subject of the film than the material that has actually been shot. They must feel free to consult the teacher, and he must feel free to control the pace of the exercise and give the optimum conditions for the success of the activity. In the kind of undirected work where the teacher does little more than make the equipment available to the children, it is impossible to predict or control whether the children will achieve what they hope to record, and failure to do so is bound to discourage them from attaining the success of which they may be capable. Yet I admit that it is the responsibility of the teacher to capture, in the end product or along the way to it, that creative spark which is the child's imprint on the film. While it may be relatively easy to recognise this in the finished film, it is difficult to structure the activity so that this contribution is not squeezed out of existence.

At this point, it is perhaps relevant to define more clearly the role of the teacher in the evolving scene in the primary school. Indeed, one of the teacher's most difficult tasks is how to adjust to the new concepts in primary education. The whole idea of children having a say in the structuring of their learning situation seems inappropriate to the traditionalist and yet when children do have a say this seems to promote a higher motivation to learn. Those who follow the theory that learning through experiment is one sure way of getting children to learn, know just how effective this discovery process is. But not all of children's experimentation is successful and not all new methods are more effective than old ones. We can use the child's environment to assist in

his development: in a group situation, we find that children learn a
great deal from each other; and working on individual studies they
learn through the use of books, reference material and programmed
activities. Where children are encouraged to use the whole school area,
the teacher is faced with new problems connected with the monitoring
of activities ranging far beyond the confines of his classroom. The
teacher is also, perhaps most significantly, concerned with emotional
and social development as well as with intellectual advancement in his
pupils.

Now that subject disciplines are becoming less clearly defined, the
teacher is faced with deciding which activities are educationally valuable
to each individual in his class at any given time. No longer is he able to
rely for guidance on the school examination, the prescribed syllabus
or even his own preconceived ideas about what should be attained by
children at different levels. The teacher using the integrated approach
who has somehow come to terms with the new methods of class management and curriculum changes, while he has contracted out of the position of the authoritarian, intellectual expert, has placed himself at the
centre of the learning situation. He has become a consultant and a
partner in the business of learning to live.

The teacher, then, will be responsible for deciding whether or not to
include film in the educational experience, and how the film resources
may best be exploited, whether by discussion, drama, written work or
art and craft, or whether by creative activity in the film medium.
Creativity means different things to different people: for example,
John Blackie in his book '*Inside the Primary School*' says: 'The creative
instinct, the desire to make something new for oneself, is universal in
man.' Such a concept is likely to be generally acceptable, and its
practical implementation in the primary school generally desirable. But
perhaps too often creativity is identified with crude self-expression,
with almost any release of emotions or eruption of words and ideas
whether or not there is any attempt at evaluation. Implicit in any
creative process is an understanding of the medium in which one works:
thus there is an essentially 'creative' element in the critical follow-up
of film-viewing if it reflects an increasing degree of understanding on the
part of the pupils, and an ability to assess what is possible and what
impossible or less effective in the art form. If film is to be used creatively,
then, it is not merely a matter of giving a child or group of children a
camera and allowing (or even encouraging) indiscriminate shooting,
nor of exposing children to films and allowing a completely free flow

of expression (or none at all) in various media after the screening has taken place. Whether one is trying to educate *through* or *in* film, for children there is learning to be done. The teacher, through his choice of films and his provision of materials through which the various responses will be made, is largely the controller of the educational values to be promoted. He selects the film material and decides at what time of the day and to how many children in the class he will show it. Viewing need not necessarily be a class activity every time and if the more modern projectors which give a good standard of illumination on front projection even without blinds are used, the remainder of the class are able to get on with their activities at the same time.

The same factors, involved in the control of educational values, affect the primary school teacher who is willing to let his children experiment in film-making. Within the current financing of primary schools, the actual amount of 'expression' in terms of finished film footage per child (or per group) will seem infinitesimal when compared with drama, or the spoken or written word: an average film exercise may provide half a minute of finished film, and even a group story-film may well be told in three or four minutes. But finances apart, this is partly connected with the nature of the medium which can compress and distil experience; and in painting, for instance, a good miniature is not necessarily less valuable as an experience because its physical area is less than that of a vast mural. With the increasing use of closed-circuit television and the possibility of allowing children to operate television cameras, further opportunities may be presented at less cost. The electronic camera produces pictures without consuming film; the children see their picture in a large viewfinder, while others in the group or class can see it on a monitor screen. If a videotape recorder is available, then the material shot with television cameras can be played back immediately, and the problem that one has with film stock of waiting for the whole reel to be exposed, processed and returned before any assessment of the results can be obtained is overcome. The running cost of such an experiment is virtually nil, and the recording tape can be wiped and used over again.

One of the basic tasks of the teacher of English is to provide concrete experience, from which can arise a really creative response. By extending experience to include the visual and aural stimuli that film provides, the children are encouraged to develop language skills through speech and writing. If the teacher will assist by gathering together their vocabulary, the fund of words can then be made available for all to use, in speech at least, and for the more able, in written work as well. Discussion is perhaps the most widely used activity following a film viewing, and while this activity is somewhat imperfect at primary level it has proved a useful way of studying both the child's and teacher's roles at this stage.

Whether the activity involves a whole class or small group, the teacher may or may not take part and can structure the degree of his participation. When taking part, I encourage the children to express their thoughts and opinions and they, in turn, strain to express themselves as accurately as possible often appealing to other members of the group or myself in their searching for the right word. When I stay too much in the background their discussion tends to become rather superficial and they are prone to skate around topics without exhausting them. I try to meet the children on their terms, to value what they have to say, and to foster a sense of security within the activity.

This seems to me to be one of the most important aspects of using films in English: visual and aural stimulus invites verbal response; and I often find myself using films where the dominant impact is non-verbal— films with special visual effects such as *Pas de Deux*, *Rail* or *Flight into Life*, films about nature such as *Between the Tides* or extracts from *The Rival World*, silent comedies of Laurel and Hardy, and animated films like *A Short Vision* or a Tom and Jerry cartoon. Film, then, becomes one of the resources of the English teacher, like painting and music and visits outside the school or visitors to the school or experiences originating in mathematics or craft or drama. If the film, like any other experience, can impinge upon the child's world or stimulate the child's imagination, this is the point of contact from which written work or discussion originates. But it would be wrong to think that a response must inevitably be recorded, orally or in writing, to every film experience; I take the view that there is a case for seeing films, as for reading literature, without feeling the need to record a response immediately.

There remains the physical problem of film: it has to be ordered well in advance, unpacked, projected on equipment that in many schools is not easily at hand and in circumstances often far from ideal; and after use it must be packed away again, and posted without delay, and the equipment returned to its store. These are real problems for many teachers, though like all problems they can be magnified unreasonably to provide the excuse for not bothering. The real issue for me is that using carefully chosen films and encouraging exercises in practical film-making are worth while, and I do not any longer see any reason why my use of the media needs justification; nor why its extension to many other primary schools need be longer delayed.

3

A secondary modern school

The function of English teaching – antipathy to
film – short films and creative response –
themes and topics – C.S.E. Mode 3 – feature
film – the Western

Philip Smith, Educational Psychologist, Durham
County Council, previously at Sherburn Modern
School, County Durham

This section inevitably expresses a personal theory of English teaching,
adapted to the needs and demands, the abilities and aspirations of
particular classes in one secondary school in County Durham. It is
not a blue-print for film-teaching (or for English teaching) but rather
an attempt to share experiences which may be relevant to other contexts,
if not immediate at least general.

My work has been based upon a need to give my subject, English,
a definition, mainly because so much of the work English teachers are
presented with could be tackled much more effectively by other members of staff as the need arises. Spelling mistakes or errors in grammar
arise much more naturally and can be dealt with more expeditiously in,
for example, a science lesson than when drawn cold from an English
textbook. For me the English teacher's role should be to add to the
child's sum of experience by presenting him with other viewpoints,
other ways of seeing life than his own restricted view. Then by using
these selective viewpoints the teacher can draw the child into life, to
help him to see and to understand and then to fit himself into the back-
cloth of society. As the most catholic of academic subjects, English
can spread into every subject and aspect of life, and question and
establish every principle for living.

Sherburn reflects the metamorphoses of many Durham villages and,
I suspect, elsewhere; twenty years ago, when its population was eight
hundred, it was closely knit, inbred and involved with its own survival.

Now, following twenty years of undisciplined council building, it has become an amorphous and currently typical Durham village of three thousand people. Originally a predominantly mining area, with all the loyalties, poverty and traditions this has come to mean, Sherburn has developed into a suburb of Durham, three very remote miles away. The pits, closed some years ago, have spread their men over the county and the country, breaking ties that have lasted generations. As the men travel further and further to work and some take their families away to the coalfields in the Midlands, so the village becomes less and less the heart of the people who live in it. No one weeps for the loss of the harshness of life; but with the loss of the meaning to life and the death of the spirit of a united village, Sherburn teeters upon the brink of the suburban sprawl without being able to compensate for its loss or revive its heart.

The secondary school, built in 1960 to accommodate two hundred and eighty children, now rarely houses more than two hundred and twenty. Bordered on three sides by agricultural land, it draws its children from a number of small villages within an area of three or four miles. Few parents work upon the land; the two per cent who do are farmers rather than labourers, working farms of up to a hundred acres. The majority of the fathers are still working in mining, light industry or transport, but outside the village. Almost two-thirds of mothers work, mainly on the local trading estate or in shops. The average size of the family is 3·3.

The classes in the school are mixed and the children are those not selected at eleven for either the grammar or technical school; they comprise sixty-five per cent of their age-group. At a later stage, because the school is a part of a multilateral unit, and if the child shows promise, he or she can be transferred to one of the other sections of the unit. Perhaps as a result of this initial selection of a third of the age-group for other schools, only one per cent of our pupils have ever made the move. Once in the school, the child is placed in one of the two streams A and B, according to his ability in English and mathematics; the flexibility of movement between the streams is only three per cent.

I came to Sherburn in 1964, engaged to teach English and a very few periods of history. The classes allocated to me were all in the upper part of the school, third and fourth year, A and B streams. For my first year I was given five periods with each class, in which time I was to follow a set syllabus embracing grammar, punctuation and other traditional skills, with periods set aside for the novel and poetry. By the time each class came to me it had followed the initial stages of the syllabus with other members of staff. As we always have a number of 'backward children' who have difficulty in reading and consequently with oral and written work, their presence inevitably affects the standard of the work and the nature of the teaching with the 'B' classes.

Though I had every intention of following the syllabus, I also hoped that the children I taught would come to understand themselves and that in their work they would find the need and the liberty to pose questions about life and their part in it. At the end of the first year, however, perhaps because I had become very sensitive to the inflexibility of my work, perhaps because I found children of fourteen and fifteen to be more conventional (and therefore less likely to demand higher standards from me) than I had expected, I realised that I must either change the direction of my syllabus or be willing to accept second-best. Towards the end of the year 1964, with my headmaster's permission, I began to plan a course which used film as both a stimulus for the creative work and as a means of approaching English in a less formal and more natural way. I hoped that what I had learned about life from my film course at Bede College could be made equally available to the children I taught, and I also saw the opportunity to put into practice my own philosophy of English teaching. I wanted to establish a course which was not wholly dependent upon rote learning and examples in textbooks, but which would allow me to use life, whether preserved in the written or filmed arts or in life itself, to help each child develop his talents and then to find a way of expressing them.

At the end of my first year (1965) all I had done was alienate the children to whom I was responsible. Every teacher knows this is possible, perhaps inevitable at times, and can be tolerated to some extent; but what I could not accept was that in addition to their work standing still, their minds remained unaware of the potential which they, as adolescents, had for living. I knew when they were 'fed-up' and depressed or when they were excited by some outburst of aggressive instincts – these levels of feeling were communicated to me, but these were really superficial aspects of their lives: to allow them to exploit only this side of their natures and not to explore a greater and truer range of the feelings and experiences that they undoubtedly had was to fail them.

I had, on a number of occasions in that first year, tried to inject interest into my lessons by using stimuli which I thought they would respond to favourably. These included a series of lessons on the First World War and its poets, discussions on records made by Bob Dylan and the Beatles, and a project on colour prejudice which culminated in a visit to '*Black Nativity*.' I feel these lessons failed (and I never received any work in return which contradicted my opinion) because I was unable to make any real contact with the classes involved; what we heard or saw was never a collective experience, the material was sandwiched between the class and myself and made more of a buffer than a point of contact.

Once I got beyond the planning stage I applied to my L.E.A. for a grant of £80 towards renting my first films; by the end of the academic year 1964–5 I was ready to begin my work. It was, however, not until December 1965 that my first rented film arrived and to bridge the gap I borrowed a number of films from the Film Library of the L.E.A.'s Audio-Visual Centre. These included compilations such as *Early Actualities* and *The March of the Movies* and films by the Lumière Brothers and Arne Sucksdorf's *Stockholm Story*. From these films I selected some technical aspect: camera-angle, the use of a static camera, single-shot films, etc., or I tried to establish the object of the film-maker, the preservation of some special occasion, for example the Black Watch going to war, the record of a daily occurrence – feeding baby, or the presentation of a little comedy, *The Waterer Watered*.

This work occupied one period per week within the normal programme of English work with each of my four classes. I would begin by showing the film, and would then talk about it, making the points outlined above; finally I would re-show the film and set a homework on it, usually involving the reiteration of the basic teaching points of the lesson:

Give one example from the film you have seen of
a an episode which used a static camera
b an episode which used a moving camera in order to tell its story.
My object was to establish with the class a basis for further study of the cinema.

But I soon discovered from the apathy that descended upon my classes that I was merely transferring to film material the structure and qualities of my former English syllabus, without even the justification that I was teaching the mother-tongue! I also learned that films I was tending to dismiss glibly as primitive examples of cinema often contained a much greater potential than at first met the eye; the films we saw were not 'just' records of events but had been selected by the film-maker with the same degree of selectivity and creativity, the same conscious artistic decision that operates in all film-making – what to isolate before the camera, at what point in time to expose the film, whether the material was to be moving or still.

Almost any film has some merit, and it is wrong to make it an easy victim of a critical method without paying adequate attention to both its qualities and the context in which it was made. The antipathy of the children's initial response is more often rooted in their inability to understand what they have seen than in any conscious criticism of the film's qualities. The teacher's problem is twofold: to help the child understand, and to help him appreciate his new knowledge. In practice, both problems are solved by the same process: by discussing the actions of the players and the sequence of events within the film, and by then reinforcing this by re-showing the film, it is possible to demonstrate that first impressions cannot always be depended upon as a true impression, which is an important discovery in the approach to any art form.

Two examples of films which created antipathy in the early stages of my work were *Bird Hunt*, an American experimental film about two small boys who, armed with an air-rifle, go hunting, and eventually to their horror kill, and Georges Franju's *La Première Nuit*, the story of a night spent by a love-sick boy in the Paris Métro. The stories of the two films are so skeletal as to pose no real problem, but the actions of the central characters and their reactions to their situations at first baffled my classes.

> If the boys' object in hunting was to kill, why was the elder boy so disturbed when he did? Why wasn't the smaller boy affected? Why should a little boy whose father is so rich as to send a Rolls-Royce for him bother with a little girl who has to travel by tube? Why in the dream-sequence are they in two separate trains and why do the two trains never meet? What has the little boy learnt when he goes back into the Paris streets after a night in the underworld?

These are the kind of questions I used in order to establish both motive in the actors' behaviour and policy in the director's decisions. I wanted the classes I taught to see the characters' problems in the light of preceding action and then to attempt to analyse these actions with reference to their own experience. I attempted to escape from the over-emphasis on cinematic technique which had dogged my earlier work.

To base the whole of my work on a film-language/grammar approach was of no greater value than a language/grammar approach in English if it did not lead beyond this and help the child to progress emotionally. In one sense it is relatively easy to justify language and grammar teaching within the normal English curriculum, because of their relevance to the normal means of communication. Film-grammar, however, serves no end but its own; it is restricted to a very limited sphere of a child's existence. Film, like any other subject, can be turned into an academic subject – in some contexts justifiably – but it was not my intention to force already dispirited children through an alternative academic jungle which was just as impenetrable, even if different, from the one in which they were already lost.

The children at Sherburn are on the whole working-class; only four per cent of their parents work in white-collar jobs. They have not, however, inherited the traditions of their parents and grandparents; the music and poetry of the coalfields have been lost with the arrival of the new prosperity and their increased mobility. The entertainment which they yearn for leaves little opening for personal creativity, and though old enough to be part of the 'pop-culture', because of their age and their lack of money they are unable to take any practical part in the music and the 'scene'. And even if these inhibiting factors were absent, there is nothing in the accepted sense of teenage entertainment within twenty miles of Sherburn. Durham, our nearest town, has none of the facilities which young people need, no discothèque, no well-run youth clubs; there are few dances and no sports clubs – in short nothing which allows young people to meet others of their own generation. One must, however, accept this sort of situation and try to offer children some way of participating creatively without their being forced away from their own world. I would never want to replace what they consider to be 'creative' – pop-music, dancing, comics, magazines, etc. – with a more acceptable form of creativity, nor do I want to revive the traditional: my aim is to create something which is an amalgamation of the old and the new and then to give them the opportunity of creating something which is part of their own world.

Five years ago when I first began working in the school I was not aware of this; only now has any pattern begun to emerge which I could call a 'scheme'. After my initial attempts to make my work academically acceptable by presenting it as a technical and historical study, and its failure, I attempted the 'thematic approach' of using related films, poetry, novels, short stories, etc. I booked a series of films, all dealing with people at work. Beginning with the classic British documentary *Coalface* (a seemingly obvious choice in an area so dependent upon coalmining, but one which generated little interest), *The Days of Whiskey Gap* and *City of Gold* – both about the Klondyke gold-rush – *En Passant par la Lorraine*, Franju's film about the steel mills of Lorraine, Flaherty's *Louisiana Story*, a film which works on both the level of the feature film and upon that of the documentary, the Shell documentaries *North Slope Alaska* and *Firefight at Ahwaz*, and finally another National Film Board of Canada documentary, *Stampede*. Of this group, *Louisiana Story* was undoubtedly the most popular, and *Firefight at Ahwaz* the least, the irony being that basically the two films are describing the same feature of oil-drilling – the blow-out. The reasons for the excellence of the one over the other is obvious to anyone who knows the two films. *Louisiana Story*, with its well-defined central characters, allows us to become totally involved in their lives and environment, of which the oil-drilling is an incidental part: we learn about the processes with much detailed illumination through our involvement with the characters. By contrast, *Firefight at Ahwaz* deals only with the processes of extinguishing a well fire, and even the main character (a real enough person) is blurred by the haste of the film-maker to capture the central event.

Of the remaining films, only *En Passant par la Lorraine* presented any of the difficulties which I mentioned earlier. Though never a popular film, its thesis that the great automatic plants were dehumanising the people of the Lorraine was accepted and generated a considerable amount of discussion. For though unemployment in our area arises from there being too little industrial development rather than from the encroachment of automation, I have always found my classes to be aware of the gradual replacement of human skills by machine uniformity, and though most of them will go into unskilled professions they nevertheless maintain an attitude that it is the machine that is threatening and supplanting their 'skill'.

In discussing the film, we noted the absence of human beings in almost all the processes, and even where we knew people must be working the director had frequently and deliberately chosen not to show them. I drew attention to the fact that in the film the only parts of the process where the human presence is necessary are where a decision has to be made. The steelmaker, like a chef tasting the soup, throws a shovelful more sand into the mixture, making or breaking a process by exercising a skill which no machine could possibly have. But Franju's optimism for man's place in the process has been significantly changed by the development of computers, able to exercise judgment and memory more infallible than any human being; and the discussion is thus able to go far beyond the film, and eventually into speculation about future societies.

Having shown each of the films, I used a wide selection of poetry and prose which was related to the central theme of work, ranging from the poetry of Robert Service written at the time of the Klondyke gold-rush, through to contemporary poetry, short stories of D. H. Lawrence and Frank Schaeffer, and each week the children produced work related to the material we had seen or read. As yet I was not successful in helping the children to write from their *own* experience in responding to the material used, and most of what I received as homework tended to be a reiteration of the narrative of the film, lacking the personal mark of the child involved, though there were occasional exceptions, such as these:

The Silhouette of Darkness
The whistling wind whistles in its ghostlike ways,
clanging of chains, the immobile tubs
all so desolate and bare, a black silhouette of memory.
No more the crowds of black dusted faces,
now the tunnels are left to the rats.

Christine

Sherburn Hill Pit
Towering pit, Bright machinery
once clanged, clattered, banged. Now all is still,
the pit is dead. No man walks here but me.
the rats hurry scurry through the decaying falling chambers.
Once green the paint flakes and falls.
Once active the heap stands alone, decaying, dead.

Barry

Though using a central theme was a great improvement on the previous approach, I found work of this quality rare. Only two children in any one class were adept enough to see connections outside the film. In addition I often found that what I wanted to use from a film was not the topic within the film which had interested the class. For example, in *Louisiana Story* my pupils were far more interested in the family than in the drilling for oil, and I found it more profitable to follow their line of thought than to drag them along mine. Since then, I have been quite content to use each film as it comes, or to book a group of films by one director, and I have found it much easier to use a man's philosophy as shown in films by Hitchcock or John Ford, than in a group of films related, often very loosely, by theme.

As I mentioned earlier, in order to establish that one approach is better or more successful than another, we must look at the work done by the child, and as my personal approach has been affected by the standard of work done, so have the methods I have used in the class-room. Every teacher becomes sensitive to the effect that any lesson generates and can adjust the level of his teaching or the intensity of approach according to his reading of the classes' moods. Both the 'grammar' and the thematic approaches to the film were preconceived notions on my part in that I went into the classroom intent upon producing a given effect and not allowing any side-issue to divert me from my aim, and I expected the class to react in a certain way, without making any allowances for their personal views. When they did not, I was forced to examine what I had done and attempt to modify my teaching methods.

Eventually I was able to reach a stage where I could treat each film individually and yet still approach it with some interest and conviction, for, as in any teaching process, I was looking for a focal point upon which my work could depend for its consistency. The first inkling of what I wanted came quite early in the course with a Harold Lloyd short, *Haunted Spooks*. In this film there is a sequence when Lloyd, intent upon suicide, is balanced upon a bridge parapet about to throw himself off. Before he eventually manages this he is approached by a number of people seeking directions or wishing to know the time. This particular scene interested my 3A class because they could not decide whether, if faced with a possible suicide, they would act any differently. Would they try to restrain the suicide or would they pretend they had not seen him? Obviously there is no right answer to this, but the very fact that the film had exposed an uncertainty seemed to prove to them that it had some value other than entertainment.

Though the discussion of our reactions to a suicide attempt, arising from the Lloyd film, was not in itself significant for that lesson or for the course, it was perhaps a breakthrough in my understanding of how I wanted to use film in the classroom. I had found a use for film which was outside the film itself and though it was some time before I got beyond this point or a film generated as much interest, and over a year before the discovery became relevant to the creative work in the course, nevertheless it was an occasion which I could look back to for justification of my work.

Obviously it is not enough to explore a situation and then simply to reiterate actions occurring in that situation upon paper; this is bald mimicry. What I wanted was that each child should leave the lesson and, with the aid of the experience, explore his own feelings and then produce something which was emotionally meaningful to him in his own situation. Towards the end of the first year of the course the children in the top 'A' stream produced an anthology of their poetry and prose. Though I had achieved a part of my aim, that of freeing their tongues, what they had written was not emotionally connected with any film I had shown them: the film and the consequent discussion had given them an excuse for releasing an accumulation of extreme verbal violence, almost invariably directed against their parents. I felt that in terms of my aims I could not justify this violence, however therapeutic it might be; I felt I needed to construct rather than destroy, or eventually I would be destroying myself in a wave of adolescent anarchy. This made me realise that what I most wanted was work which was self-analytical, in that the child was required to examine his reactions to what he had seen, and positive in the sense that at the end of the analytical process he was one emotional step up the ladder to maturity.

The films which had initiated this outburst were included in the last of my thematic collections, this one being on 'Youth' – extracts from *Tom Brown's Schooldays*, *Zéro de Conduite* and two features, Don Owen's *Nobody Waved Goodbye* and John Schlesinger's *Billy Liar*. Though the extracts made little more impact than a trailer, the two features sharpened the children's wrath. The apparent lack of understanding on the part of the respective parents in the films blinded the class to the obvious failings of the two adolescent 'heroes'. And in the discussions that followed I found myself following the same line of prejudice; I was so eager to use the class's experience that I did not make enough balance between the faults of the film-parents and their wayward sons. In addition to this I also found that the classes I showed the film to had made up their minds about the outcome of the film long before it finished. I had told them the films were about youth and they, in the belief that parents are always wrong, left no room for

C

doubt. This experience finally convinced me that the use of themes was not the approach that was going to work with my classes. I wanted each film to be a new experience, fresh and ready for an unbiased opinion. Though the children I was teaching had been able to write about the films, they had not been influenced by anything other than the most superficial aspects of the films. The emotions they described were not those which were found in the film and the film became no more than an excuse for attack and abuse, not an extension of their intimate experience.

Amongst the third-year group beginning their work with me in the second year of my course was a girl, Ruth, whose home had been shattered by her father's desertion. In addition to her normal classwork and homework she produced a large quantity of unsolicited poetry. This had an insight which was her personal vision of the Truth, a product of her circumstances; she did not produce vitriol where poison would have been justified, but wrote with sympathy and with insight into the lives of a wide range of people and situations:

Aberfan

It was peaceful,
No one had any cares in the world.
They went about their business,
Not knowing what fate had in store for them.
It was morning
The village was buzzing with children
Going happily to school,
Happily because it was a half-day holiday in the afternoon.
But it was morning
And on the hillside above the village
Loomed a pit-heap
Huge, black, wicked looking.
It watched as if human
The tiny village of Aberfan.
If someone had looked up, someone, just for a moment
They would have seen the evil approaching them.
But no one did.
One glance could have saved a generation.
Aberfan will be dead just like its children.

Ruth's poetry was mundane in that it dealt with the world around her, yet it was both revealing and acute in its sensitivity. Though her ideas were controlled by a very personal vision of life, I saw that by directing her experience, having it focussed upon one event or sequence of events, she had been helped to see her own life more clearly. Where Ruth's experience had been a real one I saw that with care I could use a film to produce a similar, though less traumatic, effect; by showing a film I was producing an experience which, freed from the conventions and routines of their own lives, could allow my pupils to see the events in the film from a position in which they were both involved and yet detached from the actual events. Ruth, because of her history, had been shocked into seeing the life of an adolescent from a singular viewpoint and she had come to express herself in a very personal and characteristic way. I hoped that presented with powerful experiences my children would respond with similar acuteness.

In the former and more closely knit village community, children would have been accustomed to share many adult experiences – birth and death, mining injuries and deprivation through strikes and lock-outs; such experiences would have contributed to a process of self-awareness and discovery. But in the smaller family units, in a world of social security benefits and a National Health Service, children have fewer opportunities for emotional development; most of all they are ignorant of their own reactions to the ordinary, their palate is so sated by the extraordinary. A film can provide an opportunity for placing life before them, life simplified by seeing it held at arm's length where they are not directly involved in the action, only in their own reaction. In a film they can see cause and effect and be emotionally involved without being physically responsible for any of the decisions the film requires.

A film which does this successfully depends upon its contribution to the ordinary life of the child. If, after having seen the film, having discussed it, possibly having seen it again and finally having written a piece of work, the child's grasp of life is in no way advanced nor his imagination touched, then the film, for that individual or for the whole class, is a failure. If after following through the process the child can write poetry like the following, then I believe I am achieving some measure of success:

> A silent town,
> The present, the future and the past,
> Fear of what is to come.

The frenzied motion of the sea
Is now in my focus.
A beginning of thought
But there is no end.

Mary

or:

My mind wanders when I am alone,
through wild lands where cold winds are blown
Along an old route in a foreign land
Towards the place where the mountains stand.

Thom

or:

I can remember when I was about seven, I used to walk around with my pram. Marion got a prop through the hood of her pram. We went to the Zoo. The elephants a baby one. The giraffe stroking them. Feeding the seals. Rain started. Yorkshire moors. Picked some heather. Anniversary Jean had a big nylon dress. Like a ballroom dress. I was sitting beside her, you could hardly see me for her dress. Everyone asleep, very frightened. Kept thinking of people I knew who had died. Grandad very bad. Allan, my brother, crashed in his van. The boy in with him killed. In hospital had stitches.

Norma

These pieces originated in a discussion of the opening of *Zéro de Conduite*, where for a very short time one of the boys in the film sits on his own in a railway carriage trying to occupy himself. In the lesson we had talked about how one could occupy a period of boredom by playing or day-dreaming and the type of play one person could indulge in or the kind of fantasies and memories they could stir up.

The selection I have quoted above are the best out of sixty pieces of work for, though I had developed both a method and an approach to teaching film, I had still not managed to get from my pupils the sort of startling improvement in the standard of their work which I wanted. It was not until the next intake of third-year pupils in 1966 that I conquered this barrier. This new group accepted the validity if not the value of the work with films, for it was relatively easy for me, as the teacher, to become involved and to understand what I intended and how far I was achieving it. Children come to their school-work with a narrower expectancy, and with a more conservative analysis of the purpose and the means and it often takes longer for them to accept what they are not familiar with.

Until this date my reasons for continuing the course had been supported by two or three accidental discoveries and a handful of inspired poems; with this group, however, I reached a point where the whole class responded, rather than isolated individuals.

Les Mistons (directed by François Truffaut) is about five adolescent boys living in a small French town who, in the space of their summer holiday, suddenly and painfully become aware of the attractions of a young woman, Bernadette, some years their senior. Though they have known her for many years, the sudden realisation that she 'is more than someone else's sister' is a violent one and their reactions equally violent. They follow her everywhere, fondling the saddle of her bicycle and going through pantomimes of adulation, vulgarity and lust. When they discover that she is being courted by a young gym teacher, Gérard (whom secretly they admire), their jealousy is fanned to excess. They plan to destroy the relationship, shouting abuse at the couple, disturbing them as they make love, scribbling insults upon the walls of the town and 'practising obscenities' in full view of the couple. They do all this without realising that the lovers are unaware of the very special attention they are receiving.

When Gérard leaves on a mountaineering trip they send Bernadette a cheap postcard depicting embracing screen lovers, signing it maliciously with the nickname the lovers have given them, 'the little Bastards' (Les Mistons), and then in the absence of their rival they set out to practise and exercise their new discoveries on new subjects, wallowing in orgies of voyeurism and lust. They are completely unmoved when they hear the news of Gérard's death, looking now upon Bernadette as an accomplice in their temptation as she has, quite unwittingly, introduced them to the 'fate and the privilege of the flesh'.

To use *Les Mistons* in the classroom, I think the teacher needs to be sure of the class in the sense that the material is emotionally close to the experiences the children are having, have recently had, or will have in the near future. The film is basic and unsentimental in its treatment of adolescent passion, exploring the normal signs of 'calf-love' and the correspondingly characteristic obsessions. The eroticism within the film is as passive as 'crushes' inevitably are, yet the symptoms, the inability to make contact (simultaneously the desire not to make contact), the need to love as a group and the urge to mock what they most need, make *Les Mistons* a valuable and sensitive film to have in the classroom.

The teacher can approach *Les Mistons* on one of two levels; firstly, it can be related to an experience which is familiar to the child and which in analysis it is able to place in some category of experience. Secondly, the film expands the primitive quality that the boys' love has, by developing and comparing the relationship between Bernadette and Gérard; it becomes apparent that Gérard's love is as destructive and basically as egocentric as that of the five boys. In the scene in which the lovers watch a mantis devour its mate, we are aware of the partial destruction of any individual when he creates such a relationship. (A perfect poem on this subject is R. H. Thomas's 'Careers'.)

This latter approach is perhaps a little more advanced in its use of concepts than the former, where there is an immediate and obvious point of contact between the boys in the film and the school audience – 'the crush'. Though I would never directly link the two in direct reference ('Did you feel like this when you were fourteen?'), it is simple to establish that the signs of the phenomena are universal by collecting the class's reactions to what has happened in the film. A child saying that 'Les Mistons' were frightened to show their real affection is in fact seeing the boys in the film within the limits of his experience and it is then simple to establish that their behaviour was characteristic.

One may also follow the many references made in the script to the Original Sin, the temptation of Eve/Les Mistons, by Satan/Bernadette and her/their loss of innocence. For the boys Bernadette is the apple, and their fall from paradise into the 'real' world marks the end of their idyllic chilhood. This line of investigation is very close to the hearts of my children; they are at an age when their childhood stretches behind them as a pageant of summer days and a life full of happiness and games. They feel that life has gone sour on them and that their exit from this paradise has left them looking at a life which has no future and little potential happiness. In a discussion such as this there is the revelation of a communal experience, and the subsequent written work is enriched by the realisation that what happened to them, and what they regarded as personal is unique, not so much because it happened but because of their view of it. Both *Les Mistons* and this class felt nostalgia for a past which had potential but had been lost before it had fully been explored. I am reminded here of the story which Gérard tells of his father who, as a young man, had 'stood up' a young girl on their first date because he had developed a boil on his nose. And now, after twenty years, hardly a week goes by without his remembering her.

To class 3A this film was a vision of reality, a Truth. They understood action and reaction and then felt that they could explore their own experiences without anyone regarding them as either being perverted or unnatural. *Les Mistons* is an exploration of love without sugared romanticism and the children in this class accepted what it said without hesitation. They reacted passionately and with equal savagery and yet the poison that came out of them came as an antidote, they attacked only themselves for their own inadequacy. They explored experiences they had never before made public and, when they wrote, it was not in bitterness, nor was it in any way directed against the world around them; what they revealed was private both in personal terms and in the sense that they as a group had it as part of their collective legend.

> Once my life was spent in playing armies
> But as I grew older I grew out of it.
> Then one day I was given a bike
> Which meant I was growing older.
> One night I went out with a girl
> I took her to the pictures,
> The film became interesting and I forgot the girl.
> When the film ended she was gone.
> That was when I realised that I wasn't really older.
> *David*

> *Other People*
> When I was young they didn't really matter,
> But now I need them.
> I want them.
> Without them life wouldn't be really worth living,
> I would be bored,
> Lost in a land of loneliness where any friendship could find me.
> *Dorothy*

Do we ever get the chance to wonder?
Are we ourselves, like those boys
who jump in puddles and chalk on walls.

Thom

Love
A woman of seventy
A man of fifty
Fell in love one day.
They sat in the park and
Feeding the ducks
What a funny way to love.
They went every day to the park
Feeding the ducks
Till one day he died
And the old woman always wore black.

Margaret

I have used *Les Mistons* since this particular occasion without the same effect or success, perhaps because I know it so well that the simplicity of my earlier reaction has been lost and the plane on which I automatically work is above that of a child coming new to the experience. This one occasion, however, taught me that there was nothing incompatible in using film as a creative stimulus as well as appreciating it as an artistic medium. Where the film had been nothing beyond a story on celluloid, it now became a stimulus to the child to ignore the barriers that fiction puts up and to create something new from his own life.

In the following year, 1967-8, knowing that it was possible for nearly all of the children in my classes to produce something of quality, I began to work on the idea that once the barriers of personality were broken down and the child had been encouraged to develop his own style of writing then it was possible for the whole group to produce work which was creative and repaid them for their effort. How, beyond the basic application of teaching skills, I achieve this is a mysterious amalgam of calculable factors and luck. Though, philosophically, I am concious of my aims, the process involved in reaching them involves a great deal more than technique. My basic assumption is that each child in a class is an individual and therefore his work and results must be regarded and treated individually and must, therefore, never be compared with the work of another child. Each piece of work is judged on previous pieces by the same child. The breakthrough comes inevitably because of the appearance of a line or an image in one poem. I always look out for some hint that the child has been carried outside the limits of his normal work. Once this has happened then I can begin in earnest to help the child to develop his insight along the lines which the signs indicate. In doing this a rapport is developed which eventually is fruitful and creative both for my pupils and for me.

Once the child has developed the skill of writing personally the greatest barrier is overcome. What I try to do then is gradually to encourage him to draw less of his inspiration from films and more from life, simply by asking him to write on any topic he likes. If the time allowed for this is made as liberal as possible, then even though the child still resorts to the film for his basic idea, any extension or elaboration must result from the effects of his own experience.

In practice this period of weaning takes most of the two years I teach these children. Only in the fifth form do they begin to use their judgment and their skills to examine their relationships and their reactions to ordinary situations. Unfortunately it is only in the past two years that children have remained for this fifth form in any numbers. However, having used C.S.E. Mode 1 for two years, in 1968 I began a Mode 3 course in English which was based on the use of film and depended largely upon the child's ability to view the world critically. The students who take the course are encouraged to select their own topics and to express them in a way and using a style which they feel is fitting for the subject. Once the school-leaving age is raised one will find opportunities for introducing this element of the work to more and more children; and it is at this level (the fifth-form work) that I found the justification of what I had been doing.

The First Night
He looked on in terror
As the sun sank below the horizon,
Only the glow of the after-light
gave a clue that light existed.
He sat, frightened of the opening heavens
and the mystic silver globe.
The heat of the ground
was drained by the bitter night.

Keith

Who Am I?
I am me.
But you are also me.
You are you

But so am I.
We are us
But so are they.
But I am me
Because of you and us.
Kath

Though I accept that the demand for literacy in contemporary society will not be met by the production of poetry – the letter to the employer, complaints about faulty merchandise, are more likely to be the norms of literary performance – I do feel that if I were to place the emphasis upon the practical, as opposed to the emotional, I should be ignoring a basic need. I feel that I must provide my children with some system for thought, some philosophical basis upon which they can begin to build their lives. The use of poetry provides them with the opportunity for exploring their own reactions to life and of establishing the validity of their personal opinions. The use of poetry established itself because in many respects it is so close to the form of the film, having the same urgency of image, suddenly juxtaposing disparate and dissimilar images and ideas. Both poetry and film can bend and twist time, place and person and yet remain ultimately comprehensible. Both can select to a fine degree and yet remain an intelligible whole, for instance an image can be shown and seen as singularly as a sculpture, and then be collected meaningfully with a number of others without losing its initial identity.

Both forms can be used fully within a relatively short period of time where a novel or play would require much longer periods of study. In addition, poetry makes fewer demands upon the writing stamina of the children I teach; it is a habit which is easier to acquire and less complex than prose writing, and, being more distinctive in style than prose, provides a personal style from the very outset. Finally, and this is really the major factor, poetry is the most personal of the forms of literature, balanced neatly between the esoteric and the universal. Even though a child's initial observations may seem mystifyingly subjective to an outsider, as the child becomes less and less involved with the narrative of the film so the poetry becomes more intelligible.

This may sound as if I am rejecting completely the teaching of conventional English, especially literature; but such an impression would be false. To reject what is offered by conventional teaching of literature in favour of a study exclusively of film would be to rob the children's minds of experiences which I regard as valuable, indeed essential. But my experience shows that to come to literature gradually having first experienced another more immediately accessible art form, such as film, is the best means of heightening and broadening the children's perception, and preparing them for the concentration required in the study of conventional literary forms.

I found this especially true with my fifth-year pupils who, having talked about a great number of films, were able and willing to read and discuss Shakespeare, Milton, Yeats and Eliot when they were eventually introduced to them. The confidence necessary to appreciate, analyse and discuss the complexities of art – whether novel, play or poem – had already been built up between teacher and pupils by earlier approaches to film; and they could begin to appreciate both the quality of the writing and the techniques by which the writers' vision and imagination had been communicated.

But if by the time my pupils are fifteen they have not reached the desired standard of literacy, and cannot achieve the easy enjoyment of literature which we tend to take for granted, then I am prepared to push this aspect of teaching into second place and to concentrate my immediate attention and theirs on preparation for the world outside the cotton-wool existence of the school; other motivations may later encourage them to acquire skills and aptitudes which have not yet been formed in the school. It is not enough to assume that the child will cope with the uncertain experiences of life by instinct and native wit, for instinct and wit (like all subjective processes) do not necessarily function adequately under conditions which alarm or confuse. The need to interpret situations and reactions to situations with some awareness and integrity is paramount. Poetry is concerned with this search for stability in chaos and with the examination of reality through personal reaction to experience.

The society in which our children at Sherburn live demands that they have more behind them than academic skill; I feel, therefore, that my work must extend further than the correction of errors. The needs of the child are both social and personal: social in the sense that the child, and the eventual adult, has the need to live and to communicate, and personal in the need to communicate with skill. Our children are disadvantaged both intellectually and culturally; they are often limited in their ability to communicate with a world grown sophisticated, which demands social skills that they lack and paper qualifications they cannot attain, and which pays little attention to their personal qualities and their integrity.

Film (and the work arising from it) can help them to understand the world and its values, and can also help them to value themselves. It gives them an opportunity to explore a world beyond their immediate existence and yet one of which they are a part. They can, if left to their own devices, drift along oblivious of their part in society, and I want them to be aware of this and to appreciate life in terms of living at more than a superficial level. They can at least begin to feel that life is there, and that they can live it according to their beliefs and abilities. Basically I want them to appreciate themselves and to become aware of themselves as having a real part to play in the society to which they belong.

Let me describe how I set about achieving some of these objectives. The film is the common experience: both child and teacher see the same things; our reactions are basically social yet simultaneously idiosyncratic. So having once watched the film I always find it necessary to go through the film event by event in order to establish what happened and why. Often both child and teacher will find that their memory tricks them; the sequence of images, even of scenes, may be confused, events misplaced, characters overlooked, relationships misunderstood. Only by this recapitulation can the true order be established; but more than this is achieved. As a group, we pool what all the individuals have seen and understood, so that when the film is viewed again (which is possible immediately with a short film), new grounds for discussion arise when original individual reactions and the compiled group response are both measured against the film. With a feature film, a relevant extract may be treated in this way and the discoveries about the extract can then be discussed in the wider context of the whole film.

The selection of the thirty or forty films used each year is of great importance to the teacher, for he must be sure of the quality of the films he is to use in order to produce the desired effect. As an example I will take an eleven-week term in which a series of unrelated films were shown to each of the four classes I taught. These were: *Corral,*

Neighbours, The Digboi Story, Distant Drums, The Flying Deuces, The Day, Simon, La Jetée, Nuit et Brouillard, Zéro de Conduite and *Les Mistons.*

Of these only *The Digboi Story* was badly received because its account of the discovery and development of a small Malaysian oil-field is spoiled by a clumsy narrative and a dull objectivity, and in no way helped by the performances which are intended to give a quasi-reality to the story. Of the other ten films, I had previously used *Les Mistons, Zéro de Conduite, Neighbours* and *Corral.* Though basically my pupils agreed with what Jean Vigo was saying about schools in *Zéro de Conduite*, their attitude was summed up by a boy who asked: 'After they rebelled what did they do?', for the film offers no continuation other than that of complete destruction.

Neighbours is a short film by Norman McLaren about two men whose pleasant lives are disrupted by the appearance of a flower on the boundary between their homes. Excess of violence follows excess and eventually the two kill each other and are buried with identical flowers on their graves. The film ends with the motto 'Love Thy Neighbour'. To tell his story McLaren uses a series of camera tricks: the men float in ecstasy across the lawn; they are suspended three feet above the ground; the boundary fence shifts at the nod of a head, and eventually the two are buried in a series of shuffling movements. Obviously this kind of technique appeals to any child and I have found an immediate sympathy amongst children for the film, which is a great advantage.

I begin by asking a number of questions such as 'What are the two men doing at the beginning of the film?', 'How can you tell they are friendly?', 'At what point in the film do their insults change to actual violence?' in order to establish certain basic chronological facts about the film. I can then move on to questions which will require the child to make certain judgments – 'Why do you think the houses are made out of cardboard?' and 'Why do the two men eventually become Red Indians?'. By the end of the lesson I hope that I would have established certain ideas about both the film and the ease with which civilised men revert to savages. This is not, of course, a statement that I would make explicitly as it would tie the subject down too firmly to allow most children to write with any freedom.

The two feature films amongst this list, *Distant Drums* made by Raoul Walsh and starring Gary Cooper, and *Flying Deuces*, a Laurel and Hardy comedy, both have qualities which make them ideal films for class use. They both have a very strong story line and follow definite patterns of behaviour according to cinema traditions. In *Distant Drums*, Quincy Wyatt, an ex-army officer who has exiled himself in the Florida Everglades after his Indian wife has been murdered by soldiers, leads a group of Indian fighters into the swamps in order to destroy a fort from which gun-runners are supplying the Seminole Indians. Having destroyed the fort and finding their retreat blocked, they are forced to make a march of two hundred miles through hitherto unexplored swamp. The final solution is the confrontation between Wyatt and the Indian chief in which the Indian is killed.

For me the strength of *Distant Drums* lies in the character of Quincy Wyatt, and in selecting suitable extracts I looked for scenes which demonstrated his ability to sway other men and the influence which he had over the lives of others. In doing this I also drew attention to the similarities between Wyatt and the strong character portrayed by the Indian chief, to make it obvious to the class that the only possible solution to the film could be this final meeting.

I used *Flying Deuces* with a slightly more 'academic' aim to demonstrate the place of pathos in 'great' comedy. Like most of Laurel and Hardy's comedies, there are scenes in *Flying Deuces* when laughter becomes irrelevant and tears would be more natural; my examples were the scene in the film where Oliver Hardy, having fallen in love with the chambermaid in the Paris hotel in which he and Stanley are staying, proposes to her, only to find she is already married; and the final scene in the film when Stanley, having lost Ollie in a plane crash, walks along a country lane, bundle over his shoulder, large flower to his nose, and meets the ever-suffering Ollie reincarnated as a horse. The relevance of these two scenes is the statement they make, both definitive in terms of the artistry of Laurel and Hardy and revealing in the scenes' contribution to our understanding of their characters as portrayed on the screen.

Of the remaining films I used in that term, Peter Finch's *The Day* generated some interest in the early scenes as the little boy, going to town alone for the first time, takes time off to explore things he must often have seen whilst driving with his father and never been able to explore. Unfortunately the interest is lost when the film wanders off into irrelevant detail about the object of his errand, to collect relatives, to see his new-born brother.

Simon struck some chords, and the central idea of an overgrown weakly ten-year-old produced some interested comments:

Simon
In a world of his own,
no one to play with,
no one will accept him
for what he is.
His mind does not think
like other boys,
and so he is rejected,
and he can't do anything about it,
For he has neither the strength
nor the mentality to do so.
And so he is left out in the cold.

Joan

Nuit et Brouillard, Alain Resnais' account of the German concentration camps, is a film which is its own mouthpiece; its comment is so violent emotionally that I was neither willing nor able to discuss it. For once I am convinced that the 'film was the message' and further discussion or writing would have been superfluous. The final film of the collection was the most surprising success; Chris Marker's *La Jetée*, which uses still photographs to suggest movements through time and space of a prisoner in World War III and makes use of concepts which confuse even adult audiences. It is a film which I found excited my children, and they were willing to speculate on a number of abstract and complex ideas, the most interesting being that if a man went back in time and in his new 'present' performed some act which affected history, would he on his return find his true 'present' altered by what he had done in the past? They also produced a number of interesting speculative poems:

The clock of life turns time.
Time dies with life
World time.
Time around the world.
Time goes quickly
End of the world. End of time.

Heather

Suspended in a life dreaming,
dreaming of the past, present, future,
dreaming of childhood,
dreaming of his marriage,
dreaming of his death.
Then all too soon
he realised that he should not have slept,
because he had died.
Dead in a silent sleep.

Shirley

Film-teaching can to some extent bridge the gap between the semi-literate and literacy. It is possible to conduct a lesson without loss if the class is backward (in the sense that their written work is below standard). One can establish the form that the film has taken and then divine what the director's intentions are, and in this way film succeeds where literature cannot, because it allows the children with lower ability to escape the restrictions of the written word. Because the film is visual/aural, it allows them to understand without possessing any mechanical skills, and also to appreciate because they have the experience of having seen many other films. However, because of the limitations of their general knowledge (which the ability to read widely would give them), they are often limited in their understanding of the background against which the film is set, and because often it is not their background, the appreciation of the film is that much lessened. Film is at once a success in that it succeeds where the printed word has not, and a failure because it depends for so much of its background on what the written culture provides.

The feature film inevitably places a strain both upon the organisation of the school and upon the teacher who is to use it. Few feature films are shorter than eighty minutes long, and many are longer; and how one justifies or arranges for the use of a whole morning or afternoon is really the concern of the individual teacher and his headmaster. The answer in my case was greatly simplified by a very sympathetic headmaster, and by having an examination timetable geared to the use of films.

Generally speaking my films arrive in time to be shown to all of my five classes at the beginning of the week, so allowing me to select suitable extracts for showing during the individual classes' lesson times. If we take as an example John Ford's *She Wore a*

Yellow Ribbon perhaps I can make the process a little more clear.

The film is set in a cavalry post in the mid-1870s, and traces the final seven days in the career of Captain Nathan Brittles (John Wayne) who has been in the cavalry since leaving his father's farm 'barefoot and in blue jeans' forty years before. Brittles, assigned to command his last patrol as escort for his C.O.'s wife and her niece, fails to complete his task. And, in the retreat from the fire-gutted stage-post which had been their destination, he is forced to leave his lieutenant Cohill (John Agar), in command.

Though refused permission to return to relieve Cohill, Brittles (now officially a civilian) returns to his troop, and after a vain attempt to talk peace with the Indian chief, stampedes the Indians' horses, leaving his men to escort them to their reservation. Satisfied at last, Brittles rides away to the new territories of California, only to be brought back by the news of his appointment by the U.S. President as 'Chief of Scouts'.

She Wore a Yellow Ribbon, though often balanced on the brink of cliché, is a Western of considerable distinction, in that it abides very closely by the conventions of the Western yet nevertheless remains a unique film on a personal level of achievement. We might open up the topic which relates this film to the pattern of film-making peculiar to the Western.

Teacher Is there anything in this film which you recognise from other films you have seen?*

Bill The hills, they're the same ones we saw in *Stagecoach*.

Teacher What else? What other connections are there with *Stagecoach*?

Dave John Wayne was in it.

Liz But he's old here.

Teacher Is there anything in the film which tells us when the action took place?

Michael It was just after the Little Big-Horn when Custer and the Seventh Cavalry were massacred.

Teacher Right! Anything else which makes it like *Stagecoach* or any other film we've seen?

---

* The material reported as dialogue is authentic in the sense that at some point it was all said, but for the sake of clarity I have reduced the number of speakers, the aim being to give an impression of the flow and direction of ideas in a lesson rather than a transcription word by word.

Dee   There were Indians.
Brian   They didn't do much. I was expecting a fight and it never came.
Teacher   Why didn't it?
Dave   There was a bit of fighting when they chased that patrol.
Brian   But that only lasted a couple of minutes.
Teacher   But why didn't they have a fight?
(*Silence*)
          Do you think the film was about the Indians or was it about something else?
Jake   John Wayne was too old to fight.
Teacher   How do you mean?
Jake   Well he was the hero but he couldn't fight like in *Stagecoach* because he was too old.
Mary   He was just the same as in *Stagecoach* though, always bossing people about.
Linda   He was different here though, he was sad. He's all alone here, retiring and nobody to look after him.

The acceptance of the central figure, Brittles, and of his power over other men is a convention, the extension of a multitude of other 'heroes', and it helps us over the initial lack of information at the beginning of the film. Ford has made him the logical development of 'the man of the West', he is the Ringo Kid forty years on, with the wisdom and experience of a man who has lived through the 'golden years of the West'. Brittles is a man with a hard past, enigmatic, yet open; inspired, and yet thoughtful; a man confused by the end of one career and excited by the onset of a new one; a nomad inextricably tied to a fort by his long-dead family.

To a great extent, Ford leaves his audience to construct the atmosphere of the army post for itself, an atmosphere dependent upon detail and gentle nuance where, within the conventions, the details are unexpected. It is important to establish this point in the pupils' minds in order that the characters we have examined are seen in some kind of context:

Teacher   Is there anything about the actual setting which strikes you as unusual? (long pause) Well, tell me where the film was set?

Michael In the desert.
Teacher Good – what kind of thing do we expect of a desert?
Brian   It's hot and dry . . . oh! there's no water.
Teacher Well?
Dee   There was a storm. I don't remember it raining, but there
         was thunder and lightning.
Teacher Can anyone remember any scenes in the film where looking
         at the horses told us something about the climate?
Dave   There was a bit when there was steam coming out of the
         horses' nostrils – that means it must have been cold.
Jake   Yes, it must have been cold – the soldiers were wearing
         their greatcoats.
Dave   And there was ice on the water.

In this way I establish a wide range of incidental information about
the lives of the men, about their women, and about the confines of the
remote desert station.

Teacher Do you think life was comfortable on these stations?
Dave   No it must have been terrible in those cold huts.
Jane   And there was no running water.
Dave   There was no hot water either, or proper toilets.
Liz   It must have been terrible for the wives.
Teacher Oh? In what way?
Liz   Well . . . boring.
Jane   But they'd have no hot water to wash clothes, or their
         babies.
Mary   They never knew if their husbands were ever coming back.
Michael Or if the Indians were going to attack the fort.

> The women are
> selfish and hungry.
> the babies
> are little and thin.
> *Jake*

Teacher What if the men weren't married?
Tim   They'd get drunk.
Teacher No, I mean what would they do for women?
(A very long and slightly incredulous silence)

Teacher   Would there be any women on the post?
Jake   Probably some prostitutes like those old bags in the film
          about the mining camp (*City of Gold*).

And though these points are unrelated to the story, collectively they
help us to construct a scale against which we can gauge the men and
their actions. Having established a general setting for the film, and some
kind of thematic thread, we can then isolate a part of the film as an
extract and examine this in terms of the theme of the film as a whole.
From *She Wore a Yellow Ribbon*, I used the scene when the patrol,
midway between the fort and the stage-depot, meets another smaller
patrol which is being pursued by an Indian war party. Their leader,
Corporal Quane (Tom Tyler), seriously wounded by an Indian arrow,
is placed in the hospital wagon. Because of the threat of further hostili-
ties, Brittles, unable to halt the patrol, suggests that the Doctor (Arthur
Shields) should remove the arrow whilst the patrol is on the move,
and that Mrs Allshard, the C.O.'s wife (Mildred Natwick), should
assist. After drinking with the half-doped, half-intoxicated corporal,
Mrs Allshard, overcome both by the fumes and by the drink, joins him
in singing a ribald version of the theme song. Once the arrow-head has
been removed, to the obvious pleasure of Brittles, the patrol continues
towards the stage-depot.

Teacher   What do you think this scene tells us about Mrs Allshard?
Jake   She was used to blood.
Mary   She knew all the men.
Teacher   Do you think they liked her?
Dave   Yes.
Teacher   Why?
Dave   She drank whiskey with them.
Brian   She sang that song with the injured bloke.
Michael   It was the theme song.
Teacher   Anything else about the song?
Jake   Yes, she changed the words. She sang 'garter' instead of
          'ribbon'.
Teacher   What does that mean?
Tim   It was a dirty song.
Teacher   Do you think that the niece would know that version?
Jane   No.
Teacher   Why do you say that?

Mary   She was a snob, she didn't care about any of the soldiers, not the ordinary ones.

Teacher   She said she was pleased about the wounded man.

Michael   She was just saying that. The Lieutenant said it was only because it made a nice ending for the stories she was going to tell when she got back home.

Teacher   Do you believe that?

Jane   Yes, she never spoke to the men, she was just interested in the young officers.

Linda   She was a snob.

Though this line of exploration, like earlier ones, may not be central to the story line, it is nevertheless of great importance in the feeling, atmosphere and values of the film – to its *meaning* as distinct from its story:

Teacher   Do you think the soldiers had anything in common?

Michael   There were a lot of Irishmen.

Jake   There was a German as well.

Mary   There was that old man, Private Smith, who had been a Confederate Colonel.

Teacher   Does that tell you anything about them? (*Silence*)
Well, had they been living in the U.S. long?

Tim   They were all immigrants.

Mary   Not the Colonel, he wasn't.

Michael   But he was different.

Linda   He was a sort of enemy.

Jane   But they were all poor.

Teacher   Does that tell you anything about the army?

Brian   It was full of poor people and immigrants.

Teacher   Why should they join the army?

Jane   It was a steady job. Secure.

Michael   And you didn't need any brains.

> It's years before you become a sergeant . . .
> and when you do,
> it's time to retire.
>
> *David*

Tim   You could work your way up to the top even if you were
           poor.
Teacher   Like Brittles?
Tim   Yes.
Jake   He was a tramp when he joined up – he said he had no
           shoes.

> You and a few others
>   Joined together to escape.
> To escape from home.
> To escape from everything.
> *Michael*

Teacher   Do you think a young man joining the army then, at the
           time of the film, would have the same chances of promotion?
Mary   No, all those young officers were snobs.
Teacher   What does that mean?
Mary   They all had money and one of their dads was a General.

Having discovered the links and backgrounds of the men, we can
move to the origins of the officers, Brittles and Major Allshard (George
O'Brien). Obviously from the 'old school', men who have worked
their way from the ranks, they mark the end of an era in which a soldier
was judged by his ability to fight and not by his parentage. When we
compare these men with their subordinates, Cohill, the son of a
General, and Pennell, 'born with a silver spoon in his mouth', we are
looking at a new army.

Teacher   We've decided that this was a sad film because Brittles
           lost his wife. Is there anything else which makes it sad?
Jane   When he leaves the fort, the way Mrs Allshard says good-
           bye to him.
Teacher   Why's this sad?
Jane   It's the end of their friendship. They've been friends for
           years and now they're splitting up.

> Only a few days to go
>   Filled with sorrow.
> Marking the days off on the calendar
>   He has nowhere to go.
> *Jane*

Teacher Don't you think they'll see each other again?

Michael He said he was going to California.

Jane He was too old anyway. He'd die soon.

Teacher Do you think that the young officers in the film will still be friends forty years later? Don't forget that would be 1916.

Tim They were friends in the film. Brittles and the Major were just like that when they were young.

Teacher How do you know?

Tim They said that they'd had to learn the hard way, and so would the two lieutenants.

Michael But they had tanks and planes in 1916.

Teacher How would that make a difference?

Beyond this point the discussion no longer clings to the film – it becomes philosophical in that the children begin to consider themselves in future relationships with those around them. Eventually, having reached no real conclusions about the film – mainly because I had reached none – the lesson is ended by the bell. The written work from the film is the extension of their own thoughts about the film, and what came out of the film.

As with many of Ford's Westerns, we are looking with regret at the passing of the good life, and are forced to ask a very relevant question: 'Are things in the new world going to be better, or are we throwing away something of great value for the sake of progress?'

> The old rest
> in peace
> The young won't.
> *Brian*

She Wore a Yellow Ribbon is both a good story and a legitimate comment upon the background to the story. It neither criticises nor postulates, nor does it ever sink into being mere escapism. Though on a very superficial level it is enjoyed for the interest of its narrative and for the natural beauty in its images, it is never just entertaining, nor does it put violence forward as a legitimate solution; the final and expected confrontation between white-man and red-man never material-ises and the only fight in the whole film, ritualistic and good humoured, ends when Quincannon (Victor McClaglen), having defeated six men single-handed, says with a mixture of good humour and regret, 'The good days are gone for ever.'

There is much in Ford and in the Western in general which appeals to me and I use a large number of them in my work. John Ford, Howard Hawks, Sam Peckinpah and Anthony Mann have a universality of appeal which offers my pupils and me a common area in which we can work, an area which can entertain and educate on and to all levels. And though I should like to use the films which I like best, films by directors such as Truffaut, Chabrol, Resnais, Antonioni, Louis Malle, Bergman, etc., I know that they are a step up a ladder of progression which my children can climb as they grow older. I know that the films which they see with me will prepare them for this and eventually enable them to see others with understanding and authority. Though watching films might be justified merely as personal contact with art, as might reading poetry, looking at pictures or architecture, or listening to music, I should expect that teaching film would carry the process from 'watching' to seeing and beyond the personal response of satisfied enjoyment or dissatisfied rejection to seeing in the film a record of someone else's vision of life.

Film study is not the cure for all the ills of society, but it has a value in that it provides a stimulus to the creative life of the child, one that will widen his understanding of himself and of other people. Though I believe that the study of the cinema as an art-form validates itself within its own forms and meanings, nevertheless I also know that within the context of English studies it must find validation outside itself, and that this must be related to the traditional English disciplines of speaking and writing. I believe that my use of lyric rather than narrative verse allows my pupils to explore the world of words and to use them in the exploration of their own emotional sensibilities, something which a traditional approach could never do.

English must remain central in the school curriculum but it must do this with some reference to society's needs, and I have tried to use film and a number of other schemes to reach this end. In a school where I.Q.s range from 70 to 130, no one approach can be the answer and each of these schemes, ranging from community service to keeping pigs, has been based upon the concept that experience and personal contacts will help the child develop and make him ready to take his place in society. Film, along with the other experiments, has helped me to offer my pupils more than just an education in techniques and I appreciate in them qualities I should never otherwise have seen. It has created conditions where relationships have been easy and have allowed us to be ourselves, unhampered by the rigid and unnatural formalities of school, and where rules of behaviour have been made from the experience of needing rather than of imposing.

In my work at Sherburn I have replaced a syllabus which I found arid and unproductive with a course which I hope will help my children to see life and a meaning to life and will eventually help them, in ten or fifteen years' time, to treat their own children with imagination, integrity and compassion; then perhaps what their generation has lost will be restored, and creativity which they regard as an esoteric view of a remote existence, will once again become a part of life.

4

A comprehensive school

Discovery of film – form and style for
imitation – symbol and allegory in animated
film – film and literature – documentary stimulus
to creativity

Keith Schofield, Librarian and English Master,
Harrogate High School, formerly at Foxwood
School, Leeds

Film came to be used in English lessons at Foxwood School some four
or five years ago, not as an act of deliberate policy, but when the
16 mm version of *Incident at Owl Creek* was loaned to us by a local
film society. It was used with a set of fifth-year boys, along lines suggested by the Head of Lower School, Mr R. Mainds, who was then
editor of a film journal and also ran courses for sixth-formers on the
making of films. The experiment, an account of which was published
in *Screen Education Yearbook 1968**, was generally regarded as successful in that the poems it inspired were effective and interesting in their
own right; but film was not taken up again for several terms, until
Mr Mainds offered us a whole succession of 'shorts' which would be
available for other purposes (teachers' courses, reviews, etc.) but which
might be exploited in the context of English lessons.

In these circumstances, our use of film was varied and extensive;
every film lesson was of necessity experimental, and the results variable
and not always related to the amount of preparation. Fortunately we
persisted in our use of film, recognising its value in making explicit
statements from which details could be absorbed, interest immediately
aroused, and to which children can respond with a well-developed
visual comprehension trained by watching television. And we rapidly
became more adept in securing better projection facilities, in building

---

* *Screen Education Yearbook 1968*, ed. Roger Mainds, p. 95, 'Owl Creek: Three
Poems by Boys of Foxwood School', Society for Education in Film and Television,
1968.

up a basic list of films with accompanying exercises, and in developing our own control and choice of material that could be exploited within our courses.

We do not confine ourselves rigidly to a set course of films within the English department, but use them as a valuable means of stimulating new ideas or recollections which can be restructured creatively for ultimate expression through the spoken or written word. Classes are presented with material in a visual form which they can generally assimilate with ease, leading to a response which can be channelled into forms appropriate to their developing skills in English. Film has been found to offer special advantages in the particular context of this school.

The school is an established comprehensive school with over fifteen hundred boys (and since 1970 it has been taking in girls), on the north-eastern outskirts of the city of Leeds. The majority of its pupils are drawn from a very large housing estate (population 42,000), a few coming from other parts of the city adjacent to this zone. Within the main zone is a great deal of social diversity, but the families are predominantly working-class with very limited cultural facilities or opportunities. Parental occupations include light engineering, service industries, transport, trading and instruments, and boys tend to follow their fathers into these jobs with little or no extra training, over half of them leaving school at the end of the fourth year. An ever-increasing number of the boys is now entering a fifth year and staying into the sixth form to convert subjects from C.S.E. to 'O' levels. A few pass through the school via the sixth form into university, or other forms of further or higher education.

The majority of the pupils have both parents at work and find little or no encouragement for academic study at home. As on so many new housing estates on the city fringes, there are few social facilities: large numbers of children play on the streets or the rather formal green areas of the estates; their parents derive their recreation from pubs and working men's clubs; and despite attempts to promote community activities through youth clubs, weekend football teams or dramatic societies, there is a high degree of vandalism. Many children entering school have a very limited vocabulary, and no literary background whatsoever. Their progress and achievement is often seriously limited by both social and emotional instability and this has to be taken into account in the organisation and policies of the school, and in the arrangement of teaching units.

The new pupils are placed in 'groups' – our technical term for forms consisting of twenty-five to thirty children representing the whole range of ability, and are taught blocks of subjects (combined studies) by one teacher. Before the school was unstreamed, groups would be split into 'sets' in which children of approximately the same ability were taught specialist subjects in various subject-rooms. The setting system still applies above the second year, though with considerable modification of rigid streaming. Sets are arranged in parallel within 'set-blocks' – four sets of equal ability in set block 1 (the top sets), three in set blocks 2 and 3, and two deliberately small sets in set block 4 (the special remedial sets). Most of the lessons described in this chapter were done in sets, and are referred to by years (A meaning first year, B second year, etc.): this avoids introducing new nomenclature arising from the changing school policy of class-grouping.

The administration is divided horizontally into three 'schools', each under its own Head of School. Lower School comprises the groups in the first two years, Middle School comprises the third and fourth years, and Upper School the fifth and sixth years. Subject departments dispose their staff across the whole range of age and ability in all three schools. The schools are primarily concerned with welfare and social problems of pupils, their subject-choices from the third year onwards, and ultimately their choice of careers; and recently year-counsellors have been appointed within the schools to give assistance with personal and domestic difficulties.

Academically, in the Lower School all boys follow the same courses, but in the Middle School increasing scope is given for subject choices. The main core subjects of mathematics and English are taken by all boys, and even those intending to leave in the fourth year are kept up with the rest of their ability set, the exception being a small group of leavers drawn mainly from the remedial 'sets' and taught by staff outside the departmental arrangement. English courses, comparatively free of the need to prepare the syllabuses of external examination boards, provide a general basis on which pupils willing to stay on into the fifth year can build up to G.C.E. or C.S.E. Both the experimental scheme of internal assessment in English language at 'O'-level (J.M.B.) and the Yorkshire Regional Board C.S.E. course work allow the continuation of our film work into Upper School.

Rooms are arranged in suites, many of which include a subject staff room where material can be discussed and freely shared, and some of the classrooms can be blacked out for films, film loops and slides, whilst one double room is now permanently arranged as a film theatre capable of accommodating three sets at a time.

The English department consists of ten full-time specialists, with a suite of classrooms, three libraries and the use of the main hall for drama. A small staffroom provides storage for communal teaching aids and apparatus, and facilitates the discussion of methods and approaches. The department has always made use of a variety of media to stimulate creative writing or discussion, and all members of the department have been involved in the film-based work. Thus, although co-operative use of teaching material and the discussion of its use with various sets is not a new development in the English department, the special problems of using film have certainly increased the collaborative process, and increased our experience of team-teaching methods to try out and develop new ideas.

Any given film may be used by individual teachers in different ways at different levels, depending on the age and ability of the children. In some cases sets may be grouped together not only for viewing the film but for closely related work arising from it. English is fortunate as a subject in that most sets have five or six 35-minute periods per week, and often 'set blocks' take their lessons in parallel, so that several of them can be shown a film together. Although all the film-rooms belong to other departments, most of them can be booked a few days in advance. The film reels are kept in the English staffroom along with prepared exercises on duplicated sheets, reviews of the films and other related material, for any teacher who wishes to use them. When sets are grouped, teachers will discuss beforehand the co-ordination of their approach and assignments.

The pattern of teaching time also allows a large number of consecutive lessons fairly close together and one whole week of English periods can be devoted intensively to the work on a film. The majority of 'shorts' can be shown in a double period of seventy minutes, and there will often be time for written or oral work whilst the all-important *atmosphere* still holds. Details of timing will be given below for each main type of study.

The need for random exploitation has taught us to experiment boldly and search for ways to adapt the lesson to any set. Staff naturally asked which film had come in and which sets it was suitable for. Exercises were devised which suggested in general terms a number of approaches or different kinds of objectives; imaginative re-creation of a scene or factual data for discussion. Material could be widely diffused in the two or three days that each film was available and sets mingled or separated as desired.

As I have stressed, no one approach has been either possible or desirable with such a variety of films, but certain very general lines of presentation have steadily evolved. Whatever their nature, most of the films require a spoken introduction which, though brief, prepares the theme in some way and gives the slower pupils some indication of what to observe. When the film is to be coupled with literary passages they are usually read before the film is shown and before the exciting atmosphere it generates totally preoccupies the thoughts of the audience. The discussion which then follows the showing of the film may either be clearing up misconceptions, fixing ideas arising from the viewing, recapitulating the subject matter in order to lead to later exercises or conclusions, or the discussion may itself be the teaching objective, in an interchange of ideas and themes arising from the subject-matter.

Some of the shorter or more complex films gain from a second show-ing. This can be used as an aid to deepen understanding or as an incentive to create goodwill before the set engages in the hard work of creative writing. It is important to judge carefully and avoid giving the impression that film lessons are time-fillers or entertainment periods. Sets soon learn to expect that there will be some kind of work and will come to look forward to it, though of course many pupils would always prefer to see the film without obligation to write after it.

The most encouraging feature of all our experience has been the revived interest and enthusiasm of both staff and pupils, evident in the growing desire of the former to recommend and try new films and to offer extra suggestions for creative work, and in the obvious involve-ment of the pupils in the subject matter, an involvement which leads to outbursts of conversation after screenings, and which results in compositions of far better quality. After the solidly factual style of most educational productions, our selection has the imaginative freshness of good literature.

The kind of work we have been doing falls into five general cate-gories which are listed here. Though it will be appreciated that more than one category may be relevant to the treatment of a particular film, exercises will be described under the scheme to which they are most appropriate. The films shown may create opportunities for:

a Imitation of aspects of film structure to achieve improvement in prose techniques and style

b Analysis and interpretation of symbolism and allegorical imagery
c Discussion
d Illumination and comparative appreciation of literary passages
e Creative writing.

One of the first films we ever used, *Pour un Maillot Jaune*, guarantees the kind of excitement essential to involve pupils in the narrative, and is still popular even with those who have seen it two or three times in successive years. The film also serves to illustrate our basic approach to films of the first category – providing a model for imitation to improve prose technique. *Pour un Maillot Jaune* is an account of a Tour de France, showing every aspect of the preparation and the event: the crowds, the sponsors, accidents, massage, the official start, time trials, the changing moods of the weather, the press reporting, victory kisses, and the final award of the Yellow Jersey in a packed stadium. Colour effects heighten certain scenes: a fiery orange tinting intensifies the mountain climb in the punishing heat, and a dark blue tint reinforces the natural greys of the crowded drive through rain and sleet.

In the period following the showing, or else the following day, the film is discussed. Such a lesson provides opportunity for collective recall of details easily overlooked or quickly forgotten. Why did the film change to monochrome sequences? What were the spectators like who lined the route? What sorts of accidents did the cyclists have? What signs were there that the French treat cycle racing as a national sport? How did the various cyclists react to the tension of the time trials?

This last question shows the value of collective discussion, since most boys notice the concentration of the red rider, but very few see the quick wiping of sweat from one anguished face, and hardly any are observant enough to see the rider who crosses himself as his bike is pushed forward, perhaps because they do not understand the gesture.

One of the teachers present would then ask how this narrative structure might be adapted to prose composition. Usually the pupils would be invited to write about any sport, and the discussion will proceed on more general lines, with references then back to examples in the film, the common experience of all the pupils. As the discussion becomes more detailed, it is perhaps better for the sets to separate and return to their own regular teaching rooms with their own teachers who will best know what encouragement and assistance is required.

It is important during this discussion to develop the idea that every sport has its own special atmosphere, and that there are many components that contribute to the feeling of 'occasion'. Until each boy has decided which sport he is going to write about it is impossible to discuss the technique by which the atmosphere is to be re-created. Arbitrary discursions to describe, say, press coverage, or accidents, or spectators, can be seen to make the compositions tedious and disjointed; such descriptive features would have to be introduced at 'natural' pauses in the narrative, and the planning of these will be related to the forms and rhythms of the sport being described. But what will by now be appreciated by the boys is that a sporting event is much more than an account of the actions of the main participants, which is the sort of composition they would have been likely to produce without these lessons.

It is not of course being suggested that the technique depends upon the film. The needs of prose are rather different and it is impossible to make descriptions absolutely simultaneous. What film does better than any other medium is to re-create atmosphere and give a fuller sense of actuality. The literary techniques of building up to a climax, suspending narration, running plots concurrently, portraying characters and making general descriptive surveys can be taught with reference to the succinct statements that film makes in a very short time. In practice a film such as *Pour un Maillot Jaune* can provide the same range of examples of storytelling techniques that we could only draw out of a set book studied over a whole term. A combination of film and book supplied the richness of material education requires.

Compared with previous contributions on similar subjects, the compositions stimulated by the film had a variety of new imaginative features, such as descriptions of the nervousness of players before an important match, the news coverage by the press, a focus on injuries, crowd interest, boardroom strategy, sponsors, machine maintenance and training. Many boys made an effort to define the atmosphere and came to realise that different sporting fixtures have different power to hold the popular imagination. Their compositions were longer and more varied in subject than had been the case on previous occasions without the carefully structured stimulus of the film. There was a sharp decline in the number of football stories and fewer examples of enthusiastic, wish-fulfilling personal heroism.

The following examples, because of the improvement they represent, seem to us to justify the time spent on them; 35 minutes viewing, 35 minutes discussion and starting to write, 35 minutes in class to write, completed for homework. Neither writer was particular noted for his interest in sport, and in the second example there is a rather pedestrian academicism in sections, especially the comments about high altitude training, but the loss of enthusiasm in favour of greater precision and deeper appreciation is not to be deplored. Spontaneous excitement, revived by the increased ability to express feeling fluently, returns later in the term or the same year.

As we looked around we could see hundreds of people milling into the stands. As the horses came into the paddock I was escorted by Jack and the Governor to Pink Rose. As I was helped on the Governor wished us good luck and said 10–1. Well that isn't good odds but they could be worse. Then we were led to the course and it was a quick trot down to the starting point. Cameras from B.B.C. scanned the whole length but there was no time to stop and stare.

At last we were all at the start, twenty-five in all. This was the tremendous moment. The flag's up. No, somebody's started off first. That was hectic. Under orders again. We're off. For a moment everybody seems frozen, then we all bunched up together. At the first jump we were lying mid-field. And at the end of the first lap we were still in that position. Already seven had fallen. I spurred Pink Rose on to the inner bend. I gained fourth position but was soon overtaken. Dirt flew like hailstones from the hooves of the leading horses, blinding us at the back. No time to worry. The crowd are roaring but I can't hear them. The jumps seem to get bigger and bigger as we came home. By now I have no idea of time, of position, of speed. But I am still behind the leaders. The last fence coming up. Oh no, she's missed her footing. That was near, we could have been under those others behind me. The last furlong, this is the most strength sapping length. It's all out or drop back. Over the line at last. Fourth only, still that isn't bad. Better luck next time.

Nigel – set block C1

It is perhaps interesting to notice that Nigel's attention has shifted from the almost inevitable glory of winning to the tension of participation, and even Roger is aware of the processes and training as well as the achievement of winning.

The strain is showing on the runners' faces, their lungs are straining

D

to keep up a regular rhythm. The stragglers are wrenching tired, unwilling muscles on in a tortured effort to keep up. The pace has been set and the rabbits are being weeded from the strong, flaggers are getting further and further behind the main body in their titanic but useless attempt at the highest Olympic awards.

This year's games may perhaps call for extreme fitness on the part of the competitors because of the high altitude at which events are taking place. Only the strongest of lungs will be able to break records, if indeed any are broken. Back on the track the race has reached halfway stage and the athletes' legs are working as automatically as pistons. None of the runners can feel the harsh cinders that are kicked up, slashing at their legs. That pain is nothing to the gnawing agony that is tearing at their lungs. Every breath taken is a rasping, wheezing, paroxysm. Only courage and willpower is dragging the bedraggled athletes on. Candidates hoping to compete in any Olympic event have to be fit in every respect. Rigorous standards must be passed. Not all training is done on the track either, a correct diet must be maintained which includes keeping away from fatty foods and confections. British athletes have to provide their own diet and train in their own time so it is not surprising that many promising young men and women give up competing because of costs. Clearly some kind of assistance must be made available to amateur athletics so that sportsmen may be better able to continue their training.

At this moment the race has not far to go and the runners are still bunched. Suddenly one breaks free from the rest, his blood pounds in his temples, his muscles knotted with cramp, only courage and a gold medal urge him on. The roar of the crowd is nothing compared with the sound of his every heartbeat thundering in his ears. The tape snaps and his knees crumple under him like straws and a wave of heat and exhaustion beats against the winner's body. He knows it was worth every minute, for he has gained the highest prize in amateur athletics.

Robert – set block C1

Another film used in a similar way was the National Film Board of Canada's *La Lutte*, an account of the all-in wrestling at the Montreal stadium – those who engage in it and those who watch it. Here again we were concerned both with what the film showed, and with the way in which similar impressions might be conveyed in prose-writing. The discussion session is always a mixture of probing and demonstrating. The teachers conducting it are trying to draw out of willing members of the audience some memories and reactions which the teachers can 'edit' in such a way as to point out or demonstrate the techniques of the film-makers. Questions about the behaviour of the spectators at the wrestling bouts will almost certainly elicit recollections of the faces and of telling moments such as the holding back of an excitable woman; and when a pupil points out that one girl was shown several times in the film some obvious staff approval and concentrated interest will almost certainly draw out more comment which can be guided by questions towards the explanation desired. In this particular instance we wanted boys to observe that the director was using shots of this fan to spin a narrative thread to which otherwise unconnected events could be attached. If the device has not been noticed then it will have to be explained.

A secondary purpose of discussion in connection with a film of this sort is to focus the attention of the pupils on the method of construction of the film and detach them, to some extent, from the subject-matter in which, in our experience, most of them have become uncritically involved. Although, if left to think for themselves, most children will ask if the wrestlers do really hurt themselves, we feel that it is necessary to bring such questioning forward to be nearer the actual experience that the film has provided.

The clue to one possible kind of prose expression is found in the third phase of the film, which is made up of sequences from a collage of fights representing many aspects of the game. Against a soundtrack of harpsichord music by Vivaldi we are shown locks and grips and footwork, both rythmic and artistic when viewed with such detachment. Collage helps to make these scenes into an art form.

There are other allusions to conscious form which should be brought to the attention of the class in discussion. The main fight of the evening, in which the obvious hero of the crowd is their local champion, Charpentier, is constructed according to an immemorial pattern. The first round goes to the heroes, the second one with some dirty play to the villians, and then the heroes make their fighting comeback. This may seem to be an unacceptable cliché, but the involvement of the spectators and the way the director projects this never fails to communicate itself to the boys who see the film. That it is a conscious form is further demonstrated by the director in two following scenes: one in which Charpentier washes and casually throws on his coat after his 'titanic' struggles; the other in which melodramatic titling mocks the outrage of the losers.

The level of discussion possible will of course depend on the age-group involved, and the finer points of film editing will be discernible only by sixth-form groups. The main items referred to above were presented to a fourth-year set block and some of the abler third-years in our school. When writing at last began the sets were restricted to the subject of wrestling, though they could well have used their experience of the film to reappraise other sports or entertainment. *La Lutte* may be set against a passage from Wolf Mankowitz's '*A Kid for Two Farthings*', and if this is included then the time pattern for this lesson-sequence would be: 25 minutes film, 35 minutes reading and discussion, 35 minutes written work (to be completed for homework). With the D2 set-blocks, the passage was read and then the film shown within a double period, and the discussion and writing completed the following day; but on reflection I feel that more time and attention should have been given to discussion in this sequence.

The following example shows an attempt to reproduce the 'collage' composition of the film, picking up incidents in the stadium and in the ring, and demonstrating at least an awareness of the sham and show-manship of wrestling, though the film's implicit indictment of the crowd's enjoyment of the infliction of pain is perhaps too much for a third-year pupil to capture.

The large hall stood silent waiting for the crowds to enter. It was the weekly night for wrestling and the last possible arrangements were being made. There were occasional tests with the collection of loudspeakers situated round the hall. 'Testing, testing, 1, 2, 3,' crackled from the loudspeakers.

The huge lights above the recently constructed wrestling ring were being tested, for they held an important position in the success-ful running of the wrestling to be held tonight.

Then when everything was satisfactory the crowds were admitted. The entrance doors swung open and in charged the night's spec-tators. Like a swarm of bees they rushed about the hall inspecting each row until they found the right one. The noise was terrific. Announcements could not properly be heard and this caused the wrestling to be delayed as the seat numbers were being announced and no one took advantage of it.

An official had to break up an argument between two women who

both claimed that a seat was theirs. In the end it was found to belong
to neither.

Eventually quiet was obtained and the wrestling began.

*   *   *   *

'Slam him Tiger!'
Tiger the 'baddy' of the bout had the Hood caught in the ropes
and unfairly took blows at him. His face was distorted by pain and
he gave rehearsed groans and moans occasionally at the Tiger. His
hands beat at the canvas so much that it seemed he was playing a
tune or rhythm.

Eventually the Tiger gave up his aggression towards his opponent
and allowed him to slump to the floor.

*   *   *   *

As usual the 'baddy' scored the first fall and continued to batter
his opponent. Then remarkably the Hood came back to get a surprising Fall. Now it was all on the last fall both taking their share of
punishment. But of course the Hood won. Only after rehearsed
bouncing from ropes, jumping over their opponents and failing to do
a proper drop kick leaving the Tiger exhausted for an easy victory
for the Hood.

Stephen – set block C1

More extensive quotation and other examples would reveal the
imitation of other film techniques such as cross-cutting, changes of
viewpoint, etc., and clearly there are many opportunities for us to
extend work of this kind in our English teaching; it is likely to become
an important area of experiment for us in the future.

What was originally only a by-product of our discussions of films
has come to have major significance in our teaching – work on the
interpretation of symbols. A number of successful short films are non-
representational, and depend upon an understanding of allegory or
metaphor. Our original purpose in using the films was to stimulate
creative writing, but the discussion often turned to questions of interpretation.

The Hangman was found to be a useful film in this context at different
levels within the school. It illustrates an American poem which tells
how the hangman comes to a small town and sets up his gallows in the

court house square. The citizens, puzzled that the scaffold is not taken
down after the hanging, are told that there will be further hangings
since the gallows have been set up for he who serves the hangman best.
The slaughter continues until, when the town is deserted, and all
except one of its citizens is dead, the hangman calls his 'helper' as his
last victim.

The poem clearly and dramatically makes the point that justice is an
instrument of the whole community and that selfishness, complacency
and turning a blind eye only result in judicial murders. He who stands
by and stares longest in the corrupt community is the one who serves
the hangman best. The pictures explain this by means of a variety of
visual symbols and superimposed layers of meaning.

The film provides fourth and fifth years with numerous examples
of the use of symbols and imagery in art, especially in literature. At
the simplest level there are straightforward equivalencies, e.g. globe
represents alien, shattered globe represents his death. At the allegorical
level are the scenes which show justice as a statue broken and defaced
by the crimes of the community. The courthouse becomes entwined in
the Hangman's many ropes and the citizens appear, like figures in
Magritte, with cloths bound round their heads carrying the upturned
L which the Hangman uses to check the angle of the gallows arm.
Their complicity is also shown in the fleeting glimpses of their feet
on the edge of the square and their hatbands of braided rope.

Second and third year classes need a second showing with pauses
for explanation at a simple level; 'the red splash on the legal document
represents the seal that is put on, but it also represents a spot of blood
because another victim will die unjustly', 'to show how empty and
deserted the town is the buildings are drawn with walls as thin as shreds
of paper'. Many boys asked why the people didn't just stop the Hangman instead of surrendering so easily, especially when no coercion was
evident. Some suggested that the townsfolk could have burnt the
gallows down, and also wondered just what crimes the victims had
committed. Why were some men wearing bandages? Was the film
only about racial prejudice? and so on. At first questions such as these
may seem frustrating, but they raise fundamental issues of how we are
encouraged to transcend literal thinking and to interpret allegory, and
I must confess that even now I find it difficult to supply good modern
examples of the injustices that the Hangman represents. Apartheid is an
obvious modern instance, but our problem is to draw attention to the
needs of our own society, such as homelessness, attitudes towards

immigrants, the treatment of alcoholics, and freedom of conscience. One third-year boy did cite the game laws of the nineteenth century as an example of legal oppression. The teacher who does not prepare his lesson in detail will find, as we did on the first occasion, that the children's questions are avoided and attention turned to abstract interpretations of the film's content instead of to an understanding of its relevance.

The poems that were written after a second showing of the film seemed to illustrate two things: that the images of the film are impressive enough to stimulate creative interest; and that some of the symbolism remains a mystery although considerable progress can be made towards an understanding of it.

> They all stood there and watched.
> Nobody would do a thing to stop it.
> The shame of it, just watching him die.
> Those round buckshot eyes,
> Straight face built to withstand blood,
> Never flinching, not a flicker of emotion.
> Who is next? Is it going to be me?
> Time passes on, better keep inside the house.
> All the town, gone, nobody left except me.
> There goes the hangman . . .
> He's seen me, he's smiling.
> He'll need some help to take down the gallows
> Me helping him,
> The rope,
> He tricked me.
> He tricked me . . . tricked me,
> Oh God, what have I done?
>
> *Philip – set block C3*

Whether or not the main point was really understood, the writer feels uneasiness at the process of punishment which he feels he is witnessing, and he conveys effectively the complacency and perplexity of the last victim . . . 'What have I done?' Here is another example:

> One day the hangman
> Came to town,
> He built a hanging tree out there.

Who are you going to take? we said
He handed us a riddle for reply
as he started on the gallows.
He grabs the alien by the hand
And takes him up the gallows steps.
Outside the courthouse door he stands
With hangman's rope in his hands.
'I will take whoever serves me best,'
The hangman said.
In days to come more men died,
And when the town is old and decrepit,
The hangman walks and calls my name.
I thought he'd come to ask my help.
We walked to the gallows,
Then up the stairs,
He grabbed me by the hand.
'You tricked me hangman.'
'I trick you, I think not,
You were the one who served me best,
So be prepared to meet your death.'

Keith – set block C2

The technique used here, three quarters of the way to being poetry, was not a product of film lessons, but undoubtedly their content has been a valuable stimulus. For the boys it is enough of a task, and sufficient achievement, to have found words and a form in which to express someone else's visual ideas. These 'poems' and others owe very little to the language of the original version of *The Hangman*, and some of the boys introduced images that were not in the film, but almost all of the 'set' felt that it had shared an experience worth retelling in another medium.

It is, of course, one of the faults of random exploitation that the work I have described above was not followed up with more studies of symbolism. We could now arrange a series of films specially to develop an awareness of symbolism in the arts, and the levels of its operation; but when we showed *The Substitute* it was not possible to build upon the interpretative skills of the classes whose work has been described above.

The Substitute presents, by means of flexible animated figures in brilliant colours, a satirical view of consumer societies which depend too much on synthetic products. The little man arrives to enjoy an afternoon at the beach with a whole range of inflatable pleasures – a car, a beach set, a meal, two girl friends, the second of which he inflates when he doesn't fancy the first – but his complacency ends in disaster, when his inflated worlds come into contact with a tin-tack. This seven-minute film was found most effective if shown twice, with a short interval, and the discussion which followed, using a double-period, with the D1 block, explored the themes and values of the film; but with the younger boys the teaching emphasis had to be placed on a more systematic evaluation of the ideas and images in the film.

Our introduction to this film only hinted that there was meaning below the surface, but that hint was taken up eagerly after a brief pause of bewilderment and amusement. Many aspects were touched upon but the main line of argument centred on these crucial issues: Where did the tack come from in such a world of plastic and rubber? (Question first asked by a fourth-year boy.) Was it the one fatal flaw, hidden and unexpected, that guaranteed eventual destruction? Was it perhaps not weakness in civilisation but death itself, alien, external and indestructible? Several boys commented on the artificiality of fishing when the fish is attached to the line before casting. It was not difficult, however, to find examples in contemporary life of this and other kinds of artificiality, e.g. the wide range of processed foods, or even of attempts to evade the artificiality through such activities as hunting, fishing and physical competition. Some realised that even the 'natural' landscape surrounding the school was more than half 'man-scaped'; grass areas specially grown, flowers specially selected, trees specially sited. Finally it was noted, by a perceptive fourth-year contributor, that the man also inflated the pump which creates the whole environment. Man is the maker of the means.

When poetry or prose were to be written they were started in the same period as the showing and without the help of any intervening discussion. Film study has only recently been used to teach some techniques of poetry, especially verse structure and rhythm, so the poems quoted here were based on methods of construction taught by means of other types of material. Here are some examples of work based on *The Substitute*.

I think that the nail in the road that the little man created at the end of the film represented reality and natural things which reduced his substitutes to nothing, and which also left him helpless and he was 'let down', showing how, without all our substitutes, modern man would be nothing.

Colin – set block D1

    'Beautiful!' said the motorist
    Sitting in his square tin car,
    admiring the mountain scen'ry
    Through his open quarter light.
    Tyres burn on molten tar
    Which covers the country road,
    On which lie massacred creatures
    Baked in the hot Sunday sun.
    No will to walk and let survive
    God's creatures crossing the road.
    Let us kill them, feed the vulture,
    Love the motor car instead.

Mervin – set block D1

My opinion is that the film is based on one object – the Atom bomb and the destruction of man.

This is shown in many ways. The atom bomb point was shown by the little fellow pushing the lever on the pump, which made things appear and disappear. This is equivalent to one man pushing ahead in e.g. the field of science, and then somebody doing a little thing which will destroy the whole object of the thing. . . . This also illustrates the object of world power. That is if one man presses a button it could put an end to most or all of the population of the world.

The most significant part is at the end where there is a nail in the road, which the blow-up car hits. This illustrates the point that there is a thing there which we do not know about like the H and atom bombs of today which we are still not sure of.

Ian – set block D1

These three pieces develop various theories of the film and are included for their ideas rather than their literary form. The last one is rather muddled, but it still reveals the nature of the attempt to understand the wider implications of the narrative. Under the impetus of the film some hurried but interesting and comparatively fresh responses were written down.

For most pupils, animated film is likely to be equated with 'the cartoon', and particularly with cartoons in which the narrative line or intense physical action is the dominant element. An ability to 'read' the meanings of animated visual images is only acquired through practice, and *The Hangman* and *The Substitute* prepare the children for a more complex piece of animation such as *The Hand* which we have come to use more recently.

A potter wakes up to find his attic invaded by a huge Hand which insists on imposing its self-image on his art. The man drives it out but the Hand insinuates itself into the room with presents such as a telephone and a television set. When these are rejected the Hand seizes the little man and manipulates him with strings like a true puppet. He is set down in a cage and made to carve a huge block which he fashions into a gigantic Hand, and when the statue is finished he is rewarded with a wreath and medals as he slumps down drained of creative energy. The little potter recovers enough to escape the cage and reach his room. Whilst trying to secure every door against the intrusion of his enemy he is killed by a falling flower-pot and the sinister Hand gives him a state burial.

The film-maker uses a wooden doll and a gloved hand to satirise the methods of tyrannous government. Not only does the Hand use mass media to put over its image, but it also insists on the continual reproduction of its ideas through every form of art and its pressures temporarily overcome the little man. Its power to manipulate, its tawdry rewards, its taste for secretive coercion and violence, and its pious observation of sentimental decencies are all given concrete symbolic expression. The man, in contrast, is represented as a simple character with creative skill as a potter and great love of plants, freedom and organic growth. Colour contributes to both the meaning and the irony of the film. The changing emotions of the little man are perceptible as colour changes, and the moods of the Hand are clearly suggested by the changes of glove. The story is told in mime with a minimum of musical counterpointing.

The film was seen by many people, in black and white, on B.B.C.-2 shortly after the Czech crisis of August 1968 so that it was easy to see parallels with that situation, but the story was intended to show the power of tyranny anywhere and at any time. Just as George Orwell insisted that his novel *Animal Farm* was not exclusively about the Russia of Stalin, so we try to point out to our fifth year that *The Hand* could be about the pressures of Western European society. The images require a basic 'vocabulary' which comes more readily by the end of the fifth year of this kind of study. Boys in the second year can enjoy the story but not until the fourth year have we found any child perceptive enough to suggest underlying meanings.

Although I have included *The Hand* in this section of films which can be used to teach pupils how to interpret symbolism, it also serves to introduce the films which we use to stimulate discussion alone. The intention being to use a visual experience as the starting point for discussion of an informal nature, in sets or set blocks at the discretion of the staff concerned.

Perhaps our most successful occasions have been those on which two or three sets of fourth-year boys, in the C.S.E. bands especially, have been put together to see a film and then to talk about the way it has impinged on their own experience in particular. In such an atmosphere, with two or three of the staff present, one idea often triggers off another and in the place of formal debate on a prepared subject there is the more informal interchange of original impressions and experiences. For several practical reasons Granada's schools programmes, *The Messengers*, were used most frequently, but the longer television film *Deckie Learner*, which tells us something of the life and reactions of a fifteen-year-old boy who leaves home to become a deckhand on a deep-sea trawler out from Hull, was more satisfactory for length and quality. Clearly any film may be used to stimulate discussion, and it would be wrong to think that no useful purpose has been served unless the showing of a film leads directly to a piece of writing. Nor, in an English course, would we think it necessary to keep the film experience 'pure' (as some film-teachers might argue). We often prefer to link the film with some literary passage, allowing the two media to complement each other.

I have already suggested the linking of *La Lutte* with the passage from *'A Kid for Two Farthings'* which also features a visit to a wrestling match. Like the film it devotes some of its attention to the crowd and focusses on a personal element, a girl spectator in the film, the little boy who is the hero of the story in the book. In the film there are several glimpses of the girl who supports the champion, whilst in the book our sympathies are engaged by the boy who is a keen supporter of the hero Shmule. We have never suggested that our pupils should imitate the chapter from Mankowitz but it can serve as a model for those who need its help.

With the B.F.I. extract from de Sica's *Bicycle Thieves* (the ending of the film) we have contrasted Alan Sillitoe's short story *'The Bike'*. The extract shows the last scenes of the film when the father, who is desperate to preserve his self-respect in the presence of his son, abandons his attempt to recover his own bike and makes a feeble effort to steal someone else's. We do not usually explain that de Sica set out to dramatise the erosion of moral values and the degradation of personality by poverty in post-war Italy. The extract very clearly portrays the man's anguish, and the furtive clumsiness of his theft implies the repugnance such an unfamiliar action makes him feel. The music reinforces the obvious humiliation of the father, as he and his son walk away from the crowd which arrested them, with a sentimental appeal for our sympathy.

The short story has a similar theme but its tone is in sharp contrast and the whole incident is less melodramatic. Sillitoe describes a young factory worker who has saved up to buy a bike from a workmate to enable him to escape from the pressures of dull work and a nagging family. Colin dreams of the country views over the river Trent, but it turns out that the bike has been stolen and has to be returned to the owner after a 'scene' in the street.

The story is very close to the social experience of the boys and its lighter tone offsets the exaggerated pathos of the film extract, and several valuable points can be made by detailed comparison of the two. In the course of discussion the leading topics would be why the two men valued their bikes, and to what extent the seriousness of the two thefts depended on their consequent effects. Some classes might explore the irony that de Sica's hero steals another bike although he must surely appreciate the pain he may be causing. Colin on the other hand is able to shrug off the episode as one of life's little defeats. For him the bike offered the best opportunity to get away from an intolerable family and it was this aspect that most classes finally wrote about. The poem quoted below was written by a second-year boy who produced it two or three days after the discussion from one of two possible themes; which of your possessions do you value most and why? and, describe an occasion when you 'escape' from home.

Escape

It's five o'clock Friday night
Suitcase packed fishing tackle all complete
Waiting for the number eight.

As I stand there
People rushing
Cars revving
Buses honking
Fumes dispersing
As the lights change off they go
Just like a race.
The bus arrives upon the scene
Luggage on the rack
Sitting in my seat
An hour later we are there.
There's the inn on the corner
Take my luggage, settle in.
A quiet meal by open fire
Leisurely stroll by the river
Fishing spot picked for morning
Back to my room
As darkness falls
Snuggled down between the sheets
Thought of the two days in front of me

Jeremy – set block B2

This poem marks, for the set concerned, an advance of technique. There is an attempt to reproduce the bustle and discomfort of noisy traffic in the short lines listing noises, contrasted with the longer and more leisurely constructions at the end when the fisherman settles in for the weekend.

Our use of Lenica's *Labyrinth* is another example of linking film material with literature, but at a more senior level, and in a rather different study-programme. We have used this film with third forms, but really it is more appropriate to a good fifth- or sixth-form group. Duplicated worksheets were prepared to begin the study. W. H. Auden's poem *'The Unknown Citizen'* was printed in full, with six questions designed to draw attention to the main features of the satire – the work of various agencies, techniques used to control opinion, and the meaning of the title. The sheet also contained an extract from Lewis Mumford's *'The City in History'*, two paragraphs of more evaluative and factual prose, with questions probing its implications – the sort of freedom which the law takes away from the citizen in the social conditions of the city, and the obstructions caused by its great complexity.

The third-year set found the questions extremely difficult, but boys were able to suggest some examples (mainly concerned with motoring) and girls might offer examples of consumer rights and protection, or controls on family behaviour in flats or council estates. Many third-year boys accepted the Auden poem as a plain description of an ideal, socially protective society, unaware of its satirical tone; and the Mumford passage and questions on the nature of law were too abstract, and beyond their social experience. I think that even with fifth- and sixth-formers, this material would need careful preparation over a longer period: we had only used two periods (seventy minutes) and a twenty-minute homework up to this stage.

Labyrinth, using stylised book-engravings of the early years of this century, describes how a man flies over the maze of a modern city, and comes to rest in deserted streets amidst imposing Victorian buildings. He hides from a roaming prehistoric beast, and fails to rescue a woman from the forepaws of another because she chooses to stay with the creature. Only a few perceptive sixth-formers are likely to associate these beasts with, for example, the release of subconsciously repressed instincts, or the fossilisation of urban social life. But the section of the film we extracted for comparison with the two passages of literature is more explicit in content and meaning.

The visiting man enters a huge palace of indoctrination, up a staircase which reminds one of the setting of Orson Welles's film of Kafka's *The Trial*. He is fixed into a machine for the control or regulation of thought, his identity number is printed on a record card, and the machine begins a deep penetration of his brain. The man escapes, pursued by the sinister machine-controller and harried by birds and bats. The last scene shows his fall, like Icarus, with skeletal wings, the last feathers drifting away. This sequence, some six or seven minutes long, was selected (and run through the projector up to the starting point) prior to the film lesson, thus leaving about twenty-five minutes of the lesson, after the film-showing, in which to tackle the final section of the work-sheets – one composition selected from three themes: advertising, life in a city, or a science-fiction story about those who rebel against conformity. A homework completed the exercise.

Although this work did partly relate to previous film and literary material – there are relevant links with both *The Substitute* and *The Hand* – the passages and the exercises were really too abstract for children lacking the basic social experience being considered. Future use of this study-programme, which does contain some excellent ideas, will probably be more closely related to a fifth-form course with some concrete examples of the application of the abstract principles, and some background reading including science-fiction.

Duplicated worksheets are obviously convenient, but it is often more economical to link film material with passages and exercises in standard textbooks. We have had some success with the sponsored film *Dial Double One* and a comprehension passage in *'Encounters Stage 3'* based on Rutgers van der Loeff's *'Avalanche!'* The film provides details of two rescue operations by aircraft, the first the rescue of an injured skier lost in the snow, and the second (which we concentrate on) the rescue of a party of villagers buried under a snowfall. The passage from *'Avalanche!'* tells of a party of boys with two villagers caught in a small avalanche, and the rescue of the orphan, Paolo, after one of the villagers stays with him instead of escaping. The implications of such generous but foolhardy action are made explicit in the film.

Both the book and the film provide many illustrations of the courage of the rescuers, the undue risks of visitors and travellers, and the techniques and organisation of rescue, and from this wealth of material we have tried out various schemes with different sets. With some, the film was used to supplement an otherwise formal comprehension exercise; with others, passages were selected from the novel and used with the film to stimulate imaginative writing. Yet another set of exercises is described and illustrated here. These come from compositions by second-year pupils on the general topic of avalanches: in addition to the material already described, we used a tape-recording of a dramatised episode from a B.B.C. Schools broadcast. The boys were required to revise their first drafts after some explanation of the purpose of paragraphing.

First version
Then I rushed along to the helicopter pad and got the things needed for the rescue and started the engine. Then my helper Pete Müler got in and we went over the mountain Ben Garves and started to descend to the place where the avalanche was. We landed near a big lump of snow and there we met a member of our team and he had with him a dog which could tell if people were under the snow. We found out that there were four people trapped so we got the dog out and it went to try to find the men. There were three men and a boy aged fourteen, then the dog started to dig and he soon found the fourteen-year-old boy and he soon recovered then we found two

men but one was still under the snow and the dog could not smell
him so we started to probe about with our big long poles. Then we
found him and we started the task of digging him out. Eventually we
got him out and gave him some oxygen and put him in the chopper
and I took him to hospital and it was another rescue for our team.

Second version
Then I rushed over to the chopper and started the motor and then
I was joined by my helper Pete Müler.

The make of our chopper was a Sikorski 24 mark II and was
made for this kind of operation. It was painted yellow and white
and was easy to handle. Then we started to rise and we could see the
hill tops.

Then we flew over the disaster spot and we could see from up
here that it had been a bad one and there were bits of houses strewn
all over the place and it was a horrible sight.

Then we started to descend and then we landed. It was chaotic,
there were people all over and we started to organise things.

Then we were met by a member of our team with a dog which
would help us to find a person under the snow. Then the dog set to
work to find the people. We later found that there were eleven people
stuck in the snow. We were hampered by bits of rubble and stone.

The first person we got out was a boy aged fourteen. Then we
were joined by two other rescue teams which ferried the injured out,
in the end there were five dead and three badly hurt and three just
bruised. Then the army were called in and they cleared up.

Stewart – set block B1

The changes, generally improvements, reveal more than the carving-
up of the first version into paragraphs. Although the technical details
of the helicopter might be regarded as padding to increase the number
of paragraphs, the other additions tend to underline the seriousness
of such disasters, and to avoid the neatly heroic ending and immediate
recovery of the rescued. The first version follows the film narrative
fairly closely, but the second incorporates ideas and attitudes from the
tape-recording. The increased information probably helps to bring
home more fully the serious nature of even the most limited avalanches,
and the cumulative effects upon the community of a large number of
these personal disasters. The writing improves not only in technique
(paragraphing) but in the richness of the ideas as well.

Not all the revisions were successful. Spontaneity may be killed off by an effort to be more precise or to incorporate new data. The following extracts suggest that the boy felt his first story to be over-dramatized, and the second version loses telling details ('my breath was slowly melting the snow and the water was running up my nose and in my mouth') and some liveliness of vocabulary ('scooping', 'scrambled', 'snowy grave').

First version
Then without a warning there was an avalanche.

Panic strickened I just stood and watched it. Great big boulders of snow came thundering down. Within seconds I was covered. The snow weighed as much as a couple of tons. The heat of my body and my breath was slowly melting the snow and the water was running up my nose and in my mouth. I started fighting for my life scooping the snow away from me. I had cleared enough away from me so that I could nearly stand up. A terrible thought went through my wet body that the snow could be ten feet thick.

The snow got thinner as I brought more away and then I stuck my head out to breathe fresh air. I scrambled out of my snowy grave. I looked around myself and saw a big mound. I flung myself on it and started digging frantically.

Second version
... the next thing we knew was that we were at the bottom of an avalanche. It came down slowly but horrifyingly then I was at least three feet under, it weighed at least a ton, well it felt like it.

I started to dig myself out from the top but when I got so far it caved in again. So I started to dig at an angle my body started to melt the snow away. Now I could hardly feel my fingers and was finding it very hard to breathe. I got frantic and started kicking the snow and digging harder and harder. I felt my life slipping away from me when just then I stuck my head out to breathe fresh air again.

Keith – set block B2

Whatever the variety of linked material (films, extracts from novels, poems, newspapers or magazine articles, and tape-recordings), the basic objective is the same: to clarify one mode of expression by means of another. Film often provides a stimulus that is more fresh, more explicit, and superficially more familiar. Individual teachers will experiment with material and with methods of presentation, and their recommendations and assessments will be shared by other members of the department, leading to more effective and systematic exploitation of the material available to us.

In developing this work, we have often in the past used film material originally ordered for other purposes; and we have found that a great variety of material can be used simply as a stimulus to creative or imaginative writing – either reinterpretations of the film material, or the development of themes digressing from it. A film suitable for fourth-year sets (though we have used it with third-years quite successfully) is *Lonely Boy*, a biographical documentary about the pop-star Paul Anka, made for the National Film Board of Canada by Raymond Kroitor and Wolf Koenig. Along with Sheppard's *The Most*, about the creator of the Playboy clubs and magazine, it allows the publicists to give their own game away, showing how uncritically they believe in themselves.

Lonely Boy is about the star Paul Anka, and has ironic overtones added by the passage of time since those resounding claims were first made concerning his greatness as an artist. Anka started as a fat boy and spent many months slimming and re-styling his hair. His manager claims that he took him up for his talent not only as a singer but also as a song-writer, but the one scene purporting to show Paul composing conveys instead the sheer monotony of a modern 'hit' and the sycophancy of the star's assistants. The usual audiences of teenage girls are shown in various stages of trance, torn between agony and pleasure. Fans beg for a sight of their idol whilst the police, armed with their night sticks, keep control uneasily, facing the hysterical mob. The film sets out to show that Anka inhabits a special world of sentiment and superlatives which is restless, pestering and full of irritants. Throughout the filming the principals remain camera conscious and adopt poses which they believe to be suggestive of the informality of a 'typical day'.

The style is a little too subtle for some third-year boys, but the following extracts show that even members of the C2 block can take a detached view of their enthusiasms about the pop world, when a comparatively remote idol is concerned, and be critical of poses, or sympathetic towards the sheer hard slog required to reach the top of the profession. Most of these poems were started during a single period and completed at home.

The Pop Star Life

A pop star life is not very gay,
It's work all night and work all day.
The manager says you're working tonight at eight and finishing at
two and get up at ten and kiss all the girls. Scream, scream, it drives
you mad, you cannot walk away or the manager goes mad.
It's all in the pop world you know, wearing clothes that are mad and
sometimes at the end it drives you insane and at the last you take a
drug. You feel gay in a world of your own but if you look at yourself
you're mad, you know he takes drugs how he will end.

Stephen – set block C2

Pop star

Every day, boring drives,
You name the city
We've been.
Down the roads, up the hills.
Every day I sing, the same old song.
What do people see in me?
Could it be my eyes?
My face?
My personality?
My boyhood ambition has come live,
I'm glad that I don't have to work in a factory.
You could call it exciting
But too active for me.
The end of the day has come,
No more shows,
Now jump into home.

David – set block C2

A very different but equally valuable stimulus came from *The Empty Quarter*, an account of Wilfred Thesiger's travels in the South Arabian desert of Muscat and Oman. An interesting contrast is achieved by presenting Thesiger's early life in London by means of a montage of monochrome still photographs, while his desert adventures introduce movement and colour from the lives of the Bedou – their camps, camel races, hawks and wives. A group of these men are persuaded to take him through the desert, a landscape of high dunes and undulating plain, where winds continually re-form the hills and drive the rippling sand into new configurations. The film examines the customs and courtesies of the Arabs, their tracking skills, and the natural beauties of the desert flora and fauna to which the Arabs living there seem insensitive.

Most of our audiences were fascinated by this film, despite its unusually slow and quiet pace, and one set asked to see it again. Writers in the fourth year (D1 set block) were asked to select aspects of the film that impressed them and develop these in any way they wished. The selection was varied and included stories of desert oil-prospecting, descriptions of other journeys, personal memories of conditions of extreme heat, and one philosophical account of life as a constant struggle:

> . . . Man, in the desert, uses his intelligence and brings water which revives life, so when the sun strikes he lives until his water has gone then he, like the animals, seeks the shade and then waits for rain or dies in the attempt to find water – life.
>
> Now the sun is losing the battle – modern man is taking over the desert and is cultivating it. He is creating life and making it permanent with continual water.
>
> Since the second world war man in his great cities has been cultivating his world making it fit for life and not war. Yet in some areas war still carries on. It is the same in the desert, areas are still left, great areas, where life is still controlled by the rain and the sun. . . .

Robert – set block D1

Some of the work was in prose and some in verse, as the following:

The Empty Quarter

The camel-dung games at night they play,
Or sometimes to the light of day,
Then its off again through the Empty Quarter
With one object in sight, to be the first,
The very first across the Empty Quarter.
From Buraimini in the north to Dhafar in the south,
Then right down to the mouth
Of the Arabian sea,

Now all to show are two bruised knees,
From caravan convoys, yes, *min qaafila qaafilaat.*
We had only one guide
But a camel he could ride, and
That is better than you or I,
Then I wished that I could fly
Leaving the desert far behind
Lost forever in my mind.
To milk a camel is quite all right,
We drunk the milk only at night.
We moved about like a small procession
We, our few possessions
A rifle, a camel and water sack
Which kept in water, like an old plastic mac.
The camel dung is sharp 'by God',
Not smooth like a small pea pod.
A good meal is what I need
Not unleavened bread and crushed up seed.
The end is in sight
Just at the time for bed tonight.

Ian – set block D1

These examples, produced in almost immediate response to the film, are rough drafts, but are promising and interesting examples worthy of further revision and polishing. Yet, ironically, *The Empty Quarter* drew to our attention a most serious failure and a fundamental teaching problem. The majority of compositions in which the desert was directly described assumed it was absolutely flat, despite the many long scenes in the film in which Thesiger's party was seen climbing considerable dunes or ridges. The simple straightforward factual statements of the film had failed to break down the deep-seated stereotype. One of the most important aims of our work with films is to draw the pupils into involvement with the events or characters portrayed, by means of the creative work they are asked to do, and identification of this sort, through some imaginative extension through writing, helps to imprint the ideas of the film more securely in the mind. More specific exercises concerning Thesiger or his companions would perhaps have forced a realisation of the true nature of the desert upon the writers. Our more general approach, whilst valid for some purposes, is used sparingly because it does not challenge fixed assumptions often enough.

Our treatment of the Peter Watkins television film *Culloden* was partly determined by the need to face this problem. To provide a high degree of critical involvement in both the viewing of the film and the writing of the compositions, we showed the film to two sets in the D1 block, requiring them to write respectively from the English and the Scottish points of view. The poems and compositions following upon this laid stress on the cruelty and wastefulness of war, in a concrete and personal way, rather than on the political and idealistic aspects of the conflict – a view largely consonant with the director's own attitudes communicated by the film.

In the context of the whole work of the English department in this school, film has proved its value in encouraging the development of better verbal communication by the pupils. Living as many of them do in unsettled domestic circumstances and culturally limited environments, the pupils need our help not only in the mechanics of speech and writing but also in the conscious structuring of their conceptual thinking. Perhaps as a result of greater exposure to television, film and advertising than to radio, conversation, books or even newspapers, their visual vocabulary seems more extensive and their response to visual images more immediate than to verbal forms. Their thinking and their spoken and written expression can therefore often best be stimulated by film.

Many teachers may be heard cataloguing the difficulties of ordering films, obtaining and operating the projector, securing the room with blackout and screen, and little comment is heard about the incidental advantages of the film-viewing situation – the value of the intense concentration upon the screen in a darkened room, more effectively insulated from extraneous sound, with the persistent distractions of irrelevant notices and charts or movements outside the windows or along the corridors effectively eliminated. Even the constant noise of the projector habituates in the ear and blankets the initial fidgeting of other pupils until the sound-track and the pictures absorb the attention. This quality of concentration, quite as much as the aspect of novelty, contributes to the unique effectiveness of the film lesson.

For this reason, viewing conditions and a proper atmosphere are important, and the harassed teacher with the reel to put on and the lights to put out should try not to forget to give attention to the small details – the seats placed too near the screen or too far to the side, the rows too cramped together and the inevitable attraction for the spectators of raised ledges (window-sills, radiators, and side-benches).

Planned timing, careful organisation, and an initial discipline of silence must be established early as the constant policy for the film lesson. In practice, the urge to make spontaneous comments on the film being watched is sometimes too valuable to be suppressed.

Carefully planned, well managed and selectively used, the film lesson is a very welcome occasion for the majority of children. They rapidly accept the classwork associated with it, and even where in other subjects the use of film material becomes more commonplace, the films used in English lessons are likely to retain their popularity by reason of their interest, quality and experiment. For our department, film is only one of the possible approaches but one with distinct advantages, correlating well with other media in a very easily controlled format. We have seen it increase the capacities of the pupils to express their ideas and experiences, and we have accepted it into our courses convinced of its high creative valency.

5

A college of further education

Literature and film compared – critical analysis
of a feature film – a thematic approach – study
of a director or national cinema – close
analysis in literature – value of genre films –
the Western – the 'art movie' – written work –
link with Film Society

Jane Corbett, Lecturer in the Department of
Liberal Studies, Kingsway College of Further
Education, London

Film-teaching has been an important part of the work done at Kingsway
College of Further Education for nearly ten years now, and is increasing
in many areas of further education. The immediacy of the impact that
film makes on the audience, its contemporaneity, the striking manner
of presenting experience, and the fine quality and range of much that
is now available on 16 mm film, all make the use of film in education
particularly valuable. Like the study of literature, it both extends the
student's experience and his understanding of that experience, and
sharpens his way of looking, and of looking critically – looking,
thinking and questioning. What the two disciplines of English and
Film have in common, and how they may feed and complement one
another, is a topic to which I shall return at more length, but we might
first consider the range of the students in further education.

The range of both age and ability is enormous. Some are fifteen-
year-old school-leavers from secondary modern schools or the lower
streams of comprehensive schools with no C.S.E. or O-levels, the pupils
discussed in the Newsom Report. Others are fifteen- or sixteen-year-
olds who for various reasons have left school but who are ambitious
to take O-level or even A-level subjects, and who have the ability to do
so. Yet others are older, already embarked on A-levels or more advanced

vocational training at the college, some with hopes of going on to University education.

Some of this range of students are day or block-release – from fifteen-year-old G.P.O. employees to legal executives or post A-level B.B.C. trainees in their twenties; and others are full-time students of widely varying social backgrounds, with a similar range of educational ability. Most students are in the college for one or two years, but block-release courses often run for only two terms full-time; and some students, both full-time and day-release, stay in the college for more than two years.

Because of this range of ability and age we make some very flexible attempts to divide film-teaching into two or three parts. Firstly, there are film appreciation courses, which are roughly divided into two groups: classes for students with O-level English and classes for those, who tend to be younger, without any O-levels. However, these two categories are flexible, and the individual character and aptitude of a student is taken into account in allocating him to a particular class. Many of the films shown will be the same in both classes, and it is chiefly the method and level of discussion and approach that will vary. Secondly, there is the use of film in English, Social Studies and History courses, where two or three full-length feature films will normally be shown each term. Each film will be used extensively where relevant over a wide range of courses, the method of teaching and treatment again varying according to the kind and academic level of the students in the group.

In this chapter I intend to concentrate upon the use of film in film-appreciation classes, because what I have to say about this will, I think, apply to the use of film in all kinds of classes and courses, and to the value of teaching film in any context. The use of film and the kind of discussion in a *film* class will not be very different from that of an *English* class, though the film course will probably provide more opportunities for the regular showing and discussion of film, encouraging greater familiarity with the film medium and the directors working in it; in an English course film will play a more occasional part, and knowledge and understanding of the medium may be more casual and less systematic.

In further education we are fortunate in not being limited to forty-minute periods. At Kingsway, the day is divided into four sessions of one-and-a-half hours (two in the morning, two in the afternoon); film classes are timetabled in the second session of the morning or of the afternoon, enabling us to run on into the lunch-break or after college hours if necessary. Thus we are not necessarily limited to ninety-minute features; and this we feel is as crucial to the serious study of film as reading an entire play or novel is to the study of literature.

I have suggested above why I think the use of film in education to be important. Like any work of art, a film at best is one man's vision and ordering of a part of his experience; and it is in encountering that ordered vision that the student comes more fully to question the nature of his own experience and environment. And it is partly through ordered, close analysis and discussion of the work of art that he learns to look more sharply and thoughtfully, and that his awareness of himself and what is around him is deepened and extended.

To compare the two art forms of literature and film is, I am aware, to do something that can easily be misunderstood. The British film industry has contributed to this misunderstanding by translating 'great books', and more recently novels and plays with a strong sociological interest (like '*Room at the Top*' or '*A Taste of Honey*'), without sufficient thought for the difference between the two media. Hence films are produced which are dull and prosaic, depending too heavily on dialogue, and representing often very simplified and shortened versions of the books from which they are derived. The visual potential of the cinema is inadequately exploited, and one is left with the feeling that the adaptation has been chosen not because the director feels that it is particularly relevant to his own times or preoccupations, but rather because it might make a commercial film, or simply because it *is* a 'great book'.

We might compare David Lean's adaptations of Dickens with Donskoi's great adaptation of the Gorki Trilogy, which is reconceived in genuinely film terms; or with Penn's *The Miracle Worker*, taken from a play which, though interesting, seems to have appealed to Penn because of his own response to its relevance to his own concerns. What he has made of the play in his film seems to me greatly superior to the original, for reasons I shall consider below.

It is a truism, but it cannot be said too often, that film is essentially a visual medium. In some senses, therefore, it is closer to painting than to the theatre which depends so much more on the spoken word. In film, the spoken word is only one element in the total work, and very often a relatively minor element. A film-maker thinks chiefly in terms of visual images, and it is through these that he conveys what he wants to express. In Arthur Penn's *The Miracle Worker*, one of the most striking ways in which we learn how the child, Helen Keller, is beginning to learn and to communicate is how we see her face and movement. For the whole of the first half of the film her movements are wild and uncontrolled, and her face is 'shut', non-communicative, almost like that of a little animal – it shows expression of a kind, anger, pleasure, greed, and so on; but when we first see her beginning to learn and beginning to achieve a concentration and a self-discipline we realise how partially she has been alive.

For example, in the scene in the little house in the grounds set aside for Miss Annie to teach Helen in, Annie hands her an egg with the chick just hatching and struggling to be born. Helen holds the egg in her hands, and feels the struggling chick breaking through the shell. Her face shows such a calm joy and concentration that we are made to feel the coming of light and understanding in her; and to realise that hitherto her face, for all its expression of passion, has been veiled, that she has been imprisoned within herself. There are other images in the film which express the same idea: one is where Helen sits in their little cottage by the fireside, a black veil covering her face, and she blows it out from her face as if to shift it a little. Miss Annie has put this veil over her head so that by blowing it out from her Helen may begin to learn to make the motions necessary for speech. The image here conveys their situation and relationship: Helen's veiled imprisonment within herself, and attempt to struggle out of it through language, which Miss Annie is trying to give her; and the dark space between them as long as Helen is so veiled. Yet whilst the image is so powerful and full of complex meaning, it is in no sense merely symbolic, but exists strikingly first and foremost on a practical and physical level, and only because of its memorable effectiveness are we led on to consider it more deeply.

Our sense of Helen's and Miss Annie's imprisonment is developed by other shots in this part of the film, where we see Annie and Helen through bars as Annie runs through the fenced-in garden trying to find somewhere for them to be alone, where she can teach Helen in peace without the terribly over-protective and self-indulgent love of Helen's parents which prevents Helen from becoming a fully human and independent being. The darkness of the big Southern house is also strikingly used, both for the way in which it evokes this particular solid, rather gloomily respectable family, and also in a larger sense the oppression of the father's paternalism, of which Helen is not the only victim, and under which it is not possible for anyone fully to grow to maturity, like a plant kept in the dark.

The very opening shots of the film, in the credit sequence, express Helen's suffering and imprisonment, and yet they have a larger and more representative significance. Great white sheets hanging on the washing line fill the screen, and Helen tumbles about within them, falling from one to the other with a kind of aimless, blind lack of control, but quite silently, just as she herself is in silence. Then we see a hill and an empty horizon. Over the top of the hill, out of the emptiness, a blind, groping figure emerges, staggering, arms spread wide, head uplifted and sniffing the air to catch what little sense she can of where she is. But juxtaposed with these images is one of the Negro servant's little children playing by the steps of the big house, and being shooed away by their mother for being there. And from their continuous background presence throughout the film, constantly being shooed away, we realise that they too are prevented from becoming fully independent and conscious human beings (as Helen is) and that they too are imprisoned by the ways of thinking and the organisation of society that the father represents.

This order is beautifully evoked in the shots of the family at the dinner table which punctuate the film. In the dark dining room the family sit around the elegant table, neatly arranged, the father at the head and each one in his subordinate place, ending with the Negro servant who hovers in the darkness beyond and excluded from the circle of the table. Only Helen is a disruptive note as she roams wildly round the table, grabbing food from the various plates and stuffing it greedily into her mouth as she passes on. The family tolerate this as the father, son, grandmother feel that the decencies of dinner time and conversation can most easily be preserved if as little notice as possible is taken of Helen – almost as if she were some badly behaved but adored dog. But when Miss Annie comes she refuses to ignore Helen and to exclude her in this way; Helen must be accepted fully as an equal, and this also means that she must be made to be able to take her place at table in a civilised manner. To do this there must be a violent and disruptive battle with Helen, and the order that the dinner table represents must be shattered and adapted in order to recognise and accommodate this live human being and give her a place.

Helen comes to represent for us in some way all those who are denied their full humanity and self-responsibility, and we see that her coming to that self-responsibility through learning both gives her a fuller humanity and necessitates new growth and self-knowledge in those around her. What it means to her to understand language is most wonderfully evoked towards the end of the film, when Miss Annie is pumping water for Helen, having dragged her from making another scene at the dinner table; and, as usual, in a vain effort to communicate with Helen she spells out the word 'water' in deaf-and-dumb sign-language as she pumps, never giving up her attempts to teach Helen language. Suddenly, Helen grasps the connection between the signs for letters that Annie is spelling out and the feeling of water on her hand. At last she understands that letters make words and words symbolise things, in fact what language is, and as she mouths sounds that are an attempt to say 'water', her face is alive with concentration and she becomes joyous, but not with the kind of merely animal pleasure of the opening of the film when she was given a doll. This time, as with the hatching chick, it is the joy of understanding, she has absorbed independence, a dignity which is new and fine, and which no words could express as intensely as the image of her that we see. Nor is the power of this scene merely dependent upon the strength of the acting of Patty Duke and Anne Bancroft, but upon the whole composition and placing of the images: the coming out of the dark dining-room into the daylight outside, Helen's grasping of Miss Annie's hand round the pump that is between them to spell out feverishly to *her* this time the word she has recognised, her face uplifted as if straining to grasp and sense fully what is around her, and behind them the neat house rising up in the background, from which they have in a sense escaped.

Growth in a human being, we perceive, does not take place in isolation but is both a response to others and affects others. Annie can teach Helen in a way no one else has been able to because she respects her as an equal human being – her very preparedness to wrestle physically with her and not merely to pet her is a manifestation of this responsibility – demanding of her what she would demand of an equal human being. She does not pity her as a cripple, nor as something less than fully human. She also learns from Helen as any teacher must learn from his pupils, for it is the very openness that is necessary for learning that is also necessary for teaching; and since to teach is to be involved in a relationship with the pupil, so there will be giving and receiving and resulting change and development for both pupil and teacher. Annie is softened by her experience with Helen, her roughness and her own suffering are softened, her imaginative understanding is deepened, and she loves for the first time since her brother died in an asylum when she was a child. One of the last images of the film is at night when

Miss Annie is sitting alone in the rocking chair on the balcony and Helen comes out full of love and gratitude and climbs on her knee, and Miss Annie holds her and spells out the word 'love' to Helen as they rock silently. And also the arrogance, pride and self-contained isolation of Helen's Southern family is questioned and modified in some way, however small, from their encounter with Miss Annie from Northern urban poverty, and the new life she has enabled Helen to find.

This commentary on *The Miracle Worker* arises out of discussions I have had with various classes, and is in a sense an amalgam of the points and perceptions most commonly raised by the students. When we first begin to discuss this film, the students are usually interested chiefly in problems raised by Helen's physical handicaps, and the problems of parents who have such a child – whether or not Helen's parents were too 'soft' with her; and also they tend to divide to some extent in their response to Miss Annie. Is she almost cruel with Helen? What special insights and difficulties do her own particular background and blindness give her? They do not as a rule mention straight away, nor necessarily seem to perceive, the larger implications of the film, the education that takes place for *all* the people who are concerned with Helen in the film.

In order to make the discussion as wide-open and inclusive of all their very different perceptions as possible, I find that much the best approach is to start with each person recalling as many specific moments or images as he can, ranging over the whole film in any order that occurs to him. The moments that remain most vividly for them are usually, in any case, strikingly significant ones or images with a complexity of meaning. The students' descriptions and recapitulation of these images enable everyone to re-see and re-experience the film to some extent, which is very important as the discussion usually takes place a week after the viewing of the film. And one person's comments will often spark off associated perceptions and memories in others so that fairly quickly a detailed memory of the film is achieved.

Above all, this process ensures that students are not closing their minds too quickly to what is really there in the film, and simply bringing their own preconceptions to the issues they discover, which can happen all too easily if they are encouraged or permitted to extract and discuss issues in isolation from the film itself. What so often happens with any work of art is that one does not in fact find there what one expects to find – it contains something that is unpredictable, and perhaps therefore disturbing, and the easiest escape route is to discuss what was expected rather than what is there.

If the students can begin to discuss what they have actually found in the work, they may become aware of the inadequacy of their assumptions and predictions. The process is not a denial of interpretation, since the students are encouraged to remember as much as possible about the film, and to say how what they remembered affected them as they watched: these recapitulations can form the basis for interpretation of the film. I often find it helpful to write up some of the questions and problematic moments or images on the blackboard so that they will not be forgotten in a free-ranging discussion, and these can then be shaped later into a more coherent account of the film as the class attempts to examine them together. By this process, I have found that the students themselves usually raise the larger implications of the film: whether Helen is merely a handicapped child, or whether she also represents a wider group and range of experience than that, and, if so, who and what; or what happens to Helen's family as she grows to fuller independence and humanity; or why Miss Annie can succeed with her when no one else can.

My function as a teacher seems to be to know the film sufficiently well to allow the students to talk about whichever parts most struck them, rather than to force interpretations upon them or to regularise the discussion into a methodical shape from beginning to end of the film. The more they range over the film, the more likely we are to get a response to its whole organic form rather than to the sequence of the 'story' or to particular issues arising from a partial context.

In this way, from the points recorded on the board, the teacher may inject into the discussion points which have already been raised but which are being forgotten in an over-simplifying process of interpretation: 'Yes, Miss Annie is hard with Helen and doesn't seem to love her like her parents do, but what about John's point that that scene where they wrestle together in the dining-room made him feel that Annie is prepared to bother with Helen and spend time with her in a way no one else does?' To which another student replies:

There is something in the way Annie takes hold of Helen roughly, like when they are down on the ground together, crawling under the table, chasing each other and pulling each other's hair, that you couldn't imagine her mother or even her brother doing. In a way they are equals.

Mary   And when Miss Annie won't put up with her goings on at the table, I was grateful because it really annoyed me the way they all let her make such a nuisance of herself like that.

Teacher Why did it annoy you? Surely she couldn't help it?

Mary   Well, it didn't seem fair somehow to Helen. What would happen to her when she was grown up? And then anyway, no one really took any notice of her, they all just sat around the table eating, and the men discussing politics, or trying to – till they lost their tempers.

Frank   Yes, it seemed Miss Annie really cared more about Helen as a human being, by trying to make her behave better even if it meant such a terrible fight. To the others she was merely a pet, like a dog – and badly behaved at that.

Teacher So you're saying that in fact Annie sees her as an equal human being in a way that her parents for all their 'love' do not. Well, in that case, what *is* their love for Helen?

And so we can continue with a discussion that leads us through to the part of the film where the parents first refuse to let Miss Annie take Helen to the little house where she can be alone with her, and then reluctantly agree to allow her a limited and quite inadequate period of time there. One student refers to the brother's visit at the cottage window where he tells Annie how God destines some people to be handicapped, and that one must accept and bow down beneath such a thing. When another student defends the brother's position, another brings up the moment where Helen first feels the hatching chick struggling out of its shell, and the wonderful alive and tender expression on her face, such as we have never seen before, and says: 'If that's what beginning to learn and control herself means to Helen, then how *can* the brother be right in what he says – leave her as a beast and pity her?'

It would be wrong for me to imply that every class works as cogently and fluently as this, or that the progression of talk is necessarily as consistent as might appear above. But everything I have quoted has been said by students in various ways, and has provoked similar responses. If the teacher encourages students to offer a detailed account of the film, then the more important critical points will inevitably emerge, many of them with every class.

During the rest of the term, students will see other films grouped

E

round a common theme. Their response to film grows more confident and enables them to talk with greater assurance and fluency about each film, but they also begin to relate the films to one another. Issues, problems or areas of experience which hitherto they had neglected now seem to merit more thought, and these are often the more important aspects of the films seen, since a number of different film-makers working in different ways have chosen to explore the same issues. This seems to me the advantage of preparing a course, at least for one term, around a common theme; though it is very important that the films chosen are chosen because the teacher thinks they are worth showing as films, and not simply to illustrate a particular attitude or point.

If, for example, one took as one's theme 'Young People and their attempt to grow to some understanding of their environment', one could include Truffaut's *400 Blows* (a useful film to start with as it is very easily approachable by students), and *Les Mistons*, Penn's *The Miracle Worker*, Schloendorff's *The Young Törless*, Szabo's *Father*, or Wajda's *A Generation*, all of which raise larger and very important political questions about the nature of the environment into which the young person is growing. To these one might therefore add several of the Polish and Czech cartoons, notably those of Jan Lenica; and short films such as Chris Marker's *La Jetée* or Polanski's *Two Men and a Wardrobe*, particularly useful since it has no dialogue and the students are forced to watch the film to discover what is happening through the visual images rather than through what people say.

At Kingsway, we are able to book about four or five feature films per term, which occupy eight to ten weeks of the term, given that the showing of a feature is followed by a week in which the feature is discussed, perhaps with an extract if one is available. For the remaining weeks of the term we would show shorts or extracts which can be discussed within the one-and-a-half-hour period. A thematic approach could be continued throughout the year, but in general I prefer to base the courses in the second and third terms on particular directors or national cinemas. It seems to me fruitful to see more than one film by a particular director, just as it is to read more than one novel or short story by a writer, to trace the artist's common concerns and ways of working, or his particular individual style and vision, discernible quite often in films dealing with very different subject-matter.

Such studies might include the films of Arthur Penn, relating him briefly to Hollywood and the American cinema, seeing two or three features plus extracts; or of Jean Renoir, relating him to the French New Wave and Truffaut in particular; or of Visconti and the Italian Neo-realist cinema; or of Kurosawa and the Japanese cinema. As my examples suggest I would try, briefly at least, to relate the particular director to his national context, and with some directors such as Kurosawa, Godard or Truffaut, to an international context.

In recounting our discussions of *The Miracle Worker*, I have tried to suggest how we experience film chiefly through visual images, and how these visual images are the 'drama' for us, and express the emotions and development of the characters, very often without words. Thus any discussion of film which does not involve close reference to what has been seen on the screen is meaningless – as meaningless as discussing a novel or a Shakespeare play without close reference to the actual words and verbal images used by the writer. The method of analysis and discussion of the two media may have much in common, and may indeed feed one another. Perhaps I should define and illustrate what I mean by close analysis with regard to literature, since the phrase is widely used but has a variety of rather different interpretations.

Any study of, say, a Shakespeare play calls for close scrutiny of the language, not for abstract academic reasons but simply to understand what is going on in the play: and to attend merely to some idea of plot or story in a play such as '*Othello*' is to all but miss the experience of the play. The full experience lies in the way in which we can discover, through a close attention to the language, how the characters develop in relation to one another, how they grow in response to what happens to them, and how far they inhibit their own growth, like Othello himself, even to the point of self-destruction. For example, we may notice how from Act III, Scene 3, in particular, Othello's language shows increasingly the same kind of coarseness and cynical brutality as Iago's, until they speak much of the time with an almost identical voice.

If we have read the play carefully, however, there have been signs of an Iago-like quality in Othello from the very beginning. In Act I, Scene 3, though no one has suggested that Othello would want Desdemona with him for any reason but his love, and she herself was the first to ask simply to go with him to Cyprus:

> That I did love the Moor to live with him
> My downright violence and storm of fortunes
> May trumpet to the world,

he, nevertheless, says to the Duke:

> Let her have your voice.
> Vouch with me Heaven. I therefore beg it not
> To please the palate of my appetite:
> Nor to comply with heat the young affects
> In my defunct and proper satisfaction,
> But to be free and bounteous to her mind.

His language here reveals what Othello as a foreigner, and black as well, has taken, perhaps unconsciously, from his relatively new and un-accustomed environment, the Venetian Court – a kind of cynical sophistication which is not native to him and yet feeds on some deep Iago-like sensual disgust that lies unrealised within him and makes love 'appetite', similar to Iago's 'merely a lust of the blood and a permission of the will' (Act I, Scene 3).

Again, arrived in Cyprus, Othello greets Desdemona with:

> Come my dear love,
> The purchase made, the fruits are to ensue;
> That profit's yet to come 'tween me and you.
> (Act II, Scene 3)

The commercial language is unmistakable here and reveals a particu-larly unpleasant quality in Othello's undoubtedly conscious way of regarding his marriage. And throughout the first half of the play, Othello's speeches reveal a self-dramatising and egotistical quality, as if he were making a public speech to an audience whatever the circum-stances:

> Upon this hint I spake.
> She lov'd me for the dangers I had passed,
> And I lov'd her that she did pity them.
> (Act I, Scene 3)

It has been far more than a 'hint' from her, and his alluding in this way to her almost open declaration of her feelings and her desire to marry him is almost comical.

If we have remarked such moments, then the swiftness and ease with

which Othello picks up Iago's extremely vague insinuations about
Desdemona's unfaithfulness, almost leading him in them in no time at
all, although he has no grounds whatsoever from experience or report
for doubting her, and the way in which he falls into such a chaos of
passion and self-dramatisation, self-pity and despair, is no longer so
extraordinary. We also have a warning of his rashness in making
assumptions and taking decisions, a decisiveness which may be necessary and appropriate in battle, but which is a foolish disregard of the
complex nature of men and events in ordinary life in the Brawl scene
in Act II which presages the storm he later undergoes in suspicion of
Desdemona's betrayal and his ultimate self-destruction. The swiftness
with which he dismisses Cassio, not waiting until the relative calm of
morning, and without any kind of trial, merely on Iago's brief evidence –

>   Cassio, I love thee,
>   But never more be officer of mine.
>   (Act II, Scene 2)

is the same rash swiftness he reveals in giving substance to Iago's
hints in Act III, Scene 3. In both scenes he refuses to trust his own
knowledge and experience of the person involved, even though he
often describes what is happening to him with more accuracy than he
fully knows; as in

>   Now by Heaven
>   My blood begins my safer guides to rule
>   And passion (having my best judgment collied)
>   Assays to lead the way.
>   (Act II, Scene 2)

Only if we attend this closely to the language of the play can we
hope to understand what happens to Othello, why it happens, and what
kind of destructive, dark despair and egotistical self-mistrust Iago
represents that is in all of the characters, and against which the only
weapons are genuine self-awareness and assuming of self-responsibility,
both of which Othello wholly refuses.

I hope I have said enough to make it clear that by phrases such as
'close analysis' or 'close attention to language' I am not referring to a
grammatical analysis or to any kind of merely abstract break-down
of the language. Grammatical terms, which clearly have their use,

can easily become a misleading distraction from any thoughtful consideration of the work as a whole and what it means or is about. So in film, too, terms like 'frame', 'shot', 'montage', 'cinéma vérité' are all useful or even necessary, but can easily become a kind of jargon which, instead of leading us deeper into an understanding of the experience and meaning of the whole film, distracts us into a pointless recital of technical details divorced from the content these techniques are being used to express, destroying the emotion of the experience we were trying to account for. There is no inherent virtue in recognising a particular type of shot – any more than a particular figure of speech – unless the function of this device in bringing about a revaluation of the meaning in that context is understood. To say this is merely to put the old point that form is inextricable from content, and that in studying film, as in studying literature, one needs to attend closely to *how* something is being said or presented in images only in order to discover *what* is being said; and that techniques and style are only means to an end, a final experience, not ends in themselves.

Increasingly, teachers of English see their role as involving not merely the teaching of literature but also an examination of the whole of contemporary culture, and particularly popular culture. Novels, plays and short stories will often be looked at alongside newspaper and magazine articles and television programmes, and reproductions of paintings and photographs are used in discussion of written material and to encourage the students' own creative writing. Film has an obvious place here, since perhaps even more than literature it straddles what we refer to as popular culture and, for want of a better phrase, 'high art' – going from the Western or gangster movie to the 'art film'. And, however arty, film must always depend on an audience and box-office takings for its survival. Film, therefore, apart from its intrinsic value, would seem to further usefully what the teacher is trying to do: that is both to include and build upon the students' existing interests and experience, and also to extend them in new directions.

Students already go to the cinema and watch a lot of movies on television and filmed television plays and series, perhaps more than many of them read. They already have a habit of watching, and so it becomes all the more important that they should watch alertly and begin to question and to some degree discriminate amongst what is available. And one of the great values of film study is that it seems to the student to relate very immediately to his own life and interests, often more readily than literature does, by including some of his existing interests and pleasures that have hitherto been relatively little included in school and in academic work, whilst at the same time much of what we, as teachers, in fact show the student may be quite new and strange to him.

As a film teacher I would certainly not see my task as one of progressing through popular films to art films. In fact I would be unwilling to make that kind of distinction at all, or to imply by it simple criteria of good and bad. A John Ford Western seems to me to be as much worth watching as a Bergman or an Antonioni movie, though the one may be a film whose strength expresses itself in the popular imagery of a genre, and the other a far more explicitly personalised vision. This very distinction between the two kinds of film-making is worth discussing in itself, and relates to the whole question of popular and minority culture, and where the strengths of popular culture may really lie. Ford, and even to a great extent, Arthur Penn, work within a highly organised film *industry*, with its own conventions, limitations and tradition. Not only is film in the tradition we still anachronistically refer to as Hollywood an entirely popular medium, but the director is also particularly subject to strong controls of box-office and the existing structure of the industry. A film is therefore far less obviously the work of a particular director in Hollywood than is, say, a Bergman or a Godard film. For this very reason certain genres in Hollywood films are far more easily recognised, for example the Western or the gangster genre, but within that genre the quality of films may vary enormously, and certain directors may also have a style and predominant concerns which are easily recognisable when one is at all familiar with their films – for example John Ford, Fritz Lang, Alfred Hitchcock, Sam Peckinpah. Thus we cannot say that because of the nature of the film industry in Hollywood the director is of no importance compared to European directors, and hence any easy distinction between the popular and the more personal work of art is immediately broken down.

The Western is *par excellence* an example of a popular form. It embodies one of the great American myths, and this myth has mainly been articulated visually. In fact it is significant how much less interesting on the whole the equivalent literature of the West is, and how so much of it has failed to be popular in the sense that the films are, and remains merely trivial. The myth the Western embodies is that of the frontier, and virtually all true Westerns are set within the short period of 1875–90, the time of the last frontier. The fact that this is a national myth can be seen in the extensive use of frontier terminology in areas like politics – J. F. Kennedy's 'New Frontier' government, Johnson the Westerner in Stetson and Western clothes, and the dude ranch, still one of the biggest holiday attractions. The frontier represents a time just before civilisation and the solidification of society – by the time the Western hero leaves the town to which he has at last brought peace, he has established it as a civilised place. But for that very reason there is no longer any place in it for him; to stay would be to hang up his gun and run a store or a farm which would be a kind of death. Nor do the people, for all their gratitude, really wish him to stay, for he represents to them a continual threat of renewed violence, both from himself – he has killed to establish peace and may therefore kill again – and from the vengeance his killing and his reputation may still bring down on him and therefore upon the town. Hence the last shot in so many Westerns of the hero riding away alone and homeless towards the next frontier town which is not yet civilised.

But the civilising of the frontier town presents a dilemma in itself. It must be rid of its bad men and this the hero must do, but not only does he thereby destroy his own position and leave no room for himself, he also enables a society to come into being which is in some ways a disappointment, inferior to the promise of the frontier. There is something tame, ordinary, self-interested and even in a sense ignoble about the civilisation that is achieved, and hence, for us, a kind of relief in the hero riding away from it all and keeping his purity. Perhaps this is the secret of the popularity of the Western myth; that America which being newly created was to be paradise on earth, just and wealthy and equal, has fallen far short of these ideals, and though the frontier has long been closed its myth leaves open the possibility of a fresh and better attempt, and yet also contains the paradox of the inevitable failure of this attempt. It is also perhaps the reason why the Western raises such important questions for an English audience too, though our own culture may be very different from that of the frontier. The Western hero is in constant conflict with, and finally rejects, the very society he maintains and furthers – but he does *not* try to overthrow it and is in no sense a revolutionary. The Western is also a completely masculine myth in a somewhat emasculated society. Women play an archetypal role: the good tending to be a blonde, virginal and civilised being just in from the East, e.g. classically *My Darling Clementine* (John Ford), and the other woman not exactly bad, but dark, sexual, often foreign (Mexican or Indian), wearing low-cut dresses and being rather wild and unladylike, yet in a way understanding better the hero and the masculine way of life; and she is often killed to save the man from a final choice between women.

In the Western, then, we get certain archetypal figures and themes of general interest and importance: the search, vengeance, the blood cycle or beleaguered warriors, and sometimes it is units rather than simply individuals we are dealing with, like the cavalry versus the Indian (e.g. *She Wore a Yellow Ribbon* [John Ford], and in a highly complex way *Major Dundee* [Sam Peckinpah]). But within this pattern or genre there is infinite variety possible, and the possibility of the director creating a strong personal voice.

What I have said suggests, I hope, that the Western is both popular and deals with serious and major themes and problems in American life, and by extension in all life. In many ways it has things in common with art as seemingly distant as classical Greek drama with its similar concerns with vengeance, justice, blood-feud and heroism. In a John Ford movie man is set between earth and sky in a landscape which dwarfs him – even a man like John Wayne – and yet with which he is in harmony. In contrast the hero in an Anthony Mann Western finds himself in a more rocky, barren landscape and an indifferent, lowering sky which in some way overwhelm him. Such placing of men within these enormous landscapes which are of such significance to the drama as a whole gives that whole an elemental quality which again relates to Greek drama. To show students and discuss with them some good Westerns can only help them to sort out the barrage of such films they see on television. Some of these are excellent; some of them, particularly the films and series made specially for television, are little different from *Peyton Place* and have much more in common with that kind of soap-opera. It is important to help the students not to dismiss the whole lot because of the worst and dreariest, which some of the more sophisticated ones are often wont to do.

The 'art movie', whatever that means, needs less of an apologia, particularly for teachers who tend to be the kind of people who go to these anyway. At Kingsway we have found that while it is important to draw on students' existing interests and on popular art forms, it is as important and as fruitful to offer the student totally strange or foreign material. Some of the most successful parts of the film courses we have held have been the Japanese movies. Since many of these are visually, technically and dramatically exciting and interesting, we have found that their impact upon the students and ability to hold and fascinate their interest quite overcomes their mere strangeness. They watch them without preconceived demands and ideas of what the drama ought to be and hence with a concentration that is unusual. They remember and ponder them both because of the memorable quality of so many of the images and because they do not fit readily into their own experience; yet there is plenty in the drama with which the student can, on reflection, connect and relate. *The Seven Samurai* (Kurosawa) is a popular example of a Japanese film that usually fascinates and entertains students of all levels, and which, of course, relates interestingly to the Western. But even the much more foreign *An Actor's Revenge* (Ichikawa) constantly returned to many students' imaginations because of the stunning quality of many of its images and the way Ichikawa makes sense of the wide screen, using only a part of it if he only needs a part, constantly giving us a sense of its space, width and depth; as for example when a rope shoots in the darkness across the breadth of the screen and pulls taut on a distant tree at the other end of the screen, or when people come running towards us through the darkness starting tiny from the very depth of the screen until they emerge and stand before us, right close to us. And this sense of depth and people travelling in three dimensions is no mere matter of close and long shots but some much more imaginative understanding of what remarkable techniques can do to create a sense of space and drama. And then there is also the whole fascinating question of our response to the ambiguous sexuality of a number of the characters, particularly the female impersonator who lives at all times as a woman to perfect his art, and yet is a strong and normal man, by no means effeminate or transvestite, but a being both man *and* woman in different ways.

I have not yet mentioned the part writing might be expected to play in film classes. We would expect the student to write regularly at home after seeing a feature in preparation for discussion of it the following week, and to keep a diary of what has been seen with film titles and names of directors plus any other notes and comments which he cares to include. Some of the students who become really interested in movies also include notes and comments on other films they have seen in their own time. Sometimes we would also require the student to write briefly immediately after seeing a short or extract and before discussion of it in class, so that in a big class everyone who may well not get a chance to speak can have a few moments to think out his response a little more fully on paper, as a basis for discussion. In addition to this we sometimes have about one session per term with no film at all when the students have a chance to write at length about what has so far happened for them in the course and about any film which has particularly interested them. There are also many opportunities for creative writing arising out of a film course. If the theme for the term was the example I have already given – 'Young people and their relationship with their environment', – the students could easily turn from a viewing and discussion of *400 Blows* to an account of their own school experience or relationship with some part of their own environment, in the form of a short story, dramatic scene, film script or piece of personal writing. The teacher can also bring in literature wherever he feels it to be relevant. Parts of Gorki's '*My Childhood*' would seem to be very relevant to films like *400 Blows*, *Father*, or even *The Young Törless*, and '*The Diary of Anne Frank*' to the latter. Joyce's book '*Araby*' and other of the '*Dubliners*' tales also come to mind.

As an extra source of film viewing outside ordinary classes we also have the Film Society. This operates in the evening about three or four times a term and is open to anyone whether they take a film course or not. For this reason the choice of films tends to be more purely popular than in the film classes but by no means exclusively so. We try to make some relation between Film Society and film classes so that another film by the particular director being discussed in the classes may be shown in the Film Society, or at least another film from the particular national cinema under discussion. By this means the interested student may get to see eight or nine features per term and a large number of extracts and shorts.

The parallels I have drawn between ways of approaching literature and ways of approaching film suggest strongly that the English teacher will in many ways be the person best equipped to discuss film with a group of students, and that film is an important addition to reading and discussion in English and also in other subjects like Social Studies and History. But I feel the need here to qualify this with what may seem to be a rather contradictory view. Just as no one would set themselves up to teach History or Literature without a thorough study and knowledge of the subjects, so a study and knowledge of film is necessary for teaching it and using it in any other than an occasional way. Any teaching of film whatsoever demands that the teacher should have seen the film several times, for discussion of a feature requires a thorough knowledge of it on the part of the teacher since he must be able to refer to specific images and moments in detail, and help the students reconstruct the film, particularly if a week has elapsed between the viewing of the film and the discussion of it. One needs to have towards film the same kind of modesty that one would have towards painting, literature or history, and the same sense that being merely interested in these arts and areas of knowledge is not enough for teaching them.

6

A college of education

Training the English-teacher – film of the book
approach – distinctions of form – communication –
document and narrative – instruction and
persuasion – film as language – subjective/
objective – impressionism – expressionism –
heightened language – film for creative writing –
child study

Roy Knight

The Newsom Report, '*Half Our Future*' (see Chapter 1: Introduction)
made clear demands for teachers to be trained to use the media of
film and television as the basis for critical study and the development of
discrimination. Bede College, Durham, was the first college of education
to offer such a specialist course in September 1964, and there are at
least two other colleges which have since begun similar courses. But
the number of students trained in such main subject courses will
inevitably be small – even in a large department probably not more
than twenty per year, and more often only half this number; so by
far the most important aspect of training teachers to exploit the media
of film and television will be the courses which are obligatory for all
students, called variously 'qualifying', 'basic', 'professional' or 'curriculum' courses. Colleges vary so much in their size and organisation
that it may be helpful to set the context of these institutions and their
students.

Colleges of education, formerly called 'training colleges', are strange
institutions. There are about one hundred and sixty of them in England
and Wales, not counting certain specialist institutions for the training
of teachers in art, music, drama, physical and technical education,
which bring the number to above two hundred. They vary from small
colleges with a couple of hundred students to large ones of well over

one thousand, though a large number now fall within the six hundred to nine hundred range; they may be sited in rural surroundings, many miles away from any similar institution, or they may be in the heart of an industrial city above the Co-op. Since 1963 there has been a vast expansion in both the number of colleges and the size of those already existing, resulting overall in the doubling of the student intake, and for some colleges the fourfold increase in their student numbers. Currently there are about a hundred and ten thousand students in teacher-training.

They are rightly regarded as institutions of higher education, and they are linked with universities through institutes of education (in some places these are now called schools of education), yet in most places, even with the development of the Bachelor of Education degree, they are not 'part' of the university, and contact with colleagues in the university, whether on staff or student level, is likely to be occasional and unsystematic, if it exists at all. In this respect, the three colleges in Durham, situated in the heart of a university city, and by a historical accident very closely linked with the university, admitting undergraduates as well as 'certificate' students, and closely associated with the social and intellectual life of the university, are uniquely privileged and rather uncharacteristic. But while providing higher education studies, now leading to degree qualifications for a small number of their students, they are also by their very nature committed to a limited professional orientation: they train teachers. There is, I think, no other kind of institution where the tensions between 'education' and 'training' are so persistent and intense. Medical schools and theological colleges with a comparably narrow professional output are much less concerned with the general education of their students; and universities and poly-technics do not constantly have to gear all their courses to the ultimate professional needs of their students.

Bede College, Durham, then, is a peculiar institution within a peculiar class of institutions! It is both a university college, with about one hundred students taking degrees, advanced diplomas, or under-taking research in the university; and a college of education admitting about two hundred students per year for courses leading to the Institute Certificate of Education (the teaching qualification) after three years, or the B. Ed. degree after four years. It is a 'voluntary' college, founded by the Church of England, which still has to find twenty per cent of all capital development costs – most of the colleges of education are controlled by the local education authorities; and it is a residential college. A little more than half of the seven hundred and fifty students are accommodated either in college buildings or hostels, and the vast majority of students are 'resident' for one or more years of their course. There is a mature day-students' annexe at South Shields, and most of these students are married women making a late entry to the teaching profession; but, apart from these, the students are men.

Increasingly, it has to be recognised that most students who are admitted to a college of education would rather be at a university. The old two-year course did offer the attraction of a quick qualification and an early earning capacity: but the present three- or four-year course, even where this leads to the acquisition of a B. Ed. degree, is the same length as a university course but does not provide the range of openings offered to the honours or general degree candidate. In some subject areas the very low academic qualifications demanded by university departments (occasionally as low as two Es at A-level) has further denuded the college of education intake; but despite this, largely because of high-pressure areas in the arts subjects such as history, geography and English, and because of the very limited opportunities for studying drama and physical education in English universities, the average entry-qualifications of students are higher now than they were ten years ago, and most students enter with one or two A-levels; though some minimally qualified students (five O-levels), particularly those with alternative experience of industry or commerce, often achieve the highest standards.

Thus, a 'typical' student, if such a body exists, will enter the college at about nineteen years of age, disappointed that his A-levels have not earned him a university place, not necessarily deeply motivated towards teaching, though willing to give it a try. At Bede College about sixty per cent of the entry will come from the North East (Durham, Northumberland or the North Riding of Yorkshire); about twenty per cent from other 'Northern' counties. These proportions have not greatly changed in recent years, and the only significant change compared with a century ago is that then, with an intake of about sixty to seventy students, only five or six of these would come from outside the Northern areas; now the proportion of non-Northerners (not necessarily Southerners since some will come from the Midlands, Ireland, or abroad) remains more-or-less constant at one-fifth.

Once here, he will meet the conflicting demands of three subject areas: first, his main subject (or, in some colleges and some courses, two main subjects); second, the Theory and Practice of Education, including courses in sociology, psychology, philosophy of education, and periods of teaching practice in schools; and third, an area of professional and pedagogic studies, designed to equip him for his teaching role. This may seem a relatively simple division of functions, which it is in theory, but, in practice, tensions and complications arise. The student aiming to teach his specialist subject at secondary level – particularly true of the science, physical education and craft students – may demand that his main course should include some guidance on the *teaching* of the subject he is *learning*; and in the pedagogic area a mere collection of 'method' lectures on the teaching of material in which the subject-matter is not known by the students is of little value, nor can one constantly base such courses with twenty-year-olds exclusively on material orientated towards six-year-olds, or even teenagers.

These, then, are major considerations of designing a basic English course, and of the use of film within it, which is the area of my concern and responsibility here. All students will attend an obligatory one-year course in English: a proportion of these will also be taking English as their main subject, though the majority will not. All the students will be required to teach English at some time during their teaching practices in both primary and secondary schools. The course, then, has to interest them in English (and retain their interest if they are already interested in the subject); it has to extend their knowledge of the materials of English – literature, drama, language; and it has to provide them with some teaching skills in the communication of the subject. These aims, it will be seen, are not very different from the aims of an English teacher in almost any school situation, since in schools, too, English will be a compulsory subject taught to pupils of widely ranging commitment and interest.

The course runs for twenty-six weeks within a timetable-slot of two and a half hours each week: two terms of eleven weeks, and then a four-week wind-up after the first-year teaching practice in the third term. Most students will continue with the English course in their second year, but it then splits mainly into a series of options, personal preferences and specialist professional areas; and it is in the first-year course that the major infusions of film have taken place.

The decision to introduce film into the basic English course arose primarily from the interests of those concerned with it: without conducting any very detailed analysis of motives, we felt that (a) film would be of value in directing study towards areas of English experience we considered important; (b) teachers should be made aware of the value and function of film in English studies; and (c) film would provide an immediate impact-interest with students expecting, probably, to be taken through the intricacies of English grammar and the critical subtleties of Jane Austen novels. As 'English' teachers, our immediate reaction was to turn to the *film of the book* approach; and though we abandoned this approach about four years ago, I think that a consideration of its advantages and limitations is relevant to many levels of English teaching.

Films used in this way included *The Cruel Sea*, *Great Expectations*, *Billy Budd*, *A Kind of Loving* and *Saturday Night and Sunday Morning*. The basic requirement of any film/book (or film/play) approach must be the intrinsic artistic qualities of both the film and the book – and one would expect it to be a comparatively easy task to select from the three thousand five hundred films* made from novels, short-stories or plays a case of a 'good' book made into a 'good' film: it only gets difficult – perhaps impossible – when you try. The first elimination takes place on technical grounds, since of the vast number of films made, only about ten per cent will at any moment be available in 16 mm distribution. For example, a comparison of Defoe's '*Robinson Crusoe*' with Buñuel's film would be exciting and profitable in evaluating the qualities of both Defoe and Buñuel, and facing the characteristics of the two media; but only recently has the film become available on 16 mm. And so we are forced to consider a list of a few hundred films, most of which we eliminate, since *from the point of view of English literature* their origin would not be thought worthy of consideration. Just glancing down pages of Mr Enser's book, though Bryan Forbes' *King Rat* and John Huston's *Key Largo* may be very interesting films, as are Hitchcock's *Psycho* or Mark Robson's *The Prize*, one would not necessarily wish to begin an English course with a study of the work of J. Clavell, Maxwell Anderson, Robert Bloch or Irving Wallace. In a way, the interest of the films is primarily the way in which they extend and transcend their origins.

So we are reduced to, perhaps, about fifty available films based on novels or plays which would be regarded as valuable material in an English course at school or college; but this list is likely to be further reduced by instances in which the *film* material is regarded as at best inadequate or at worst meretricious in its treatment of the original material of the play or novel. The final list is likely to comprise no more than a couple of dozen films. This is taking an extremist and

* ENSER, A. G. S. *Filmed books and plays, 1928–1967*. André Deutsch 1968.

pessimistic view of the situation: but it is not far from the truth when one conscientiously performs the exercise, and probably accounts for the inclusion of strangely poor material in our experiments, and for the decision to abandon this approach. It also accounts for my earlier comment (Chapter 1) that the most profitable comparisons can often be made between a book or play and a film *on a similar subject*, rather than the attempt to film the book or play under consideration.

Of the films and books which we actually dealt with in this manner, it is fair to comment upon our experiences. We would usually require the incoming students to have read the novel or story before coming to college: what decisions would govern this choice? Should we expect and require them to read a work they would be unlikely to know, or should we choose a work which they might know which we should subject to a different approach? Stan Barstow's '*A Kind of Loving*' and Alan Sillitoe's '*Saturday Night and Sunday Morning*' would come within the latter category: many students would have read these as paperbacks stating a point of view about 'protest' with which they might find some sympathy. Here, I think, our expectations were generally justified: students did know these works, and have a direct response to them. Or if they had not been read already, then there was an immediate response to their subject-matter and attitudes.

'*Great Expectations*' and '*Billy Budd*' were regarded rather differently. These would be works which not all students had met, and which we regarded as key-works of their authors: here, reading might be extended, and the comparison with the films might be used to illuminate the qualities of their originals. The barriers were the rambling and complex plot structure of the Dickens novel, and the stylised remoteness of language of the Melville short story: many of the students, the majority out of touch with a systematic study of 'classical' literature, just found they could not read, could not really understand the original works – certainly they did not know, if they read them, what they were about, other than the basic narrative of the story.

The Cruel Sea was an exceptional case, since it was chosen as a film which would contribute to both the English and the religious knowledge courses: perhaps religious knowledge gained the greater benefits? Few could regard Nicholas Monsarrat's novel as other than pretentious, and Charles Frend's film may be said to have done justice to the qualities of the original (without achieving any particular distinction as a film). But one can hardly advocate the use of less-than-good material, whether in literature or film, to begin a course on the assumption that the weaknesses will lead students on to a demand for better things: if they sense the weaknesses, then they are dissatisfied from the start; and if they do not sense the weaknesses, they are likely to be unsympathetic to your attempts to demonstrate them. Thus, the main asset of *The Cruel Sea* whether as novel or film is the beautiful construction of its plot whereby Miss Prism's dictum that 'The good ended happily; the bad, unhappily' is ably worked out; and if her definition of 'what fiction means' is acceptable to teachers of literature, then '*The Cruel Sea*' would be an admirable beginning. If there is any concern with values in the novel, then it is at the level of 'Can there be – indeed, must not there be – a lesser of two evils?', and this may indeed be a very relevant argument for the religious knowledge department which shared the film with us; but when, in the novel and in the film, this is reduced to the level, after the depth-charging of the men in the water, of 'Still there are thoughts; and for thoughts there is gin', one wonders whether the moral complexities are adequately reflected in the characters; and it becomes difficult to assess what is subtle irony and what is mere inadequacy.

Great Expectations raises more difficult problems, which perhaps spotlight the difficulties of the comparative book/film method. I accept without reservation that Dickens is one of the great English novelists – one of the great novelists in any language; and regard '*Great Expectations*,' for all its flaws of plot-structure, as one of Dickens' great novels. I see it as a persistent and powerful attack upon snobs, both social and intellectual; and a mounting indictment of the stratification of society under an increasingly rigid Victorian class-structure. 'My sister [Mrs Joe] having so much to do was going to church vicariously; that is to say, Joe and I were going.' Uncle Pumblechook ('*I* was not allowed to call him uncle under the severest penalties'), Drummle, Startop, Miss Havisham, Herbert and the Pockets, Jaggers, Estella, the Hubbles – we are presented with a series of portraits of the narrow-minded, the pretentious, the arrogant, who gradually absorb and infect Pip, all characterised by Dickens with shrewd understanding and verbal brilliance. From this parade, one character alone stands apart – it is Joe Gargery, ever kind, ever concerned, the natural gentleman (though denied the attribute because he is a blacksmith). Whatever the strains of the plot, again and again the characters come at us with the fullest force of description and dialogue: 'Be grateful, boy, to them which brought you up by hand' . . . 'What is detestable in a pig, is more detestable in a boy' . . . 'Why he is a common labouring-boy . . . He calls the knaves Jacks, this boy. And what coarse hands he has! And what thick boots.' . . . 'Though he called me Mr Pip he still could not get rid of a certain air of bullying suspicion; and even now he occasionally shut his eyes and threw his finger at me while he spoke as much as to express that he knew all kinds of things to my disparagement if only he chose to mention them.' Condemned from their own mouths by Dickens' uncanny eye and ear.

When we move to a film treatment we immediately accept that the complexities of plot are likely to be simplified, and in this process certain minor characters eliminated: such changes though significant quantitatively need have no significance qualitatively. As George Bluestone comments: 'They provide statistical, not critical data.'* The only relevant question we may ask is whether the total experience of the film is akin to the total experience of the novel or play. And if we ask this question with reference to David Lean's film of *Great Expectations* we are likely to end with a rather strange answer. We are likely to conclude that '*Great Expectations*' is a novel of frustrated lovers who, despite the clumsy interventions of good-humoured rustics, like Joe Gargery, and malignant figures on the fringe of the story, like Magwitch, eventually triumph in the cause of true love, and walk hand-in-hand to a happy future as the end-credits roll. Perhaps the key sequence is that in which Pip, resident in Herbert Pocket's chambers, is visited by Joe Gargery. (Chapter XXVII in the novel.) The whole context in which Dickens presents this incident is one of Pip's shame: 'If I could have kept him away by paying money I would certainly have paid money. . . . So throughout our life, our worst weaknesses and meannesses are usually committed for the sake of the people whom we most despise. . . . As the time approached I would have liked to run away. . . .' And finally, ashamed of his treatment of Joe, 'As soon as I could recover myself sufficiently, I hurried out after him and looked for him in the neighbouring streets, but he was gone.' And Joe's management of his hat is treated within a context which makes Pip's conventions look small, and Joe's concern seem natural:

> With his good honest face all glowing and shining, and his hat put down on the floor between us, he caught both my hands and worked them straight up and down, as if I had been the last-patented Pump.
> 'I am glad to see you Joe. Give me your hat.'

* BLUESTONE, George. *Novels into film*. University of California Press, 1961 (C.U.P. in England).

But, Joe, taking it carefully up with both hands, like a bird's nest with eggs in it, wouldn't hear of parting with that piece of property and persisted in standing and talking over it in a most uncomfortable way.

And, later:

Here Joe's hat tumbled off the mantelpiece, and he started out of his chair and picked it up and fitted it to the same exact spot. As if it were an absolute point of good breeding that it should tumble off again soon.

If we *read* the chapter, the shame and embarrassment and lack of breeding are essentially Pip's; if we *watch* this scene in the film, the shame and embarrassment and lack of breeding are essentially Joe's. He is played as a bumbling clown; the business is invented with all the imagination of a Jerry Lewis comedy sequence, and only half the taste: the whole emphasis of the chapter (and of the characters) is totally reversed. The ironies of the situation are eliminated for the sake of easy laughs, which is exactly what Dickens refuses to do.

Here then, in the film and the book of *Great Expectations*, we have an almost unmanageable critical clash, from the point of view of English teaching. Those who like the book must be offended by its treatment in the film, and may conclude that the essential quality of film, as a medium, is to eliminate all subtlety, to crudify literature and reduce all ironies and linguistic tropes to stark contrasts of black-and-white or grey shadows of mediocrity. But those who respond energetically to the obvious qualities of the film are unlikely to be tolerant of the richness and dexterity of the novel: it will seem to them to be fussy and pretentious and tedious. Thus, with these particular contrasts, we lose out on both sides. The opportunity to obtain a response and make progress critically with either the film or with the novel is virtually jammed by the conflict created over the wide range of interests and responses to the material. One can successfully appraise the technical competence of the opening sequences of the film, or perhaps discuss the performances of Martita Hunt or Valerie Hobson or John Mills as pieces of film-acting; or one can discuss the descriptive powers of Dickens in the novel, and the rich characterisations of minor characters eliminated from the film – but there can be little interrelationship of the material, and little if any progress from one to the other.

Billy Budd is a far more interesting case. For one thing, the narrative structure is infinitely less complex. The moral conflicts of the characters are portrayed in the film directed by Peter Ustinov, with almost agonising respect, culminating in the long discussion at the court martial which defies most of the traditional canons of film-making with almost Godardian insolence. Although many critics discounted its painstaking accuracy to history and locale – it was largely filmed on board a ship – many people do respond to its claustrophobia: the lack of privacy of thought, the constant awareness of tensions, the injustice and deprivation, the floating empire of authority and protocol. However one regards the performances of Terence Stamp, Robert Ryan, John Neville and Ustinov himself, and some flawless performances of smaller parts, one can never escape a feeling of the actors' integrity. The film offers little substitute for Melville's verbal flamboyance and quaintness, but it in no way underrates his major preoccupations.

As I have already suggested, the students found the Melville text difficult, and we must concede that his particular brand of poetic prose, occasionally dropping unconsciously into blank verse, is probably an acquired taste; and a taste difficult to reproduce in cinematic terms. Where Melville is warm, throbbing and impassioned, Ustinov's film is cool, ticking and intellectual: where Melville's tale loses its sense of reality, and grows into a sort of mystic allegory, Ustinov's film constantly brings us down to the physical rather than the meta-physical, time present rather than timelessness, the personal conflict rather than the abstract debate. The comparison here is, therefore, the contrasting style of handling source material, regarding the 'source' as the basic story subsequently treated by Melville in the novel (or short story) and Ustinov in the film: each has integrity and style and technical facility, and we can begin to appreciate the qualities of each – but, again, it becomes difficult to extend comparisons from one form to the other, or to make judgments about the nature of the novel or the nature of film. The two works are, in their way, too personal as works of art to admit comparison except of the artists.

The two modern novels, '*A Kind of Loving*' and '*Saturday Night and Sunday Morning*', probably provided the most valuable contrasts between novel and film. Time will tell, and may prove me wrong, but I suspect that Stan Barstow and Alan Sillitoe will find their place in the history of literature as 'good' writers rather than 'great' ones, at any rate in respect of the two works under consideration. Their subject-matter is direct and personal, their style assured, the context is a 'real' one with immediately recognisable locale and characters – we have all met Ingrid's mother and Arthur's Aunt Ada. One does not feel that one is wasting time in reading either work; nor is one overwhelmed into incoherent silence by the impact as of the greatest literature: neither is a '*Wuthering Heights*' nor a '*Middlemarch*'!

And the film versions have comparable integrity. Both John Schlesinger and Karel Reisz are directors who command respect at most times, and admiration at their best: and these were the first feature films of each director after having established their reputations with short documentary films. It would be possible to extend examination and analysis from the novels and features to the short stories and short films of the respective writers and directors, to attempt to trace the evolution of style and establish a consistency of attitude to subject-matter: but in the time available in our courses we were not able to do this.

In these two examples, then, we really were able to examine on a more-or-less equal and adequate basis the distinctions of *form* between novel and film, an examination aided in the case of *Saturday Night and Sunday Morning* by a fairly extensive discussion of the problems of the transition from one medium to another contributed by Karel Reisz to the N.U.T. Conference on Popular Culture and Personal Responsibility in October 1960. Reisz, for instance, explained the valid distinction between writing and reading about a physical process (being sick, beating up) and filming and watching this process on a screen. Reading about someone being sick in your lap is one thing: we can distance ourselves, take time to adjust, and soften our response by contributing just that degree of imagination to the incident that we need to control it. But this is not possible in film, and the 'control', the 'distancing' has to be contributed by the director rather than by the spectator. Although MacLuhan would argue that print and film are both 'hot' media, there is clearly a distinction to be made in the degree to which we can 'cool' them by injecting or rejecting 'information', and the very high definition of the film medium does not allow much cooling to take place.

Thus, in the scene where Arthur Seaton is beaten up by the Squaddies (pp. 151–3 in the Pan edition), the process is described very much 'in close-up', almost blow by blow. In the film the sequence is taken at night (hence in darkness) and in long shot. Students are free to discuss what may be seen as a distortion of the novel, but some will see this process as a valid distinction between the media. They may also note that Reisz provides a sort of objective correlative in his earlier treatment of the fairground, developing a virtuoso passage of filming from the roundabout in order to build up the *threat* of the beating-up rather than the actual physical process of beating-up.

A more complex distortion occurs in the elimination of the family nexus in the novel, or rather its reduction to Arthur's younger brother and one friend, Bert. Throughout the novel, even where the characters play no major role, one senses the presence of brothers, sisters, cousins and nephews, Fred, Eddie, Pam, Mike, Dave, Jane, Ralph, 'The Tribe' as indeed they are called: these provide a sort of collective experience upon which the family draws from time to time, a great variety of contacts and levels of confidence. In the film the lonely Bert is obliged to act as the 'feed' or stooge for all Arthur's private and public thoughts, a role no character can adequately fulfil, and this is a whole change of emphasis which alters the quality and degree of relationships and characters. Similarly, Ma Bull has to stand in for a whole range of neighbours, and so, in the film, achieves a dominance by frequent appearances in scenes in which in the original novel she plays no part – the incident of the drunk and the smashed window, for instance. It is sometimes difficult to account for shifts of this kind which do not really seem to be intrinsic to the narrative structures of the medium; and even more difficult to see why in *A Kind of Loving* Vic's father who is insistently presented in the novel as 'nobbut a collier' is transformed by Schlesinger into an engine-driver: this simple change moves the Old Feller into the aristocracy of the working-class, and correspondingly eliminates many subtle overtones in the father/son relationship.

In a college of education, studies of the kind described above will be done by a year-group of between one hundred and two hundred, and for most practical purposes the total number will be broken down into groups of about fifteen to twenty for discussions, seminars, or tutorials. Some of the work may be written – compiling detailed lists of distinctions between novel and film, preparing check-lists of character traits or details of locations represented in both novel and film. As discussions develop, it may be necessary to check back to a sequence in the film or the pages in the novel, and unless the film is to be retained over a period (many distributors will allow a week's hire at fifty per cent above the charge for a single showing), there is a distinct advantage in having a large block of time for concentrated work upon the film.

Comparative treatment of book and film contains many hazards.

It is only too easy to get side-tracked into discussing relatively minor departures in plotting or to get involved in elaborate discussion of technical points, and thus lose the major thread of the critical examination of the ideas presented by the two media; and I think that these dangers increase the higher one works up a value-scale of book or film. Thus the most irrelevant discussions are likely to emerge in discussing a Shakespeare film, where someone will surely have been counting every line and every word of text missed out (something they will rarely do in the theatre) with such concentration that they will have missed the qualities of the film that *replace* the words. For this reason, my ideal Shakespeare film is undoubtedly *Throne of Blood* (Kurosawa's retelling of the *'Macbeth'* story) where verbal comparisons are impossible!

As I indicated earlier, we abandoned the comparative approach partly because of the limitations of material, partly because of the difficulties of getting the 'right' points made, and partly from a total reorganisation of the structure of the English basic course to throw greater emphasis upon the concept of *communication* and *style*, and less upon specific works of literature.

Over the last four or five years the course has begun with film, but not with a feature film. We start with the axioms that *not all word-exchanges are communication* and *not all communication is word-exchange*. People can read without understanding, listen without hearing, hear without comprehension, and not infrequently talk without meaning: it is rather important for students who are going to be teachers to be introduced to these ideas very early in their course lest they assume that all knowledge must or can be communicated by telling things to the children, or by getting the children to read them.

We usually begin with Norman McLaren's *Rhythmetic* which, once past the credits, is completely non-verbal. Lines of figures perform animated calculations, adding, subtracting, jostling each other, edging along until an arithmetic crisis is reached and resolved. The film has logic, which one might expect of mathematics; and within mathematical terms it has a narrative progression. But the students also find, and in discussion recall, that it has emotion, the power to involve them (they join in the game), and perhaps most remarkably, humour (they laugh). If it is discovered that animated figures can, through the art and wit of the film-maker, do all these things, then our basic point begins to be established. And we usually follow this with one or two other McLaren films, largely to show the range of his techniques and imagination.

We next consider three distinctive areas of communication: giving facts (information), telling a story (narrative) and giving instruction (orders or persuasion). In the first section we use early silent material (*Early Actualities* and the original *Lumière Programme*). There are two major reasons for this: first, it is relevant in a programme dealing exclusively with communication in film to consider the origins of the medium, and what its purpose was conceived to be; and second, we later in the course show Truffaut's *Les Mistons* which contains at least two 'homage' references back to the Lumière material, and thus we are providing the source material for subsequent quotation and allusion.

Silent film can easily be dismissed as crude and naive, whereas its relatively simple quality can focus attention more rapidly on key qualities or techniques too easily taken for granted in more complex and sophisticated film material. The sense of film being a recording medium, providing a permanent historical record, is one that needs to be established (the Funeral of Queen Victoria, or Lord Roberts returning from the Boer War); but there is also the factor of film creating the event – I am sure that in the early years of the century the fire brigades turned out more frequently for the film cameras than for fires! And thus the problem of the nature of cinematic truth arises at this early stage of discussion.

But by far the most interesting point to arise, from the Lumière material, is how easily 'documentary' turns into 'drama', fact into magic. The waiter who appears in the *Game of Cards* sequence is clearly determined to be more than a 'documentary' waiter: he, at this earliest point in cinema history, knows that the camera is on him, and he is determined to 'give a performance' – and people have been 'performing' in front of movie cameras ever since. And the Lumière brothers create a performance, too, when the demolished wall reinstates itself by the reverse motion of the camera.

Drama invades the documentary, too, in *Watering the Gardener* (*L'Arroseur Arrosé* – I cannot think why we do not call this episode 'The Waterer Watered'; though even this would not capture the irony of the French pun, since *arroser* can also mean 'to treat' in colloquial French, and the scene thus becomes 'A Treat for the Gardener'). Here the whole scene is constructed as a comic narrative, and quite clearly the Brothers Lumière had their eyes on their audiences in providing a range of items within the programme. In fact, the whole history of cinema is contained in these eight minutes of film: the personal toy of the home-movie maker (our workers, our baby), the historical record of an unrepeatable event (the wall demolished, the photographic congress), the first comedy (the gardener sequence) and the first drama (the boat leaving the harbour – will it survive the storm-tossed seas beyond the harbour bar?).

Leaving the area of information, which so easily slips into dramatic form, we consider story-telling, and the beginnings of narrative structure in film. Again we use at least one early silent sequence – *The Great Train Robbery* (1903), *Rescued by Rover* (1905) or *Rescued from an Eagle's Nest* (1907). Any of these marks a significant development in technique – a variety of camera set-ups, some indication of parallel events involving the manipulation of time, the creation of tension by cutting. And one of these early films is juxtaposed with a more modern narrative sequence – we usually use an extract from Clouzot's *The Wages of Fear* in which the four men, driving two lorries of nitro-glycerine, negotiate a hazardous bend in the road. We ask what techniques are used in the 1953 film that were not used in the earlier example; what is the balance of narrative content between pictures and dialogue, between actors and camera.

These may seem naive exercises and pointlessly simple questions; but they are necessary stages in any course-work involving film. Most of the students, at least up to O-level and many beyond, will have been systematically taught to form some sort of analytical response to the spoken and written word. Unfortunately in some instances this process will have meant their being told *what* they should respond. Faced with film, which most of them will never have discussed, will never have been invited to treat seriously or critically, they must be trained to look, then to see, and then to analyse what they have seen and how they have responded to it. Since the whole point of the work is ultimately to sharpen their responses to literature as well as to film, the earliest course-work must offer reasonably simple material with just enough ambiguity to challenge the easy, stock response.

Thus, in the next section dealing with instruction and persuasion, we do not take a simple 'instruction' film about how to make a mortise-and-tenon joint, or how to breed rabbits: we have often shown *Painting a Chinese Landscape*. The sort of questions asked would be: Is this narrative (the creative event) or information (recording what is happening) or instruction (how to do it)? There will usually be a difference of opinion, and various bids for compromises – it does not really matter, and we cannot assume that there is a 'right' answer.

To conclude this section of the programme, we show one of Robert Brownjohn's Midland Bank advertisements, *Money Talks*. This is just a superb piece of graphics, and of imaginative animation, and has something in common with the McLaren film which we showed first. In advertising the various services offered by the bank, many basic aspects of film technique are employed: there is a narrative voice, though one is more likely to recall *how* something was said rather than what was said; words are used on the screen, but so animated that the power of the word is carried by a visual rather than a verbal stimulus. For instance, when recommending that the bank can pay instalments on your car, the word 'automobile' on the screens drops its two 'o's (aut$_o$m$_o$bile) and drives off the screen like a monstrous American car, on its own wheels; and the 'o' in 'holidays' becomes the setting sun of the travelogue, and sinks below an imaginary horizon to the twanging of Hawaiian guitars; or in discussing foreign currency, 'money' suddenly acquires a proliferation of foreign accents, 'ṃôñè̓' as foreign voices jabber on the track. The inventiveness turns words into pictures, and pictures into other words: some take on the force of ideographs rather than phonetically constructed words, while at other times the nature of screen space is exploited as the final 'w' of 'grow' (strategically placed in the bottom left-hand corner of the screen) extends to become the jagged graph-line, as we 'watch our money grow'. Word, picture, sound-track, music, timing and space cram the short two-minute film with an intellectual and emotional richness that exploits, and thus reveals, much of the power of the film image. Again, its wit and compression make it a stimulating talking-point.

This film forms a suitable bridge to the final film in the programme. Much film, indeed most film, does in some way relate to physical reality: someone was actually present at Queen Victoria's funeral, even if we were not, and film transported us through time and space to get us there; Rover was a dog (Cecil Hepworth's own dog, Blair) and a baby was rescued (Cecil Hepworth's own infant daughter); someone did paint a Chinese landscape. But when we show Walerian Borowczyk's *Renaissance* we are forced to appreciate that here the event is created on and by film, and could have no existence outside the medium. In *Renaissance* we see a scene of absolute desolation – the walls of the room blackened, torn books, battered junk, piles of unidentifiable rubbish, the result of an explosion. Then, as the film progresses, each item in the room gradually reconstitutes itself: the shattered remains of a basket are rewoven into shape, a battered flugel-horn appears almost reinflated as its missing parts are restored and its dents blown out, a bare stalk acquires a complete bunch of grapes, the torn pages of the books reattach themselves to their bindings, a shattered table staggers to its legs from the floor, a stuffed bird re-collects its feathers from the debris, a quite incredible renaissance is achieved, to be completed by the reassembly of a grenade and clock forming a crude time-bomb which, once reconstituted, begins to tick away again until it explodes leaving a scene of absolute desolation. . . .

The students are asked to conceive *Renaissance* as a short story, or a poem, or a comic strip, or a piece of sculpture, or as and in any other art form. Of course, one can narrate what the film is depicting (as I have done for some parts of it above); one could produce still pictures illustrating various stages of the reconstruction; one could write a poem about destruction: but only in film (using elaborate techniques akin to those of animation, and working backwards in real time to achieve effects which when projected appear to move forwards in film time) can you create this film.

The assignment associated with this film programme is to ask the students to communicate *one idea* (or concept) in *two different ways* (or media). At the simplest level, this might mean buying a picture-postcard of a place and then describing in minute verbal detail all that is depicted in the postcard (virtually impossible when you try to do it); or one might take a process and describe it first in words, like those elaborate instructions that sometimes accompany a piece of machinery or kitchen gadget, and then in pictures, as are sometimes devised for international instructions. As with any assignments set for a very wide range of ability, there is great variety in what is attempted and in what is achieved. We have, for instance, received a baked cake and the recipe for it; mysterious constructions and the algebraic equations which provide the key to their spacial relationships; working scientific experiments with the chemical formulae depicting the reaction. (This is not an exercise that could be done by postal tuition.) Some students do not get the point; or sometimes we do not get their point – it is difficult to tell. But in the vast majority of cases we receive proof that they have achieved some understanding of 'media' and some awareness of the variety of 'communication' that can be achieved. This seems to be a useful starting point for a course which will ultimately focus attention on language and literature, and upon the means by which it may be taught and ideas about it stimulated.

The English course continues by considering the qualities and functions of speech (communication by the spoken word), of mime (communication by movement and gesture, without words), and various aspects of descriptive writing – descriptions of people, places, scene-setting (written and spoken word), and there are individual and group assignments arising from each aspect of the work, sometimes written, sometimes oral, and sometimes dramatic. The next injection of film into the course comes either late in the first term or early in the second – the pattern varies slightly from year to year. As before, film is used to open up a new area, a new pattern of thinking and writing, and to help towards the definition of various critical terms such as subjective and objective, impressionistic and expressionistic, metaphor and symbol, allegory and parable. The 'tone' of the course is shifted from the more objective and exterior aspects of communication to subjective, interior and more extravagant forms of communication.

We would usually begin with a fairly conventional attempt to portray in film subjective attitudes or feelings. We have in times past used Stan Brakhage's *Desist Film* in which, with staggering hand-held camera techniques, he attempts to capture the frenzy and tensions of an adolescent party. Although the film does ably illustrate the problems and inadequacies of subjective-camera techniques, it is really such a dreary and boring film, and so repetitious, that the point is blunted by the sheer agony of watching. We also tried using *The Gentleman in Room Six* in which characters visit a man in a seedy South American hotel, and entering into discussion with them as it were through his eyes (we never see him until the last shot) a picture of his identity is gradually built up: but again the rather crude technique, and the weakness of the final revelation which has now, twenty years later, lost even more of its point (the man is shown at the end to be Adolf Hitler!) did not really satisfy us. Most recently we have used Howard Blake's *A Few Days*. A girl narrates on the track a love affair, which we see on the screen as in her memory; and within the narrated tale there are a number of quite extravagant, and obvious, subjective-camera techniques. She is 'head over heels' in love – so the camera turns head-over-heels; 'Try and catch me,' she says – and the camera chases after her; 'Why isn't he interested in my legs?' she thinks – so the camera manifests a discreet interest in them. The techniques are rather obvious, but this is not necessarily a drawback; what we discover in viewing the film, which has no small degree of integrity and charm, is that the whole treatment appears *thought out* rather than *felt in*, so that the inward feeling of being in love is not really captured on the film.

We therefore proceed to examine other styles of conveying mood and feeling, and show Arthur Lipsett's *Very Nice Very Nice*. This uses an Impressionistic technique, at times almost subliminal, by juxtaposing and manipulating, through distorting lenses and dissolving techniques, many hundreds of still pictures, images which flash past, striking patterns of pictures and an elaborately edited sound track, partly verbal, partly natural sound, partly 'abstract' sound, with a chorus punctuation of applause and a complacent voice saying 'Very Nice, Very Nice'. The seven-minute film encapsulates many images and moods of Canadian (and American) society, with a cruelly ironical glare.

To contrast with Impressionism, we show an example of Expressionism, Robert Wiene's *Cabinet of Dr Caligari* (the B.F.I. Extract). The settings, costume, lighting and make-up all project outwardly the inner feeling of insanity, distortion, unbalance, which characterises the tale. This is a fairly straightforward exercise mainly to provide data (either by duplicated hand-out or by lecture) on the technical critical terms used, whether in painting, film or literature. But the real purpose of this session is to develop the notion that the subjective camera finally becomes a reality (in André Bazin's words) 'not thanks to the puerile kind of identification of the spectator and the character by means of a camera trick, but, on the contrary, through the pitiless gaze of an invisible witness. The camera is at last the spectator and nothing else.' Thus the camera's ultimate subjectivity is best achieved through its complete and relentless objectivity, because by this means the greatest degree of psychological involvement of the spectator is brought about, leading the spectator to perform the subjective analysis of the content of the film.

We then proceed to test this theory, examining an extract from Louis Malle's *Le Feu Follet*. The film recounts the last twenty-four hours in the life of a suicide, Alain Leroy (Maurice Ronet). The opening sequences of the film introduce us to Alain and Lydia, his mistress who wishes him to divorce his wife, Dorothy, living in New York. Their conversation also makes reference to Lydia's friend, Francesca, whom we do not see. Lydia is leaving for New York, hoping that Alain will join her, arrange a divorce, and marry her: and the conversation immediately preceding the extract under consideration goes:

Alain: No, Lydia, I shan't come to New York; I shan't marry you.
You'd be unfortunate, another Dorothy. . . . And, in any
case, you can do nothing for me. Too late. . . . (To the taxi-
driver) Take Madame to Paris, Hotel Raphael, Avenue
Kléber.

The sequence which follows is too complex to describe at length; but
the script is published (in French).*

The point about this sequence is that Alain is hardly ever out of
camera: even when we are not looking directly at him we catch his
reflection in the mirror, we see his hand reach into frame, we never
lose his presence even in the rare moments when he is out of shot –
thus, by technical definition, our viewpoint is objective. We regard him,
rather than regarding objects through his eyes. We cannot orientate
ourselves to the situation, to the relationships, to the objects.

He has returned to the nursing home (Lydia's first remark in the
film has been 'Alain, you're ill' and his reply 'For a long time') where,
we must assume, he is a voluntary patient: but being treated for what?
Who are these people, involved in an elaborate discussion of Thomism,
Racine, Proust, Cocteau, Genet? How can one enter their world?
How is Alain placed by the other characters? (There is the enigmatic
conversation with Mademoiselle Farnoux: 'You, you are "difficult" . . .
if you weren't, you wouldn't be where you are!') The doctor is called
away by a whispered message, and leaves to perform an unknown
function: and when Alain leaves the room and stops on the balcony,
who are the children? What is the ambulance for – delivery or discharge?
Mademoiselle Farnoux questions Alain about his parents, as they
move into the billiard-room – 'They live in the country. They're very
old. I don't know them any longer.'

Alain enters his room through a door which is not a door: again,
for a moment we are disoriented – is this, even, the room we saw
before? And the long sequence in the room begins. Which objects
belong to Alain, and which belong to the room? What significance
have they for him? We cannot adjust, define, resolve: photographs,
newspaper cuttings, a cheque, a date scribbled on the mirror, a pack of
cards, an unfinished game of chess, the statuettes and the flag, the
mini-bowler, the doll, the cigarette packets, the objects multiply but
without definition. We share Alain's lack of purpose, lack of contact

* *L'Avant-Scène du Cinéma No. 30* (October 1963) Paris.

(though clearly some of these objects must possess connections and meanings which we cannot fathom). But in this process our psychological involvement and orientation begin to parallel his psychological involvement and orientation: he cannot motivate and connect (witness his dissatisfaction with and amendment of his writing – we, too, are dissatisfied because we cannot enter into an understanding of what it means to him), and nor can we. Thus, throughout this sequence we are gradually drawn into an identification of feeling with Alain – a subjectivity which arises from *our* psychological response rather than being presented with *his* psychological response.

With *Le Feu Follet*, we have sometimes contrasted a totally different subjectivity in the closing sequences of Antonioni's *L'Eclisse* (The Eclipse). The film begins with Vittoria (Monica Vitti) breaking off an affair with one lover, Riccardo; during the film she enters into another love affair with her mother's stockbroker, Piero (Alain Delon). They spend a night together at his office; she leaves, walks down the street, and we are presented 'with a rapid succession of visual images, at times realistic, at other times abstract'. (There are about eighty of these images in the last five minutes of the film.)*

We are at the street intersection where Piero and Vittoria met: but it is not at all clear whether she (Vittoria) is also here, observing what we observe; or whether the images are those of her memory which we share; or whether we alone are presented with images which are designed to take *us* back over events and achieve a personal psychological response which is parallel to, though different from, hers. Some of the images, whatever their function, operate on an objectively factual level: the street intersection has a place in our experience of their relationship, as has the stadium which they have passed many times; and the matchbox floating in the water-barrel was thrown there at the time of the first encounter between Vittoria and Piero. Piero and Vittoria have agreed to meet 'Tonight. At eight o'clock. Same place.' And as shadows fall we wonder whether time has passed and their meeting is imminent: a blonde girl arrives at the street corner, but it is not Vittoria. We hear footsteps, but neither comes into view. A bus draws up, but neither Vittoria nor Piero is among the alighting passengers. Others wait, and we wait with them: but no one arrives.

Are some images to be accepted at the level of symbol? The water runs out of the barrel, and down the street-drain; faces peer from behind

* *L'Eclisse* in 'Screenplays of Michelangelo Antonioni', Souvenir Press, London (Orion Press, New York) 1963.

F

gratings, from balconies; the nurse pushes a pram, and children play in the shower from the water-sprinkler, till that too is stopped. What are the eyes, behind the spectacles, watching? The images grow more and more threatening; commonplace objects acquire an intensity of texture, a brooding importance which we cannot penetrate; again we constantly fail to establish a pattern of relationships, any sequential response to the events. Again, as in *Le Feu Follet* (though without maintaining contact with Vittoria) our response is becoming geared to the doubts, uncertainties, tensions of her relationship. And at times the images themselves lose connections with reality to become abstract, formal designs; the effect is more like collage than montage (which usually invests a series of shots with some logical or emotive connection). To analyse this sequence by means of an aesthetic of content is not only meaningless but irrelevant to their effect, to our response.

Significantly, if we search for literary analogies to these two film sequences, in which a high degree of subjective involvement is achieved, we are most likely to turn to stream-of-consciousness writing within the narrative novel. What we will find in Virginia Woolf's '*To the Lighthouse*' or in Joyce's '*Ulysses*' or in Beckett's '*Watt*' is, interestingly enough, *not* the conventional subjectivity of first-person narrative in the present tense but, for the most part, a similar, objective, minutely categorised description of events, objects, sounds. The controlling qualities are formal and contextual, rather than technical, in the literary form as in the film.

The other film which we regularly use in this section of the course is John Krish's *I Think They Call Him John*. It is a film of unique power which defies conventional comment or discussion: one student's comment upon it may give an indication of its quality:

> *I Think They Call Him John* has several qualities which make it as good a piece of documentary as anything I have ever seen. Its principal virtue is that it never strays from its subject and that within its acknowledged limitations (length, documentary quality, small budget and a sponsored film) it does everything that could be done. In short it approaches perfection.
>
> The film is a compassionate and absorbedly unrelenting examination of a day – a Sunday – in the life of an old man. Within less than half an hour it packs a lifetime of experience. Its single character moves faultlessly through actions that are second nature to him, watched remorselessly by the camera – and us. The use of sound –

and more importantly, silence – is brilliant. Krish's main aim has been restraint and the pacing is slow and observant. The strange and wonderful thing is that in conveying the boredom and the trivia of the day, Krish and his team never bore us.

The film might have been inspired by Arthur Miller's famous line 'Attention must be paid'. It is work which does not ask our attention, rather it demands it. It foresees a deep look into our own hearts. As we watch John, the temptation may be to make excuses. Say that it is not too bad, he has a television, a comfortable home, a caged bird. And yet we fool no one, least of all ourselves. As he searches for the minutiae that will fill his day – and every day – we are forced to take sides. Quite unsentimentally Krish observes and, through his observation, comments.

John, searching for dust in the unused rooms, making a cup of tea and eating his lonely meal as the sound-track recalls his mother's comment on the crowded Sundays of his childhood – 'you never know who might come' – thrusts us into an awareness of what his life was, is and will be. Krish has learned something from Bresson, from Ozu and from de Sica's *Umberto D* and produced economical and pithy comment on the problem of human communication.

The next area of study is the ways in which language (whether visual language in painting or film, or verbal language in the spoken and written word) may be heightened to accommodate feelings that cannot be adequately expressed by direct description – the areas of metaphor and image, symbol and parallelism, allegory and parable. These are concepts which thirteen years of teaching have often left very confused in the minds of many of our students, and since they are destined to be teachers they are likely to transmit their confusion to their pupils. We cannot guarantee that all get the concepts clear after viewing the films, but at least they have been obliged to exercise their minds along original channels, to try to come to grips with these terms through another door.

We use the short Israeli film by Aline and Yoram Gross *We Shall Never Die*. Unless we accept a symbolic force in the film it can only be a film about candles, because that is what in terms of physical reality it is. Candles burn down, striped candles splutter and flicker but other candles take their place, the flame never dying; we hear marching feet on the sound-track, glimpse railway lines and improvised toys among the images. Whether the stripes are seen as prison bars, or as the pyjama-stripes of prison uniform (an idea specifically reinforced by the 'labels' as well), or more vaguely as the 'stripes' of suffering, does not seem to me to be vital in the activity of response. Whether the railway lines are a specific reference to movement from ghettoes to concentration camps, or more vaguely a symbol of dispossession, wandering, and persecution, does not invalidate the force of the symbol. And whether we carry the analogy of the guttering candles to the point of identity with bodies being melted down to provide soap and fertilisers, or see it merely at the level of extinction, again does not affect the inherent nature of the interpretation. The all-important aspect of the film is that though candles are the *material* they are not the *subject-matter*. When Macbeth talks of having 'scotched the snake, not killed it', or of 'letting the frame of things disjoint, both the worlds suffer', or of needing to 'lave our honours in these flattering streams And make our faces vizards to our hearts', we do not for the moment imagine that he is discussing snake-hunting, cabinet-making, astronomy, bathing or fancy-dress balls! Yet such is the *material* of his imagery. If film were indeed tied by its nature to the material aspects of its *real* content then it could not possibly make metaphorical statements, exploit symbolism, create allegories. Yet highly sensitive writers such as Gavin Millar can assert, writing on 'Metaphor in the Cinema':

> It comes to this: the cinema is a vehicle for observing, primarily, the appearance of the visible world. No one is under the illusion that this vision will be an objective one. But in this pursuit, the film-maker tampers with the natural flow of life and ignores the image's constant particularisation at his peril.

Those candles, on film, will for ever be candles! Yet in discussions of the film with students, none has ever suggested, having seen the film, that it is *about* candles – all have agreed that it is somehow connected with the human spirit, or imprisonment, or extermination, and most take the point that it is about Jews (there is a Jewish lullaby sung on the sound-track).

To examine more elaborate forms of metaphor, we would normally use one of Roman Polanski's short films, either *Two Men and a Wardrobe* or *Mammals*. Here again, if these films are not accepted as allegorical in form, if we must accept directly the evidence of our own eyes, then *Two Men and a Wardrobe* can only be about two men who actually walk out of the sea, carrying a wardrobe, meet with hostility from restaurant proprietor, hotel manager, tram-conductor, girl, keeper, etc., and walk back into the sea with their wardrobe: this must be the film, because this *is* the film. And *Mammals* is no more than a story of two men and a sledge ride? At this level it is hardly satisfying, since there is so little narrative climax, and the journey seems pointless. And how, at this level, can we respond to the moment when one 'wounded' man receives such attention and so much bandaging that he quite disappears from view against the snow-white background? Is the lesson to be learned that in a snowy landscape coloured bandages should be used? Or are we nearer to the truth in believing that we can so overwhelm another man with attention and concern, as manifestations of our own self-righteousness, that we can virtually annihilate him? I know which 'truth' I prefer.

One of the things about metaphor or allegory or parable is that they express ideas which could not be expressed otherwise. It is therefore important in discussion of films exploiting these forms (or novels or poetry) not to drive a group towards a rigidly defined meaning, message, specific truth. Is *Two Men and a Wardrobe* about Poland, carrying the burden of its oppressors on its back; or the burden of history; or are the two men Germany and Russia carrying the Polish wardrobe, at first creating Poland from the sea of European states and ultimately submerging her again?

Questions of this kind want gently (or if necessary, violently) to be redirected: if the wardrobe was, in fact, Poland and we were meant to know this, would the film-maker not have painted 'Poland' on it? Do you think he left the tale ambiguous because he did not know how to make it specific? Does an allegory have to have one unique interpretation? Is it more or less valid, and valuable as an experience, if it has more than one possible interpretation? Is there a distinction to be made between a thing being complex, and its being complicated? Between ambiguity and obscurity?

Because one rejects *the* explanation or *the* interpretation, this does not mean that all discussion of meaning has to be rejected: an interchange of ideas, a group-grope may well illuminate an idea or an image that was obscure. John may not accept Bill's interpretation, but it may focus attention upon a factor which John may re-evaluate to reinforce *his* interpretation. Even where a director or writer has set down in an interview or article what was in his mind or what his intention was in creating a film statement of this kind (and, in fact, Polanski has refused to elucidate these films; or like Hitchcock has accepted any elucidation offered in order to gratify the offerer!), this does not mean that it is the only interpretation: it merely means that this was an interpretation in the mind of the creative artist, but once the art has been launched upon a public, it grows and its interpretations must grow as it is received. I must bring my own experience to a work of art, and *for me* that work of art is bound to be the sum of my experience plus the artist's communicated experience. Discussion of film is particularly valuable in that words can never *define* the experience of film – there is no appeal to the words in the text (nor even to those in the dialogue or the film script) because these can never be *the film*: thus those engaged in the discussion are free to speculate, to offer words, without the danger of being put down, which is especially important for weaker students, or for weaker pupils in a class.

In all this work, which has been established now for more than ten years in the basic English courses at Bede College, we have five fairly well-defined aims. Ten years ago, these aims would have been much vaguer, but as we have grown more familiar with the use of film in our own English teaching and have assessed more systematically the students' responses to the material, we have been able to change the programmes, rearrange the order and the presentation of the material, gradually introduce new material to keep ourselves 'fresh', and formulate our aims more distinctly as:

(1) to increase our students' familiarity with film as a medium
(2) to make them aware of the formal structures and techniques of film, and to make comparisons with literary forms which reinforce both the similarities and the differences
(3) to accustom them to the use of film in our English teaching in order that they may be encouraged to use film in their English teaching
because we find (for the students) and believe that they will find (for the pupils) that film is a means
(4) to help the less coherent student to express ideas about art and ultimately ideas about himself
(5) to stimulate the abler student by challenging his experiences by the originality of a new medium, in which he is less likely to have had training in perception, or to have been given the 'right' answers to the questions asked.

There are eight lecturers working full-time or part-time in the department, and though the choice of films and the preparation of notes, information sheets, etc. is my responsibility, all members of the department are involved in discussions, seminars, the assessment of assignments, and an analysis and evaluation of the course. All regard it as a valuable part of the course, and, in fact, the number of film sessions has steadily increased during the years, in face of the ever mounting pressures to include this or that element in the basic courses – a reasonably encouraging sign that the film material 'earns its keep'.

The points made in (1) and (3) above are perhaps the justification for this chapter of the book, linked as they are with (4) and (5): almost all the material we use we would regard as having an equally valuable place in the classroom. Approaches, teaching methods, organisation of material will change, and clearly complex ideas and highly sophisticated films such as *Le Feu Follet* and *L'Eclisse* could hardly be used below sixth-form level. But I would reinforce the point made earlier – that in these courses we get, willy-nilly, students of a vast range of ability, aptitude and interest, most of them with commitment to subjects other than English. Their response to this material and these methods leads me to hope that they would have value outside colleges of education.

There are other sessions of film within the English course which I shall record, but with little comment or analysis. One session uses film material purely for impact as a stimulus to creative writing: if you provide material powerful enough in itself, ideas, emotions, even techniques can be liberated; and saying 'Watch this, and then write something' is often a richer stimulus than saying 'write about this'.

This programme varies considerably, and has sometimes included *Blacktop* (washing down a school playground – good for textures, patterns, movement), *Corral* (breaking in a young colt – skills, movement, tempo), *Night on a Bare Mountain* (Alexeieff's version of Mussorgsky's musical vision – fantasy and horror), two George Dunning cartoons, *The Apple* and *The Flying Man* (good imagination, and flexibility of narrative structure). The programme has *always* included Alain Resnais' *Nuit et Brouillard* because of the overwhelming intensity of its cold impact, and for the interest of its treatment of time and memory (as in all Resnais films). I would use all of these films in schools, though the Resnais only with a senior form whom I knew well; but the other films have been used successfully in primary schools and at the junior levels of secondary schools. The use of films to stimulate creative writing is discussed in some detail with examples in other chapters (Chapters 3 and 4 above).

Our other programmes, sometimes one, sometimes two, are usually devoted to films about children, and are used 'professionally' or pedagogically to orientate students towards classroom situations, thought and language processes in children, and as examples of material which, dealing with child experiences and attitudes, can often be used with success in the classroom. Such material has included extracts from *Whistle Down the Wind*, *The Fallen Idol*, *Bicycle Thieves* and *The Childhood of Maxim Gorki*, short films such as Franju's *La Première Nuit*, Truffaut's *Les Mistons*, Vigo's *Zéro de Conduite*, Richard Hawkins' *Bird Hunt*, *Terminus*, *Thursday's Children* and *The Red Balloon*. A number of these are discussed elsewhere in this book; and I have written elsewhere about the use of *Les Mistons*.*

* *English in Education*, Vol. 2, No. 2. Bodley Head, for N.A.T.E.

APPENDIX A

Practical problems

Film, of its very nature, is a practical subject whether we are considering the practice of showing film in the classroom or the practice of making films in 'studio' or on location. Like other practical subjects, film probably makes greater demands upon the ingenuity and resourcefulness of the teacher, and upon the financial and accommodation resources of the school, than some other subjects such as history or religious studies. It is foolish to ignore or underrate the problems of using or making films but equally irresponsible to exaggerate the difficulties. As writers of the chapters in this book have repeatedly stressed, the cost and trouble of using film has to be weighed against the value of its use in English teaching: they and many other teachers have found using film worthwhile and 'cost effective' in educational terms.

The notes in this Appendix are not intended as a comprehensive guide to the choice and use of film and film-equipment in school or college; they merely set down for the teacher who may not be experienced in the use of film some advice about selecting and showing films for classroom study, problems of space and timetabling, and comments upon costs.

SELECTION, ORDERING AND CHECKING

Films are usually selected from distribution catalogues either of commercial distributors such as Rank, F.D.A. or Contemporary or more specialised educational distributors (British Film Institute, Sound Services, British Transport Films, foreign embassy sources, etc). There are about two hundred agencies distributing films: a comprehensive register of these was published in the last *Screen Education Yearbook* (1969) which is still usable although out-of-date, and an annual survey of sources of factual films is published by *Film User* (P.O. Box 109, Croydon, Surrey). The major distributors advertise regularly in most film periodicals (see Appendix G). Most catalogues provide brief (and not always accurate) summaries of the films they offer, but if you do not know the film you are selecting it is worth the time and trouble to seek further advice and information from someone who does know and has used the film, from reviews published in *Monthly Film Bulletin, Film User*, or the *British National Film Catalogue*, or from accounts of film-teachers in S.E.F.T. or B.F.I. lists and publications. Remember the descriptions of films provided by the distributors are designed to persuade you to book the film rather than as a guide to its usefulness in the classroom.

Essential points to check in selecting and ordering films are:

the gauge – 35 mm, 16 mm or 8 mm (even 9·5 mm in some lists)

the ratio – whether 'standard' or 'scope' (which requires a special anamorphic lens, which may be hired, and probably a larger screen than that in normal use): some 16 mm films may be available in either ratio

colour – many 16 mm versions of films made in colour may be black-and-white copies

running time – which may differ from the version originally shown commercially

sound – some silent films are now available in sound versions; and some amateur-made films have magnetic (and not optical) sound tracks which can only be used on projectors with a magnetic track head

cost – which will be discussed below

The most important (and most difficult) point about ordering films is to do so sufficiently far in advance. Some films are booked for *two years* ahead, and it is often difficult to get the film you require at shorter notice than six months. For this reason, wherever possible, you should give either alternative film choices or alternative showing dates. Most booking-forms make provision for this, but if ordering by letter or in some other way (by L.E.A. requisition) set out your order as clearly as possible with alternative choices or dates precisely indicated. Some film libraries work by index-numbers rather than film-titles: double-check the index numbers in such cases (it can be both harassing and embarrassing to receive the wrong film!).

Most film distributors send confirmation of bookings, but not all; some operate on the principle that your order is confirmed unless they notify you to the contrary. Most film libraries refuse to accept telephone enquiries or bookings, but do not hesitate to follow up a written enquiry by telephone if confirmation has not been received within a reasonable time (say a month).

If you do not wish to act as your own booking agent you should take out Educational Corporate Membership of the British Film Institute

(£5 p.a.). This entitles you to use the services of the Central Booking Agency. The agency make a booking charge on almost every film, but if you are ordering a very large number of films from different sources, with complex alternatives of films and dates, and if you require additional information about films, programme notes, credits, etc., then it may be worth your while to place your bookings in the hands of the Central Booking Agency which has the resources and expert knowledge for complex booking orders. Educational Corporate Membership also provides *Sight and Sound, The Monthly Film Bulletin* and use of the Institute's book library and information services.

However you have selected and ordered your films, check the films as soon as you receive them. This means checking the film-leader or film-credits on the actual film, not merely the film-can since the transit case will not always contain the film-cans listed on its label; and the film-cans will not always contain the films listed on their labels. If you have not seen the film you have ordered (or if you have not seen it recently) *always* run through the film at a private viewing before you show it to a class: this is an essential aspect of film teaching and not an indulgent private luxury. It serves to check both the quality and content of the copy you have received.

Whatever you have selected, whatever you have ordered, the final responsibility for what is shown in the classroom is yours; and this will probably have involved checking the selection, checking the order, checking the confirmation, and checking the receipt of the film before showing it in the classroom. And the involvement of others (a colleague in the department, a clerk in the L.E.A. office, a booking agent) is more likely to increase your responsibility, though it may have reduced some of the administrative chores of the ordering process.

SHOWING THE FILM

Pupils or students will be accustomed to two viewing situations: either the highly specialised presentation of the cinema or the familiar comfort of the home, for films on television. Few classrooms will provide the equivalent of either. Nevertheless, the teacher or lecturer should have *as an ideal* the closest possible approximation to the best professional facilities for film viewing. There are three factors involved: picture quality, sound quality and comfort.

Picture quality is affected by four factors, all of which can to some extent be controlled by the teacher, though none of them entirely so – the quality of the print, the quality of the projector, the quality of the screen, and the distance between projector/screen/audience. Keep films in cans when not in use: film will collect (electrostatically) dust and grime from the atmosphere, particularly in the dusty conditions of classroom and stockrooms. Careful handling of the film will reduce this. Film distributors are very conscientious about the maintenance and cleaning of their prints, so if you do get a poor copy (dirty, scratched, defective in any way) do complain immediately and precisely to the distributor; and if there is real cause for complaint, the hire-charge may be reduced or waived. But there are only grounds for complaint if you have taken the maximum care of the film.

Do look after the projector (if, as is likely, there is no cine-technician to maintain it): know how to clean the film-gate and the condenser lens; keep the projector covered when not in use; send the projector in for professional maintenance and servicing during vacations. It takes about an hour to learn how to thread and use a film projector, how to safeguard damage, and the emergency drills involved with blown bulbs, damaged film, slipping and jumping. It takes only a few evenings to complete and qualify in a course on the use and maintenance of a great variety of projectors, and such courses are regularly organised both by local education authorities and by commercial firms in most areas. Even if there is a lab-technician or a colleague or a pupil regarded as 'responsible' for using projectors, the film-teacher needs to have a degree of expertise himself.

Use the best screen that you can afford: it will probably be in a better condition if it is a fixed screen than if it is portable, but a portable screen will be better than even the cleanest wall. Use the *smallest* screen that can effectively be used in the classroom in which you are operating, and position the projector to *fill* the screen (without spilling over the edges on to walls, blackboard or furniture). A small bright picture will be more effective than a large dim one, and a science colleague will explain the *inverse square law* if you are not already familiar with it.

Given a good print, a good projector and a good screen, still the major factor affecting picture-quality will be the blackout of the classroom. No temporary blackout is effective – neither curtains, nor shutters, nor blinds: the only effective conditions for good viewing are found in a room without windows, or a room with permanent fixed blackout. But short of the ideal (which in a large school or college should not be too difficult to obtain – a specialised darkened room will be in almost continuous demand) you can make temporary arrangements as effective as possible. Make sure that curtains, shutters or blinds fit properly and are not damaged (torn or holed); persuade the caretaker or head teacher into repairing damage as soon as it occurs, or replacing defective equipment. Have the room blacked out *before* beginning a film lesson, and keep it blacked out throughout the lesson if you are going to re-show films. It is much better to teach (question, discuss, write about) film in a blacked-out room using artificial light than to show film in a hastily and ineffectively blacked-out room, having to take time to draw curtains or lower blinds, to check for light-leakage around the edges of the windows, through tears in the black-out, etc.

Despite the difficulties involved in obtaining good picture quality, as a general rule the picture-quality in most classrooms is likely to be better than the sound-quality. The reasons for this are partly technological and partly physiological: the eye is a more tolerant and accommodating organ than the ear, and the optical systems of most projectors (and film prints) are significantly better than their sound systems (and sound tracks). Here again a permanent (fixed and wired) system is likely to be preferable to a portable system. The loud-speaker (or speakers) can be positioned and acoustically matched to the room to provide a much more satisfactory sound-system than will ever be possible with a small portable speaker. Nevertheless, experience achieved by trial-and-error will in time reveal the best position for the speaker (usually below or next to the screen, and always as close to it as possible) and how maximum volume and resonance may be achieved with minimum vibration. As a general rule, a better result will be achieved by having the class strain to listen to a quiet track than by deafening and deadening them with a blasted one. Not only will loud volume blur the quality of speech and effects on the sound-track, it will also increase the noise caused by scratches and dirt, the distortions of sound, and the general vibration of the system.

Having done one's best to achieve good blackout, good picture quality and good sound quality, these will be minimised if the class is uncomfortable or unable to see the picture or hear the (best) sound. Classrooms with flat floors, rows of desks, fixed desk-benches or hard chairs – in other words, most school classrooms – are the worst places in which to show films! It really is worth the trouble to spend time carefully arranging the classroom, either before or at the start of the lesson, to achieve the best possible viewing conditions. This probably means getting the projector and screen as high as possible and the audience as low as possible – this, after all, is the basic design of a movie-theatre; grouping the class (=audience) as tightly as possible, with chairs in a semicircle as equidistant from the screen as space will allow; perhaps letting some children sit on desks (or benches at the side of a classroom or laboratory) as well as on chairs. Showing a film is a distinct, practical, specialised classroom operation: it is not something added in to a 'normal' classroom situation and environment, and it therefore demands the same attention to use of space, disposal of equipment, discipline, planning and control as a P.E. or drama or science lesson.

In time, schools and colleges will have a tiered auditorium, with comfortable (padded) seats, isolated projection facilities, permanent screen and sound installation (and professional technicians to maintain and control the resources). Until such a time, it becomes the teacher's responsibility to make the very best use of what he has – and this can be quite a satisfying context for work. Too many teachers using film begin with a series of excuses for the inadequacies of the film, the equipment, the environment and their own lack of competence instead of using comparable energies to get the best out of all these factors.

PROBLEMS OF TIMETABLING AND FILM AVAILABILITY

The film lesson must be seen as similar to other practical, specialised lessons such as art and craft, science or games – this is to say it ideally demands a double-period allocation in a secondary timetable. In primary schools, where class activities are likely to be less rigidly timetabled, this is less of a problem. Even short films and extracts usually have a running time of 15–30 minutes, so that up to an hour of lesson-time may be occupied in showing, rewinding and reshowing a film or films. And contributors to this book have emphasised the value of immediate discussion and analysis, and the value of being able to re-show film material while ideas and opinions are fresh. Little progress is made if we show the film in one period, discuss it a day or a week later, and then (if we can afford it) re-book the film for a second showing at some later date.

In broader terms of timetabling it is clearly desirable to have film-study lessons concentrated on one or two days in the week with a number of forms. Almost all film distributors charge *by the day*: show a film to six forms in one day and you pay for it once; show it to the same six forms over three or more days, and you pay for it several times (though there is usually a percentage reduction for showings on consecutive days); show it to 3A this week, 3B next week and 3C the week after, and you might even find it cheaper to *buy* the film than to hire it!

There are clearly additional advantages (if space permits) in showing a film to several forms or sets at the same time, and then letting several teachers develop their work from the film either independently or collaboratively according to an agreed plan. Mr Schofield has discussed both of these systems in Chapter 4. In smaller schools, whether at primary or secondary level, it may be most effective to show the film outside class time – at the lunch-hour break or in assembly time – in order that more than one class may view the material to be discussed at a later time with one or more teachers.

Extensions outside the class timetable become even more important when dealing with feature-films, the shortest of which tend to have a running time of 85–90 minutes, and which allowing for reel-changes will probably overrun even a double period. Given the understanding co-operation of head teachers and colleagues over such matters as alloca-tion of space and registration, it is sometimes possible to begin a film-viewing session a little before the official start of afternoon lessons, or to extend the last period of the morning or afternoon by a few minutes into the pupils' free time: there are very rarely any objections to this practice from the children, who would prefer it to interrupting the continuity of an exciting and absorbing film.

It is possible to teach film in 35 or 40-minute timetable slots; it is possible to teach film to a single form in the school; it is possible to run a film course without showing a feature film: but the possible is not necessarily desirable, and certainly not the most desired. The greatest advantages accrue from an extensive and varied use of film with several forms over a wide curriculum; from the sympathetic timetabling of film-study periods; and from imaginative flexibility in the grouping of forms, the exploitation of extra-curriculum time, and the most effective planning and co-ordination of the work.

COSTS

It is impossible to generalise about the cost of using film, since the cost-factor is not entirely an objective one: one school will regard a pottery-kiln costing perhaps £2,000 as an expensive luxury while another will regard it as an essential item of equipment; another school will provide instruments for a school band or a full symphony orchestra whereas another may choose to invest in a swimming pool. Varying priorities will be established with regard to textbooks, art materials, scientific equipment, travelling expenses for visits and expeditions. It is against such a background that the financing of film study within courses must be argued.

The range of hire-costs is very wide. Some full-length features may cost £25 or £30 for one hiring, yet it is still possible to hire some feature films from specialised libraries (Central Film Library, certain embassies) for a purely nominal handling charge, and even commercial features by major directors such as Hitchcock and Ford can be traced in the lists of some of the smaller distributors at one-tenth of the maximum hire-cost of 16 mm features. Despite the attractiveness of short films and extracts from the point of view of timetabling, these are often relatively expensive film forms; and anyone who has run a film society knows well enough that a two-minute short can often cost half the hire-charge of a two-hour feature.

Not unnaturally, teachers often have recourse to 'free' film libraries; but one must immediately issue a word of caution. No films are completely free to the hirer or borrower. He must inevitably meet the cost of returning the film, and must usually pay postage or transport costs both ways. Most free film libraries now charge a booking or service fee usually between 25p and £1, though such a fee often covers the booking of a whole series of films; and in some cases there are additional costs of compulsory insurance. In all dealings with film libraries, whether 'free' or 'educational' or commercial, the hirer or borrower does well to read the booking instructions and conditions (including the small print) with great care in order to budget realistically for the cost of obtaining and returning film, and to establish clearly whether the (now quite high) cost of film postage is to be regarded as a departmental expense or borne on the school postage-fund; to determine which category of school-account will pay for the purchase of film catalogues (in many cases the cost of the catalogue is deductible from the first order placed with the library) or for the membership subscriptions sometimes necessary to secure the use of a film distribution library.

Such services suggest other ways in which film study may be incorporated into the curriculum without necessarily hiring films every week. Though the hire or purchase of individual film-stills is relatively expensive (indeed prohibitive on most school budgets), the B.F.I. Stills Library does provide at a nominal cost thematic collections of stills to almost any order (e.g. the Western, the gangster film, national collections, work of particular directors, particular periods, the animated film, documentary, etc.). Such a collection hired for a short period either for display or study can effectively reinforce projected film material, and form the basis of a series of lessons preparing for or following up extracts, short films or features.

There are also a few suitable film-strips and slide collections (usually for purchase rather than hire) which the regular user of film for study purposes may find useful as an alternative to film hire occasionally. And the increasing number of well-illustrated books on film will provide lesson-material as well as library reference.

But even exploiting these alternative sources, the main film element in any course must be film itself, and most local authority film libraries, even where these exist, tend to be collections of visual aids material – much of it very poor – of only limited value to the English teacher. Such sources, however, must not be neglected: it is usually a matter of intelligent and knowledgeable reading of the library lists. A film in the geography or natural history or anthropology section may well be excellent material for creative writing; an industrial documentary may reinforce a thematic study; the most unexpected treasures may be unearthed. There are many examples in the chapters of this book of lessons or courses based largely or even exclusively on 'free loan' material or films likely to be available in L.E.A. centres.

The effective use of film, like any effective teaching of any subject, will depend upon the skill and knowledge of the teacher; and if the teacher does not have the knowledge it must be acquired. Teachers' centres should be (and some already are) useful sources of such knowledge: many film libraries will loan programmes of films without charge for viewing sessions of teachers, and a group of schools could probably secure the same facilities if not within reach of a teachers' centre. The Federation of Film Societies arranges both national and local viewing sessions, and some regional film theatres would be prepared to mount special viewing sessions if enough teachers would demonstrate their interest and make their demands known.

FILM-MAKING

Once the capital cost of equipment has been met, one of the cheapest ways of 'using film' is making films. Not very much has been said about film-making in this book for two reasons: first, because most aspects of film-making are likely to find a more congenial place in books on Film in Drama Teaching or Film in Art Teaching; and, second, because comprehensive accounts of this aspect of film teaching have already been published, notably '*Film Making in Schools*' by Douglas Lowndes (Batsford 1968) and a symposium on '*Film Making in Schools and Colleges*' (British Film Institute, 1966). Both of these contain much practical information about equipment and costs, and are rich in ideas about the place of film-making in school and college curricula from infant schools to teachers' colleges.

Much of the school and college film work shown at festivals and in competitions does, indeed, originate within English departments; and, as John Bennett clearly indicates in Chapter 2, film-making is valuable not merely as a creative activity but also as a discipline, exploiting and reinforcing many of the disciplines which would be the basic aim of any English teacher.

The kind of flexibility of organisation and sympathetic timetabling which I have outlined above as desirable if not essential for film study will clearly be as necessary (and probably more so) if film making is to be part of a course; and the process of film editing really requires the special allocation of space for both practical work and storage.

THE TEACHER

The conclusion to be drawn from the foregoing notes upon practical problems, as indeed from every chapter in this book, is that the English teacher who wishes to introduce film into his courses will have to be a 'better man' than his colleague or neighbour. This is not to exercise a contentious judgment or make an odious comparison; it is to state a fact. For he will of necessity need to be an effective and imaginative teacher of English before contemplating the introduction of film.

From this point on, he will have to establish relationships with his colleagues and the more senior staff that will secure an effective response to his special pleading for helpful timetabling, for good equipment, for money, for viewing facilities, for a degree of flexibility that will enable him fully to exploit the film that he gets for study or the stock that he obtains for film-making. He will become both diplomat and politician; he will probably have to become something of a technician as well as a creative artist and critic; he will need to know as much as the care-taker and the cleaners about the impossible positioning of electrical sockets and the mysterious availability of extension leads and plug-adaptors; he will soon know better than the school secretary the vagaries of postal services and train connections and where to find the string and the scotch-tape; and if his film bookings go through the normal processes of L.E.A. requisitions, he will become as skilful as his head teacher in dealings with the Divisional Office.

He may become loved by his pupils and hated by his colleagues, and may pass through a period when these attitudes are reversed (particularly if he has promised his class a film which doesn't arrive, or if he has a film which has arrived and which will plug a gap in someone else's syllabus).

But when he persists through adversity, meets the problems and surprises with the calm wisdom of experience, accomplishes the chores with routine skill, he will begin to enjoy the discoveries and rewards which the teachers contributing to this book and many others at all levels of education have found arising from their introduction of film into English teaching.

> The lyf so short, the craft so long to lerne
> Thassay so hard, so sharp the conquering.

But Chaucer wrote also a '*Treatise on the Astrolabe*', thus establishing an early link between literature and technology. The English teacher who assays the use of film follows worthy precedents; and may fondly yearn for comparable fame.

R.K.

APPENDIX B

Film in the Humanities Project

The Humanities Project is not concerned with the teaching of film nor with the teaching of English. It finds its place here as a very precise example of the inter-disciplinary, often multi-media, enquiry-based work grouped around themes which has become an important element in the secondary school curriculum. The use of film within this or similar structures is likely to be the first experience for many teachers and children of serious classroom work with the kind of film material usually associated with film teaching proper. Done well, the kind of work envisaged by the Project can constitute, as a by-product of its main purpose, a valuable approach to film study (as well as to English, history, social studies and so on).

The Project arose out of the prospect of the raising of the minimum school-leaving age in Britain from fifteen to sixteen years. It was felt that new teaching strategies were called for.

The context for this work had already been set:

To set a class to study a carefully defined problem in human conduct and human relations into which boys and girls can project themselves and work out the various implications of different courses of action – this is realistic teaching.   (*Newsom Report*)

The problem is to give every man some access to a complex cultural inheritance, some hold on his personal life and on his relationships with the various communities to which he belongs, some extension of his understanding of, and sensitivity towards, other human beings. The aim is to forward understanding, discrimination and judgement in the human field – it will involve reliable factual knowledge, where this is appropriate, direct experience, imaginative experience, some appreciation of the dilemmas of our human condition, of the rough-hewn nature of many of our institutions, and some rational thoughts about them. (Schools Council's *Working Paper No. 2*, on the raising of the school-leaving age.

With this background the Humanities Project was set up in 1967 in order to research into the problems that this approach raises for teachers. Its brief was to:

> ... offer to schools and to teachers such stimulus, support and materials as may be appropriate to the mounting, as an element in general education, of enquiry-based courses which cross the subject boundaries between English, History, Geography, Religious Studies, and Social Studies.

It stated that:

> ... the claim of the humanities in the curriculum rests upon the assertion that their study enhances understanding, and hence judgement, in those areas of practical living which involve complex considerations of empirical data, values and cultural traditions.

The Project, financed by the Schools Council and the Nuffield Foundation, ran until 1972. During its last two years the Project's materials have been published, in 'pack' form*, while the Project itself has been concerned primarily with dissemination and evaluation. The themes or topics chosen for the experiment were war, education, the family, relations between the sexes, city life, poverty, work and leisure, law and order, and race relations – all in one way or another, considered controversial areas of universal human concern. Film is only one element in the Project's materials, and before discussing its place it is necessary to explain something of the theory of the approach as a whole.†

By definition a controversial issue divides society – including pupils, parents and teachers. In a democracy we do not expect everyone to hold the same views. We value a dialogue between informed views. (In any case, teachers are not, in fact, free to express their moral positions in schools, unless those positions fall within the generally accepted norms.)

---

* Packs are published by Heinemann Educational Books Ltd. Titles published so far are: *War and Society, Education, The Family, Relations Between the Sexes, People and Work, Poverty,* and *Law and Order.*
† The approach is described in greater detail in *The Humanities Project: an Introduction* (Heinemann, available separately).

If different teachers, pupils and parents have views ranging over the whole spectrum of opinion, teaching in these controversial areas should be based on open but disciplined discussion rather than on formal instruction. The Project is committed to responsibility (the acceptance of one's own accountability) rather than to authority (depending for justification on others).

Teaching must permit and protect divergence and maintain respect for individual opinions. The teacher cannot be an 'expert', cannot have the 'right answers', cannot solve by authority all issues about values arising in discussion. But discussion must be disciplined and the teacher must understand his purely *procedural* authority – as the 'chairman' of the discussion – in the classroom. The Project aims at a form of discussion in which the teacher should be a neutral and impartial chairman and a resource consultant. He should help a discussion group to find its own way to an understanding of the issues at stake, and should try to moderate social group pressures on students to conform. 'Neutrality' means that the teacher does not propagate his own view and is prepared to see the students treat all views according to consistent critical principles. 'Impartiality' means that in normal circumstances, all students within the discussion should be treated alike.

To teach controversial matters well, a teacher must believe the issues to be important, implying that he has deep commitments of his own. He is not teaching neutrality so much as the nature of responsible commitment. If education is to move away from the idea of custodial containment to the desire to help students to cope with life after they leave school, it must at some time wean them from dependence on teachers' authority.

Neutrality and impartiality is not only a professional ethic in controversial areas; it is also important in what happens in the classroom. The chairman of a discussion can breach his neutrality in a number of ways. By responding more favourably to some student contributions than others he may endorse a particular view, just as he may if he asks questions in a leading way. The danger is that a chairman-teacher may destroy a discussion by redirecting it from a genuine attempt to understand the issue in question into a guessing game about what is in the teacher's mind (instruction in disguise). The purpose of neutrality is to put the responsibility for gaining understanding on the pupils.

If the teacher maintains neutrality, the source of information or 'evidence' for discussion must come from somewhere other than himself. To avoid the typical situation in which discussion becomes an exchange of prejudices and opinions, the Project assembles, supplies and recommends materials for discussion. These materials include printed matter (extracts from novels and plays, poems, newspaper articles, leaflets, letters, material from books on history, sociology, anthropology, philosophy, etc.), taped materials (drama, songs, interviews), photographs, and films. The essential points about these materials are:

a they are from existing sources, not specially manufactured;
b they are designed to represent a range of different views on as many issues as possible;
c they cover both fact and fiction, data and experience;
d they are not intended to be definitive – schools are expected to add to them;
e they are supplied in multiple loose copies so that each student can have in front of him a copy of the evidence under discussion.

How is this sort of evidence used in discussion? The Project's research in its thirty-six experimental schools shows that students tend initially to look to a chairman for authority, assume that he knows the answers, and try to guess what he wants them to say. They will see the 'evidence' as material from which they are expected to make a clear-cut case. They will expect that evidence produced is designed to foster consensus. They will often be sceptical and make the least of conflicting evidence.

At first they often regard documentation as evidence only about facts and events. It takes time for them to understand that fiction or poetry can be evidence for a mood or emotion, and that a piece of didactic prose can be evidence simply for the *existence* of a point of view rather than *proof* that it is right. Skill and judgment in these areas need experience before they can be developed. While the teacher-chairman risks harming the discussion if he asks questions to which he thinks he knows the answers, he can point out ambiguities which he himself cannot resolve. He can help the students to interpret evidence. He can encourage pupils to clarify their arguments. By introducing new pieces of evidence he can either help students to see what may not be clear in another piece, or discourage easy consensus. By refusing to break silences in discussion himself, he can encourage the students to take responsibility for their own discussion. By his sensitivity to student discussion he can suggest and stimulate outcomes, or follow-up work, which may further extend the understanding gained in discussion.

The Project does not think, nor does its research show, that the change of role required by this kind of teaching is easily achieved. It needs some retraining, dedication and, sometimes, painful experience, but if successful, it can bring considerable rewards in terms of the intellectual level of work achieved. The method is not intended as a way of teaching other classroom subjects, but, as Lawrence Stenhouse says, it 'radically changes teacher-pupil relationships and has profound implications for the authority structure of the school'.

Film is only one kind of material among others. As with the printed material, the films range from newsreel and documentary to fiction, from ten-minute extracts and short films to feature-length works. Feature-length fiction films are regarded as especially important since they offer complete and complex experiences, where so many other materials are in extract form. The films are selected for their relevance to a number of basic issues, and their representation of different attitudes. Thus, a selection of films on war may include films in which war is accepted as necessary or even glorified, as well as films which are anti-war in intent, documentary or newsreel films made about actual wars as well as fictionalised personal experiences of war. In the context of an enquiry into a particular theme, film may be used in a number of ways:

a to begin the enquiry, by raising issues which can then be explored either through the film or through reference to other materials;

b to be introduced at a particular stage of an enquiry, to provide material for the discussion of a particular issue (though it should be noted that problems of booking make this very integral use of film difficult);

c to sum up, by showing a film, possibly a complete feature film, at the end of an enquiry to help draw together or synthesise various pieces of evidence discussed and issues raised.

Every different kind of evidence, whether artistic, historical, scientific or sociological, poses its own disciplinary problems: what *kind* of evidence have we here? how do we assess it? It is not always easy to see that there *are* problems of this nature since, clearly, in discussion of *issues* various problems about the nature of the evidence are accepted implicitly. Equally clearly, certain kinds of evidence do not pose these problems as obviously as others. The experience with film has been that the most favoured kinds of film are documentaries and the most naturalistic fiction. The tendency here would be to forget that what we are seeing is artificially created, and to treat it as if it were real, a slice of life, so that we discuss life rather than the artist's response to it. However, if all we want is issues, then why use art?* Film is used in the Project partly because it is an important mass medium and art form, but also because it raises issues in a special way, a filmic way, different from the way other materials raise issues. The issues it raises are not something separate or abstractable from the art object. Issues and comment upon issues are not simply *there*, self-evident and unambiguous. In exploring art evidence and considering issues in it we are called upon to consider also the way the art work embodies those issues.

The aim of the work in the Humanities Project is not to teach film (or literature, or sociology), but questions will arise which may need to be decided on filmic (or literary or sociological) grounds. Those concerned with the value of teaching film as a subject valid in itself may have justifiable grounds, in practice, for suspecting the Project's use of film guilty of being, at best, utilitarian and, at worst, impoverishing, though this must be put against the evidence that groups seem to be able to come to a level of understanding of art works which may be superior to that gained by a fundamentally artistic approach to them. Again, though, this fact does not dispose of the undeniable problems.

In order to give some idea of these problems, a few (random) examples might be taken. This discussion of them is unreal in the sense that in a classroom situation a group would normally come to these film examples in a very precise context. A short film recommended in the war theme would not be seen in isolation. Rather a group might come to it having explored other kinds of evidence in the same thematic area, and therefore bring to it relatively precise concerns which will influence what they both see and look for. The new piece of evidence might be introduced, for example, to explore in greater depth an area already touched upon or to throw a different light upon it.

Listen to Britain
A short propaganda documentary made in 1942. It is made up of sights and sounds of wartime Britain in such a way as to act as a morale-booster.

Documentary film may be compared in many ways with written journalism or history. There is usually a core of fact which the film

---

* This question is raised in an acute form by the pamphlet *'Films for General Studies'*, compiled by the Association for Liberal Education and published by the National Committee for Visual Aids in Education, 1971. For example, a teacher using Resnais's *Hiroshima Mon Amour* to teach about war complains that there are 'too many flashbacks' and the film is 'too verbose', implying that the style 'gets in the way' of the message.

wishes to communicate. Ethnographers will testify to the value of film as record, and documentaries about famine, courtship habits or education can provide recorded factual evidence of great use to the enquiry being undertaken. As with journalism, beyond the level of raw fact (in so far as this ever exists) there will be considerations of bias and attitude expressed in tone and selectivity. Such considerations may be especially important when dealing with propaganda. In addition, as with *Listen to Britain*, there are problems of meaning in art.

At the raw-material level *Listen to Britain* offers in its images and sounds evidence that certain activities are going on in the midst of war: people work in the fields, planes fly overhead, a dance is going on, men and women work in factories, troops march in the street, and so on. But this does not take us very far into the film – we could gain as much from a series of still photographs. The particular force of this film is in its artistic ordering of images and sounds to present a composite picture of a nation at war. The nature of the ordering of these elements is such that it creates an overwhelming impression of unity, strength, harmony and of a carry-on spirit. This is not something which would escape an unwary audience, of course, but in order to consider what the film is doing, precisely what it is saying, students would be forced into a consideration of the total effect which stems from particular juxtapositions of images and sounds, the use of music to unite conventionally separate activities, the effect of composition and lighting on things photographed. Differences of opinion in discussion could be settled only by reference to the film. This process may be a perfectly natural one, but once engaged upon it one is into a kind of film teaching.

Extract: *Up the Junction*

This television play is built up around scenes of life in the Clapham Junction area of London. The extract consists of the opening sequence in which three girls meet three boys during a dance at a pub. They go to a swimming pool, are discovered there, and run to avoid being caught. They drive away in a car. Rube and Terry get out to go for a walk. Ron and Sylvie stay in the car. Dave and Eileen make love in a derelict building. The extract ends with shots of workmen demolishing homes.

The first half of the extract is very 'busy' and basically naturalistic, with its snatches of character observation and natural conversation. One could use it as if it were 'real': What kinds of characters are they? How do they feel about each other? Why do they say the things they do? Are these the sorts of encounters you recognise in your own lives? And so on. But the second half of the extract cannot be treated in the same way. Compared with the first half it ceases to be naturalistic – the dialogue becomes non-synchronous, the narrative line breaks down, as narrative action is intercut with non-narrative and music is used not as a natural background but as a form of commentary. It is no longer real in the same way; one feels very strongly the influence of the artist saying something *about* the action, at a remove. At this point, if one is to make sense of what is going on one is forced to consider how the material is structured, what relationships are implied between different sets of visuals, what 'comment' the music intends, what the mood is. Whereas in the first half one might be able to talk about people or life, here one must talk about what the artist is saying about them. In doing so one is, again, into a kind of film-teaching, although, again, one would not imply that this would be unnatural or opposed to the needs of the enquiry. We may be more used than we think to effects of style, to reading the visual language, though we may not be used to analysing and we may not have the vocabulary necessary for such analysis. Without it, however, the film evidence would remain obscure or in the way – which would constitute a serious obstacle to understanding part of the evidence which must alter quite substantially our response to the more immediately accessible evidence. It is in the nature of Project teaching strategy that the teacher cannot have an agenda of points about the evidence which he insists his group must work through – a comprehension exercise is out of place here – but it is important that the teacher and his group are aware of these dimensions in the evidence and prepared to grapple with them if the need arises.

Extract: *A Generation*
The film, set in Warsaw 1942, follows the experiences of Stach, a boy who joins one of the underground groups of the Polish Resistance, and who is matured by his experiences and relationships in the struggle.

    In the extract Stach learns how to join the Resistance. On Sunday he is taken to church, where a wedding is taking place, to meet Dorota, the girl leader of a resistance group; they part within a photographer's heart-shaped frame. A meeting of young people takes place; Dorota talks of the aims of the Resistance and the members swear allegiance. Next day Jacek sees the crowds staring at the bodies hanged by the Germans. Back at work, frightened, he refuses Stach's offer to join the Fighting Youth. Stach drives the lumber truck into the yard, stopping as he encounters a group of Jews being herded along by German soldiers. At the yard he is warned against the German sentry at the gate

who later stops him and calls him into the office where he is accused
of stealing, beaten, and thrown out, now on the verge of tears.

The extract (and the feature) are recommended in the thematic area
of War and Society concerned with morale and attitudes of people in
wartime and especially around the ideas of resistance and the problems
of an occupied people. (This is not to say that this is all *A Generation*
is about: art is not created to supply materials for teachers exploring
themes with their pupils.)

In this thematic area one might ask a general, almost an abstract,
question: Why do people join resistance movements? In employing art
in thematic enquiry work we must accept that understanding general
issues comes from understanding particular manifestations of them, so
in this instance one would ask: Why does Stach join the Resistance?
What do he and the others we see gain from belonging to it? What does
Stach learn from his experiences in the film? These questions are framed
to be as open as possible. Questions with in-built answers defeat the
purpose of placing responsibility for understanding on the pupils.
The questions themselves refer one back to internal evidence, to the
evidence of the film: Stach's behaviour and expressions, the way the
Resistance group meeting is filmed, the changing moods and rhythms,
and our responses to all these. Disagreements in the group about
response and meaning – without which discussion of general issues is
fruitless – must take place through understanding of what is happening
in *film*.

It will be seen in these examples how work in the Humanities Project
(in film as in other media), while pursuing 'understanding, discrimination and judgment in the human field', can on the way contribute to an
understanding of the nature and processes of art and to 'imaginative
experience'. It is in this that the work links up with the aims of English
and film teaching.

                                                                                      Jim Hillier

APPENDIX C

Film in the C.S.E. examinations

There are cogent arguments against bringing the study of Film or Screen Education into the examination arena. These notes, however, are intended for the teacher who feels he can take advantage of a liberal examination structure to safeguard the position of Film or Screen Education in the upper part of the secondary school while at the same time minimising the deleterious effects of examinations.

A teacher wishing to offer his fourth- or fifth-year pupils the chance to let their work in Film count towards an award in the C.S.E. examination has basically two methods open to him. If within his region there is a Mode 1 syllabus in English or Art which allows scope for work in Film, he may take advantage of this. Alternatively if there are no such suitable openings then he may devise and submit for approval his own Mode 2 or Mode 3 examinations.

MODE 1
Some examination panels, in preparing their syllabuses for English, have recognised that teachers of English frequently go outside written texts to analyse and discuss issues and attitudes with their pupils. In connection with work on the set theme, 'Conflict', which was prescribed recently as alternative to the set-book section of the English syllabus, the English panels of the Metropolitan Regional Board panel listed the following films as material which teachers may find useful:

(1) *Neighbours*
(2) *Paths of Glory* (extract)
(3) *They Were Expendable* (extract)
(4) *The War Game*
(5) B.F.I. Film Study Unit No. 2, 'War on the Screen'.

Other Boards are less explicit but offer some openings. For example one Board includes within its English syllabus the following possibility:

Questions of a general nature will be asked on special topics from a set list, the purpose of which is to promote study and discussion in schools of a range of interests relevant to English studies, especially those where personal judgment and expression of views are involved.

Its 'set list' includes 'Radio or Television: uses and abuses as a mass medium, balance of programmes, "influence on people's minds" ' and there is provision for a teacher's choice of 'other topics closely related to English studies' to be notified to the Board. This provides an opportunity for some study of the cinema. Another Board has a similar provision:

The questions on special topics and themes will be of a general nature and their purpose will be to promote study and discussion in schools on a range of interests relevant to English studies.
The topics include 'Radio and Television' and 'Theatre and Cinema'.

MODE 3

If the Mode 1 syllabuses do not provide a suitable opportunity the film teacher must consider drawing up and even examining his own syllabus. He can either offer his own syllabus for an orthodox subject which also includes film (e.g. English and Film) *or* alternatively he can submit a distinct subject called Screen Education (as it has been in the two or three syllabuses already accepted) or Film.

One Oxfordshire comprehensive school offers a Mode 3 examination in English which makes reference to film. The various activities which a pupil may pursue include course work on some aspect of 'the mass media', including contribution to a folder on literature and film of not more than one piece of writing on film. The syllabus suggests that his comments might include: 'the success or failure of the film in telling a story, illustrating a theme or portraying relationships; the director's use of visual imagery to point up meaning; the art of effective editing; the use of camera movement and angles, alternate use of long shots and close ups and other devices in order to create tension, drama and point of view; the use of sound as a means of intensifying atmosphere; the importance of the performance of the actors and actresses.' The course allows for the viewing of a variety of feature films and extracts including *The African Queen* and *Les Mistons*. The C.S.E. candidate is orally examined on this folder of work and is 'expected to back up and support arguments, assertions, statements and views presented in his folder. He will be expected to speak clearly and thoughtfully and in a continuous dialogue between himself and the examiners.' The film aspect of the English course is allocated two periods a week in the fifth year.

Greater freedom and concentration is, however, offered by Mode 3 syllabuses which are concerned wholly or principally with film. These are already being followed in schools, usually on an option basis, with the pupils choosing between (say) Screen Education and Music or French. Since it is this form of examination which offers the greatest challenge to orthodoxy an example is given here. It illustrates the form of syllabus already approved by an Examination Board.

SCREEN EDUCATION

Initially extracts which demonstrate the art of film will be shown. From these will follow a study of the impact of motion, picture and sound in film. Thereafter will follow a brief consideration of the basic functions of the cameraman, director, editor and actor. The major part of this work will be approached through practical film-making, theoretical conclusions being drawn from practical experience.

This will lead to a closer examination of the part played by the director. From one specific example (e.g. Eisenstein, Ford, Lean) the particular vision of a director and the ethos in which he works will be studied in conjunction with his personal idiosyncrasies of presentation. Any palpable developments in his work will also be noted.

Visual persuasion, particularly in propaganda and advertising, will be studied in consideration of selection of material, insinuation, symbolism, exploitation of emotional reaction, commentary and music in relation to the aims of the film.

The work of Norman McLaren will be the basis of a study of animation, since this will lead to pupils hand-painting their own film. Other forms of animation will be considered in relation to their function and the element of fantasy. In contrast, documentary will illustrate the realistic use of film, its social comment and its own peculiar demands.

The particular aims and methods of film-makers will be studied in the context of the history of film. This will be linked to an examination of television, its particular limitations and advantages, its immediacy, social impact and effect on the film industry, technically and economically.

Most of these ideas will be presented in conjunction with thematic study. For example, material on war will be discussed both for subject-matter and methods of persuasion. This emphasises the fact that the course aims to study film as an organic whole and the particular aspects already mentioned will only be isolated to obtain a better understanding of the whole medium.

OTHER APPROACHES

The syllabus examples quoted here are not intended as 'model' syllabuses which all should seek to emulate. Their compilers would be the first to agree that there is a need for continuing research and development in the methodology of Screen Education. New and different syllabuses should be designed and tested and the resulting conclusions shared with interested teachers. We are clearly only at the beginning of such research and it certainly should not be confined only to examination syllabuses. To suggest this is not to belittle the achievements of pioneers in the field. However, what are needed now are experiments which move out of the stereotype of the Screen Education syllabus which at times has attempted too much, too superficially. There is a very strong case for those who wish Film to be an important element in the final years of a secondary education to offer it in its own right as a Mode 3 C.S.E. subject and within that context to work in a narrowly defined area and to work in *depth*. Of course, a spurious academicism is to be avoided at all costs and the central concern must be to extend the imagination and sympathies of young people. The aim of concentration, however, is to enrich response and to avoid the dissipation of effort over a hopelessly large area. A carefully chosen topic provides the framework on which points about the cinema as a whole can be made. Some outline sketches of what such Mode 3 syllabuses might contain follows:

(a) Themes

Any discussion of *any* film will want to concern itself centrally with the director's attitude to human experience. The questions we must in the end ask of all art which objectifies human experience in fiction – what values are implied here? what comment is made about personal relationships? what does it all have to do with ME? – have always acquired a particular force in discussion of cinema. Hence the examination of several themes (e.g. Family, Work, Heroes) that can be traced in both film and supporting written texts makes good sense. Jim Kitses' book 'Talking about the Cinema' offers some well-documented suggestions.

(b) Film-making and the documentary cinema

The most accessible genre in which a young film-maker can work is probably documentary. He observes and records. Embarrassing actors can be avoided; costume and props are not required. Simple ten-minute documentaries with or without striped sound can be made for £5 on black-and-white film. Moreover, there is a massive and lively tradition of documentary in the cinema and in television. The aim of such a syllabus would be to make valuable connections between the pupil's own film-making, the documentary tradition and current practice. Having worked on a short film about, for example, an area of his town soon to be demolished in the course of urban renewal, he will not only more clearly understand the social problem which is the subject of the film but will also more clearly recognise the strengths and weaknesses of (say) *Listen to Britain, Le Sang des Bêtes, Very nice, Very nice, Seven Up, Phoebe, Nice Time* and *The Chair.*

(c) National cinemas

The British and American traditions in the cinema are both sufficiently well defined and accessible to make this a fruitful course. The aim naturally would not be to offer an absurdly superficial sociological and cultural history of either Britain or America, but to select films (either for showing specifically on the course if one has the budget to allow it, or for showing at the school film society) which are rich and significant films *in themselves* and also incidentally illustrate the main concerns of film-makers, either in Britain or America. For example if one chose the latter for special study then a viewing of *Guns in the Afternoon, The Big Heat* and *Hell is for Heroes* would set out three areas of special concern in the American cinema as well as provide three films of considerable relevance to the discussion of personal values in a corrupt society.

(d) Directors

That the director is the distinctive *author* of a film has been one of the major tenets of recent criticism. Within some of the syllabuses quoted above the idea of looking at the work of particular directors is already emerging as being one way of concentrating critical attention. It might be a good idea to extend the principle to provide the whole of a year's

G

study. The work of three contrasting directors could be looked at: (say) John Ford, David Lean and Orson Welles. Again the work of these directors would be attractive to film societies, likely to appear on television and possibly might be added to during the course. Their films will bear close examination both as individual works and as part of a pattern of development.

Conclusions

Film-teaching does not *need* external examination to discipline it; there are arguments against such examinations. However, examinations designed and controlled by the class teacher might help both teacher and class to order their priorities. If courses compete for attention at the upper end of the secondary school, examinations might be one of the criteria of survival. Experiments in all kinds of courses should be encouraged. There is a need for the exchange of information and experience which can be met in part through the Society for Education in Film and Television (63 Old Compton Street, London W1) and the Education Department of the British Film Institute (81 Dean Street, London W1V 6AA). In addition teachers should be willing to report their experience to others who might wish to try something on similar lines. Above all what is needed is a conviction that film and television *matter* – not as a threat but as an opportunity which any teacher who cares about the personal development of young people would be unwise to ignore.

Roger Watkins

APPENDIX D

Some film courses

There are inevitable difficulties about setting down any courses or syllabuses, especially in film. Few teachers present exactly the same course-material to any two forms or in any two years – courses invariably evolve and are transformed, and by the time they have been taught, assessed and set down, they have probably been changed again; and, indeed, some of the course-material may be no longer available.

It is essential, therefore, to regard the courses set out below merely as providing ideas which might spark off new courses suited to other teachers and other pupils. In most cases, they are little more than film-lists, with the minimum of annotation, not to obstruct their effective adoption by other teachers, but rather as a repeated warning that each teacher must select, preview and plan his own course materials, perhaps with the sort of critical and pragmatic advice found in the earlier chapters of this book, and in occasional articles and commentaries in film and teaching periodicals.

R.K.

(a) SOME FILMS FOR THEMATIC WORK AND STIMULUS IN JUNIOR SCHOOLS

Most of the films in these lists are short films, and most come from 'free-loan' sources (though see Appendix A for warning about 'free' films).

See also the catalogue of *The Children's Film Foundation* and *100 Films for Juniors* (S.E.F.T.).

Animals

Vanishing Prairie
Seal Island
Bear Country
A to Zoo series
40 minutes at the Zoo

Dream of Wild Horses
Die Kreuzpine
The Living Pattern
The Rival World
Crin Blanc

Birds
Zoo
The Colourful Marsh
Armand and Michaela Denis
  on Safari
Water Birds

Churches, Castles and Markets
Coventry Cathedral
Castle and Country (Scotland)
An Artist looks at Churches
Stockholm Story

The Countryside
Off the Beaten Track
The Great Adventure
The Wind on the Heath
Secrets of the Marshland
Wild Highlands
Journey into Spring

Effects (Sound and Colour)
Listen to Steel
Let's go to Birmingham
River of Wood
Colour of Life
Prince Electron
Mirror of Holland
Colour
The Inconvenience
The Revealing Eye
Getting Warmer
Snow
Rail

Entertainment
Kermesse Fantastique
Holiday
Ski on Water
The Smoking Machine

Men at Work
Manouane River Lumberjacks
Sewermen
Every Valley (coal-mining)
Under Night Streets
The Real Thing
Herrings for Sale
The Big Mill
Night Mail

Mountains and Volcanoes
Antarctic Crossing
September Spring
Wild Highlands
S.O.S. Notlandung
Sing of the Border
Mountains and Fjords

People in Other Lands
Louisiana Story
Corral
Chuk and Gek
The Oil Rivers
Traders in Leather
Giuseppina
The Boat People

Rivers and Lakes
Mekong
The Captive River
The Lake District

The Seashore
Surf Boats of Accra
Between the Tides
The Question Tree

The Seasons
Journey into Spring
Speed the Plough
Spring in the Mountains
Flight into Life
Wiesensommer
Twilight Forest
Snow

Sport
The Home-made Car
Sport in Germany
World of Sport (series)

Special Occasions
   (Christmas, Easter)
Amelia and the Angel
On the Twelfth Day
Christmas in Germany
The Star of Bethlehem

Weather and the Elements
Snowdrift at Bleath Gill
Snow
Fire Below
Praise the Sea
Life Boat Coming
Hook Line and Sinker
Fire at Dukhan
Fire Fight at Ahwaz

Villages, Towns and Cities
Whistle Down the Wind
Rhythm of a City
Pembrokeshire, my County
Capital Visit
Hull Now

Children on the Screen
Louisiana Story
Chuk and Gek
Giuseppina
Amelia and the Angel
One of them is Brett
Thursday's Children
Whistle Down the Wind

(b) FILMS USED AT SHERBURN SECONDARY SCHOOL*

The main purpose of these film-lists, representing three years' work in film related to English studies, is to emphasise:
(a) variety – few choices are duplicated
(b) individual choice – only one teacher could successfully pattern courses in just this way.

Spring 1966 – Comedy
The Decorator
Double Whooppee
Haunted Spooks
The Lady Killers (extract)
A Marx Brothers feature

Children and Young People
Giuseppina
Thursday's Children
La Première Nuit
Bird Hunt
Fan Fever
Lonely Boy
A Few Days
We are the Lambeth Boys

Summer 1966 – Film-making
Pacific 231
Glass
Film-making in School: Planning A Film Script
Telling a Story in Pictures
Film-making in School: Shooting the film
Harry's Half-crown

Autumn 1966
History of the Cinema
Crin Blanc

Le Grand Méliès
Monsieur et Madame Curie
Neighbours
Vox Pop
Tramps
The Last Laugh (extract)
Metropolis (extract)
Alone with the Monsters
Seventh Seal (extract)
Guns in the Afternoon
Desist Film
Los Hurdes
Lonely are the Brave

Spring 1967
Three Lives and a Rope
Le Pilier de la Solitude
Rain
Sausalito
Tomorrow's Saturday
The Big Heat

Growing up
The Pumpkin Eater (extract)
Tom Brown's Schooldays (extract)
Zéro de Conduite
Young Chopin
Nobody Waved Good-bye
The World of Apu

---

* The use of some of these films is discussed in Chapter 3: some half-term units have a clearly defined theme, but others could only be regarded as 'films a teacher found useful'.

Summer 1967

Time out of War
Corral
Billy Liar
Strangers on a Train
Les Mistons
Seven Samurai
Window on Europe
Nothing but the Best
The Wages of Fear
The Ipcress File
Lord of the Flies
Twilight Forest
Traders in Leather
Surfboats of Accra

Autumn 1967 – Comedy and Documentary

The Adventurer
Towed in a Hole
Happy Anniversary
Coalface
Days of Whiskey Gap
City of Gold
En passant par la Lorraine
Louisiana Story
North Slope Alaska
Firefight at Ahwaz
Stampede
Ashes and Diamonds (extract)
Giuseppina
Floating Around
Way out West

Spring 1968

Stampede
Terminus
Hancock Extract (TV)
Steptoe Extract (TV)
Z Cars Extract (TV)
Paths of Glory (extract)
Le Caporal Epinglé (extract)
The Gunfighter (extract)
Room at the Top (extract)
A Kind of Loving (extract)
Les Yeux sans Visage (extract)
Third Avenue El
Bird Hunt

Summer 1968

They Caught the Ferry
Yo-Yo
La Première Nuit
Winchester '73
Paul Tomkowicz
Nahanni
Night
Ambulance
Sunday
The Builders
The Haunting

(c) FILM STUDY IN A COMPREHENSIVE SCHOOL

This work was done nearly ten years ago in Wandsworth School, London SW18 by two members of the English staff, John Bakewell and Ralph Billington. A great variety of film study continues at the school, and this course is included mainly for historical interest, to show how film studies were introduced with two fifth-year classes. A more detailed discussion of the course is available from the B.F.I.

Term One: Establishing a theme

First three weeks – study and discussion of certain extracts from novels (40 min. per week):

1 *'Key to the Door'* (Alan Sillitoe)
   'Catcher in the Rye' (J. D. Salinger)
2 *'This Sporting Life'* (David Storey)
   'The Day of the Sardine' (Sid Chaplin)
3 *'Key to the Door'*
   'The Wolf who went Places' (James Thurber)

Remainder of term – three feature films dealing with youth: (3–4 periods per week: films shown at two- or three-weekly intervals)
The Childhood of Maxim Gorki (Donskoi) – Russia
Les Quatres Cents Coups (Truffaut) – France
Five Boys from Barska Street (Alexsander Ford) – Poland

Term Two: Introduction to film-making (2–4 periods per week)

1 *Telling a Story in Pictures* and some film exercises made by a previous group at the school
2)
3) Kodak films on *Film-making*
4 *Oliver Twist* (extract)
5 *Kameradschaft* (extract)
6 *Battleship Potemkin* (extract)
7 David Lean *Openings*
8 *The Devil Came to Drink* (school film made at Wimbledon, King's College)

Term Three devoted to film-making

(d) A LITERATURE AND FILM COURSE IN A COMPREHENSIVE SCHOOL

This programme was prepared for fourth-year pupils of Wilsthorpe Comprehensive School, Nottingham, by Adrian Done of the school's English staff and used in the academic year 1971-2. The material is arranged thematically, according to the inclinations and level of the group of students concerned. The films are chosen primarily as experience and emotional stimulus, not just as evidence to initiate discussion. The literature is suggested to complement the films.

Programme

A. Conflict and Loyalty: aggression and peace

September 8
Film
Bread and Circuses – 14 min. – colour. Bullfighting and carnival, and scenes of bedlam and dignity in contrast. Fiesta – the film suggests the bullfighting acts as an outlet for the violent and brutal feelings of those involved.

Literature
'*Death in the Afternoon*' – Ernest Hemingway
'*Mountain Lion*' – D. H. Lawrence
'*Shooting an Elephant*' – George Orwell
'*Travelling through the Dark*' – William Stafford
'*Original Sin*' – Robinson Jeffers

September 15
Film
A Time out of War – 22 min. An image of man's true nature – the naturalness of good (a seminal idea of medieval thought – see Boethius: '*De Consolatione Philosophiae*'); a truce between two Union soldiers and a Confederate.

Literature
'*The Red Badge of Courage*' – Stephen Crane
'*A Poison Tree*' – Blake
'*All Quiet on the Western Front*' – Remarque (ext.)
'*A Precocious Autobiography*' – Yevtushenko (ext.)
Note: music, natural sounds.
Listen/watch: Radiovision: 'In the Trenches.'

G*

B. Conformity and Protest

September 29

Film   *The Greater Community Animal* – 7 min. – colour.
                      Animated. How individual idiosyncracies have to
                      be processed out for a man to become acceptable
                      to society. (Relates to unison of mob in *Bread and
                      Circuses*, and individuality of *A Time Out of War*.)

Literature   'The Machine Stops' – E. M. Forster
                      'The Pedestrian' – Ray Bradbury
                      'Dooley is a Traitor' – James Mitchie (in 'Here
                         Today')
                      'The Fable of the White Horse' – Jiri Filip

October 6

Film   *Red Stain* – 14 min. – colour. Anti-war protest.
                      From the stain of the Martyr's blood grow red
                      flowers that eventually overwhelm the war machine.
                      Note: contrasts of shape, movement and colour
                      in drawing.
                      Record: 'What Passing Bell'.
                      Write: 'A Ballad of the Red Stain' – perhaps based
                      on a Donovan, 'The Universal Soldier', or Dylan,
                      'With God on Our Side'.

October 20

Film   *The Hangman* – 11 min. – colour. A mysterious
                      hangman, gaunt and black, arrives in town and puts
                      the inhabitants to the gallows one by one. No one
                      has the courage to protest. A powerful film, a
                      'compelling disturbance'.

Images   Like Chirico's.

Literature   From 'Conflict 2' and 'Themes' – Rhodri Jones
                      From 'Off Beat' (short stories) 'No Witchcraft for
                      Sale' – Doris Lessing; 'The Killers' – Ernest
                      Hemingway
                      From 'Black Boy' – Richard Wright

C. **Contemporary Life: loneliness and friendship: family and home**

November 24
Film   *Let's Have a Party* – 28 min. Concerns the love
                        of a high-school pupil for a girl in another class.

Literature   '*A Kind of Loving*' – Stan Barstow
                        '*Young Mother*' – Josephine Kamm
                        '*The L-Shaped Room*' – Lynne Reid Banks (extracts
                            available).

December 1
Film   *Cathy Come Home* (ext.) – 11 min.

Literature   From '*The Heart of the Hunter*' – L. van der Post
                        ('a primitive home')
                        '*Odour of Chrysanthemums*' – D. H. Lawrence.

December 8
Film   *Match Girl* – 25 min. – colour. Study of loneliness:
                        references to Hitchcock, Monroe, the cult of the
                        motorbike; colour, mood, Christmas. Fantasy/
                        reality.
                        Note: *A Taste of Honey.*
                        '*Hobson's Choice*': BBC Drama series: Monday
                            11.25; Tuesday 2.00.

Literature   '*The Boarding House*' – Joyce ('*People and Dia-
                        monds*').

D. **Observation, Perception – how do you see your environment and
    people?**

January 12
Film   *L. S. Lowry* – 16 min. (The artist himself provides
                        the commentary).

Literature   '*My Important Grandparent*' – by a pupil (dupli-
                        cated) Sillitoe, Naughton, Lawrence, etc.
                        Richard Wright's '*Black Boy*', or M. Gorki's
                            '*Childhood*', etc.
                        Looks forward to next film.

E. Conservation, Environment
January 19
Film
        End of a Street. A tele-recorded programme about the demolition of a slum street in Oldham (refers back to *Cathy* on track), and the reactions of its inhabitants to the end of their old way of life.
        See: 'Conflict 1' – selection on 'The Home'.

February 2
Film
        The River Must Live – 21 min. – colour. River pollution – biological process and cycle, and how it breaks down. Beautiful photography. Closely observed.
        Reference: Trent River Board, Derwent, local canal.
        Writing: objective and subjective modes.

F. Crime and Punishment
March 8
Film
        12 Angry Men (ext.) Eleven of the jurors are certain of the boy's guilt, but one isn't.
        Reference: *Birdman of Alcatraz*, Sacco and Vanzetti, Timothy Evans.

Literature
        'The Proverb' – Marcel Aymé ('Recent Short Stories').
        'Tickets Please' – D. H. Lawrence ('Modern Short Stories').
        Listen: Chorus from the Gallows – Ewan MacColl, ballads.
        One of the Virtues – Stan Barstow (record).
        On Seeing a Beauty Queen Home – Bill Naughton (record).

G. Strange Places: enigma, contrast
April 26
Film
        23 Skidoo – 9 min. Ominous; climax, enigmatic, a 'ghost town' haunted by . . . .
        Note: music on tape.

Poems
        'Your Attention Please' – Porter
        'The Responsibility' – Appleton
        'I am not yet Born' – MacNeice.

May 3
Film
The Labyrinth – 15 min. Loneliness – an eerie city inhabited by monstrous beings.
Note: music and use of colour.

May 17
Film
City of Gold – 23 min. Recalls the Klondyke gold-rush – Dawson City (relates back to *End of a Street*).

Literature
'*Venture to the Interior*' – L. van der Post (ext. in 'Modern Adventure': Finn).

H. Conservation: exploration

June 14
Film
Beyond the Missouri – 30 min. – Story of the Western Settlement – the myths and legends, the facts.

Literature
'*Ordeal by Hunger*' – G. R. Stewart (The Donner Party, 1848, in the Sierra Nevada).
'*The Searchers*' – Alan le May.

June 21
Film
The First Americans – 30 min. The decline of the once proud Sioux – dreaded warriors. Today they exist, almost forgotten, on reservations, with one of the lowest standards of living in America today.

Literature
'*The Spirits of the Slippery Hills*': 'The injury the coming of the Europeans had done to the being and spirit of Africa. Samutchoso's gods were dying of a contagion brought by me . . . now to whom and to what could he turn?'; from 'Modern Adventure': Finn.
Parts of '*The Lost World of the Kalahari Desert*', e.g., ch. 9.

I. Comedy

June 28
Film
A l'Assaut de la Tour Eiffel – 20 min. Could look at Beano/Dandy humour; or the tadpoles in the Wellington boots episode in '*A Kestrel for a Knave*', etc.

(e) A THEMATIC COURSE IN A SECONDARY MODERN SCHOOL

Film is taught under the 'umbrella' of English, and the courses include not only films and extracts but also television material, newspapers and magazines, illustrative material (pictures and photographs), gramophone records, and novels, poetry and drama. Themes for study are almost always social issues.

Outline for a study of WAR

Feature film	*King and Country* (Losey) – Futility of war, effect on the human personality, dilemma of loyalties, physical conditions, etc.
Short films	*Neighbours* (McLaren) – Animated parable of petty jealousies which cause war.
	Hotel des Invalides (Franju) – Documentary contrasting the legend with the reality.
	Dieppe 1942 – German newsreel record of Dieppe Raid showing mood of defeat, despair and humiliation, contrasting with heroic attitudes.
	Guns of Navarone (extract) – Heroic view even without glory.
Records	'Universal Soldier' (Donovan) – Oversimplification: if there were no soldiers there'd be no wars.
	'With God on our Side' (Dylan) – Ridicules the political excuses for wars.
	'Oh What a Lovely War!' – Variety of material, originally contrived patriotism.
Books and verse	Wilfred Owen and Siegfried Sassoon are obvious poets. Extracts from novels and war biography. Book which made most impact was '*The War Game*' (script and stills from Peter Watkins B.B.C. film).
Press cuttings	There's always a war somewhere – reports and pictures.
Drama	Act and tape-record from '*The Long and the Short and the Tall*' (Willis Hall) and '*Hamp*' (basis for *King and Country*).

The above material was used over rather more than a term with fourth-form pupils. It is interesting to compare the material and the approach with the war-theme curriculum outlined in Stuart Hall and Paddy Whannel's '*The Popular Arts*'.

(f) FILM AND LITERATURE IN AN AMERICAN HIGH SCHOOL

This work was done at Lillis High School, Kansas City, and is described in '*MOVIES: Universal Language*' by Sister Bede Sullivan, o.s.b. Teachers in England might wish, or need, to choose different examples.

How a screen play differs from a stage play

'*Raisin in the Sun*' – play (and film-script) Lorraine Hansberry (Methuen) film directed by D. Petrie (U.S.A. 1961). (Film cast same as original stage cast.)

How a screen play differs from a novel

'*Barabbas*' – novel by Par Lagerkvist (Four Square paperback); film-script by Christopher Fry, directed by Richard Fleischer (U.S.A. 1962).

Documentary

Nanook of the North – Robert Flaherty (U.S.A. 1927).
The Quiet One – Sidney Meyer and Janel Loeb (U.S.A. 1948).

Biography

Monsieur Vincent – life of St Vincent de Paul, film directed by Maurice Cloche (France 1947).

Ideas for examples more directly relevant to British (and to Protestant) experience might be obtained from A. G. S. Enser's '*Filmed Books and Plays*' (André Deutsch), though this deals with no films later than 1967; and ideas for treatments may be stimulated by George Bluestone's '*Novels into Film*' (University of California Press). A particularly interesting British example is, perhaps, '*Billy Liar*', originally a novel by Keith Waterhouse (Michael Joseph 1959), then a play by the author and Willis Hall (Michael Joseph 1960), who then scripted the film, directed by John Schlesinger (1963).

(g) A ONE-YEAR FILM COURSE AT KINGSWAY COLLEGE OF FURTHER EDUCATION

This material was used by Jane Corbett during one year's work at Kingsway.

Autumn Term: Theme – Young people and their attempt to grow to some understanding of their environment.

Week

1 *Two Men and a Wardrobe* (Polanski) – short
2 *Bicycle Thieves* (de Sica) and *Zéro de Conduite* (Vigo) – extracts
3 *400 Blows* (Truffaut) – feature
4 Stills collection from British Film Institute
5 *Les Mistons* (Truffaut) – short
6 *Iron Helmet, Attention, Labyrinth* – animated shorts
7 *Young Törless* (Schloendorff) – feature
8 *M* (Fritz Lang) – extract
9 *La Jetée* (Chris Marker) – short
10 *Father* (Szabo) – feature
11 Stills collection
12 *The Miracle Worker* (Arthur Penn) – feature
13 *The Miracle Worker* – extract

Easter Term: A director – Jean Renoir (first half); Georges Franju (second half).

1 Slides of Auguste Renoir's paintings
   Extracts from *Boudu Sauvé des Eaux* and *La Règle du Jeu*
2 *Une Partie de Campagne* – short
3 *La Grande Illusion* – feature
4 *La Grande Illusion* – extract
5 *Le Caporal Epinglé* – feature
6 *Le Caporal Epinglé* – extract
7 *Hôtel des Invalides* – short
8 *Le Sang des Bêtes* – short, with slides of surrealist painters (e.g. Chagall, de Chirico, Dali) and work by Soutine and Rembrandt.
9 *Eyes Without a Face* – feature
10 *Eyes Without a Face* – extract
11 *Thomas the Imposter* – feature
12 Stills

Summer Term: Japanese cinema (Kurosawa and Ichikawa)
 1 Extracts from *Ugetsu Monogatari* (Mizoguchi) and *An Autumn Afternoon* (Ozu)
 2 *Seven Samurai* (Kurosawa) – feature
 3 Stills collection
 4 *Rashomon* (Kurosawa) – feature
 5 *Rashomon* – extract
 6 *Tora-No-O* (Kurosawa) – short feature
 7 *Burmese Harp* (Ichikawa) – feature
 8 *Bridge on the River Kwai* (David Lean) – extract
 9 *An Actor's Revenge* (Ichikawa) – feature
10 Stills
11 Written analysis of reactions to year's work, plus detailed response to one or two particular films.

Earlier examples of film courses taught at Kingsway College (by Jim Kitses and Ann Mercer over the five years 1960–5) are contained in *'Talking about the Cinema'* (B.F.I. 1966) and the supplementary pamphlet *'Film and General Studies'*.

Further suggestions appear in the D.E.S. Pamphlet *'General Studies in Technical Colleges'* (H.M.S.O. 1962) including a Communities and Relationships first-year course based on films, reading, television programmes, visits, plus writing and discussion.

See also: F. D. Flower's *'La nguageand Education'* (Longman 1966) which discusses the basis of 'English Study' within a General Studies course whatever the medium (books, films, newspapers, etc.) and whatever the course-content (social, political, artistic, practical).

(h) A MONTH'S FILM STUDY AT THOMAS DANBY COLLEGE OF FURTHER EDUCATION

At this Leeds college film study and film-making reinforce work in several aspects of General Studies, including English, Social Studies and Liberal Studies; about four hours per week are available for this work.

Week One – a programme of short films chosen from the following:

Giuseppina – a young girl's view of national stereotypes as life passes at an Italian village petrol station.

The Home-Made Car – rebuilding an old bull-nosed Morris.

Dial Double-One – two mountain-rescue operations by the Swiss Air Rescue Guard.

A Child's Guide to Blowing up a Motor Car – a behind-the-scenes look at a sequence from the James Bond film *Thunderball*.

Stable Door – a carefully planned warehouse raid pointing the message of crime prevention.

Strike Action – a school film of a revolution against milk in favour of tea.

Rhythm of a City – a day's events in the city of Stockholm.

Week Two – documentary film chosen from the following:

Thursday's Children – an early Lindsay Anderson film about the Royal School for Deaf Children at Margate.

Time Is – Don Levy's film attempting an analysis of Time.

Nanook of the North – Robert Flaherty's early documentary record of Eskimo life.

Man of Aran (extract) – a later Flaherty documentary.

Between the Tides – an effective documentary of the sea-shore.

Terminus – John Schlesinger's account of a day in the life of Waterloo station.

Inheritance – the aftermath of the Algerian war.

Our Daily Bread – a primary school project on the Freedom from Hunger Campaign.

No Limit and *Challenge* – two films about the work of the Le Court Cheshire Home.

Week Three – industrial and scientific films chosen from the following:
Water in Biology – water as an environment for living things.
Physics and Chemistry of Water.
The River Must Live – a study of river pollution.
The Nature of Fire – its characteristics, prevention and control.
The Radio Sky – the development and use of radio-telescopes.
Analysis of Mass – principles, construction and use of the mass spectrometer.
Forth Road Bridge – planning and building.
Revealing Eye – the use of cinematography in scientific study.
The Rival World – the world of the insects.

Week Four – animated films
The Power to Fly ⎫ histories of flight and the motor-car.
The Moving Spirit ⎭
The Energy Picture – how man found and harnessed various sources of energy.
The Great Synthesis – the part played by petro-chemicals in the modern world.
House Warming – the history of home heating and modern developments.
Dreamland in the Sky – puppet-animation, promoting Air India.
Man in Flight – animation and live action together present a history of aviation.
Dots and Loops – a Norman McLaren experiment drawn directly on to film.
Drawings that Walk and Talk – a compilation of historic animated material.

The above programmes are compiled mainly from 'free-loan' material, with some material from the British Film Institute. Though clearly designed to provide film experience, the programmes created a base of interest for a variety of oral and written work (critical, historical, technical, imaginative, thematic).

The college has also used B.F.I. Film Study Units (see Appendix E) and film material designed for thematic treatments.

(i) A COLLEGE OF EDUCATION COURSE RELATING FILM TO LITERARY AND DRAMATIC FORMS

This course was devised by Dan Millar and Roy Knight for fourth-year B.Ed. and other advanced students at Bede College, Durham: the course-time available was one afternoon per week over three terms.

1 **Definitions – I**
   What is 'drama' in film, radio and television? What elements are common with theatre and 'literary' drama?
   Tous les Garçons s'appellent Patrick (Godard)
   In Two Minds (David Mercer)
   L'Eclisse (Antonioni) (extract)
   Paths of Glory (Kubrick) (extract)

2 **Definitions – II**
   What differentiates 'drama 'in the various media? Formal distinctions, historical elements, social relationship and function.
   Extracts from *L'Atalante* (Vigo), *La Peau Douce* (Truffaut), *8½* (Fellini), *Sawdust and Tinsel* (Bergman), *Ugetsu Monogatari* (Mizoguchi) and *The Blood Donor* (Hancock).

3 **Shakespeare – I: Naturalism**
   Macbeth (Orson Welles) and extract from *Citizen Kane*.

4 **Shakespeare – II: Poetry**
   Throne of Blood (Kurosawa) and extract from *Rashomon*.

5 **Shakespeare – III: From stage to screen – Realism**
   Henry V (Olivier) and other Olivier Shakespeare extracts, and from *Julius Caesar* (Mankiewicz).

6 **Modern Drama – I: Brecht's Epic Theatre and Social Function**
   Threepenny Opera (Pabst) and *Caucasian Chalk Circle* (Schools TV: B.B.C.)

7 **Modern Drama – II: John Osborne**
   Look Back in Anger (Richardson) and extract from *The Entertainer*.

8 **Comedy – I: The Vaudeville Tradition**
   The Cure (Chaplin), *The Immigrant* (Chaplin) and *The Music Box* (Laurel and Hardy).

9 **Comedy – II: The Silent Screen**
   The General (Buster Keaton).

10 **Drama of Movement**
Un Jardin Public (mime: Marcel Marceau), *The Rink* (sport), *Corral* (work), *Chinese Theatre* (convention), *The Day Manolete Died* (ritual).

11 **Melodrama – I: Dickens, Griffith and the Film today**
A Griffith film.

12 **Melodrama – II: Eisenstein**
Feature and extracts of Eisenstein.

13 **Popular Theatre (Renoir – I)**
French Cancan

14 **Sophisticated Comedy I (Renoir – II)**
Eléna et les Hommes.

15 **Sophisticated Comedy – II**
A Bergman comedy.

16 **Theatre/Cinema: Comedy (Dreyer – I)**
Master of the House.

17 **Theatre/Cinema: Drama (Dreyer – II)**
Ordet.

18 **Theatre/Cinema: Tragedy (Dreyer – III)**
La Passion de Jeanne d'Arc.

19 **Artifice – I: Mechanical, puppets, ballet, opera**
Short films and extracts.

20 **Artifice – II: Animation**
Work of McLaren, Disney, UPA, Hubley, Pintoff, etc.

21 **Non-Theatre: Documentary**
Work of Jennings and Franju.

22 **Anti-Theatre: Bresson**
Mouchette and Bresson extracts.

23 **A Theatre: Godard**
Les Carabiniers and Godard extracts.

24 **Director as Auteur: Vigo**
L'Atalante, Zéro de Conduite, A Propos de Nice.

(j) A 'FORMAL' INTRODUCTION TO FILM AND FILM STUDY IN A COLLEGE OF EDUCATION

A one-term introductory course to film form, and various approaches to film study – one afternoon per week.

1 **Cinema – I: Industry or art?**
   The Big Heat (Fritz Lang).
2 **Cinema – II: Homage to Hollywood**
   A Bout de Souffle (Godard).
3 **Auteur – I: Hitchcock**
   Psycho.
4 **Auteur – II: Hitchcock**
   North by North-West.
5 **Movement – I: Italian Neo-realism**
   Umberto D (de Sica).
6 **Movement – II: Italian Neo-realism**
   Bandits at Orgosolo (de Seta).
7 **Documentary – I: Humphrey Jennings**
   Fires were Started and *A Diary for Timothy.*
8 **Documentary – II: A question of style**
   Thursday's Children (Anderson).
   The Vanishing Street (Vas).
   Together (Mazzetti).
   Lonely Boy (Kroitor and Koenig).
   Rhythm of a City (Sucksdorff).
9 **Documentary – III: A question of tradition**
   Work of Flaherty, Grierson and Basil Wright.
10 **Experiment – I: Animation**
   Examples from Emile Cohl to Norman McClaren; and the work of Bob Godfrey.
11 **Experiment – II: Avant-garde**
   Time Is (Don Levy), *Pas de Deux* (McLaren), *Sang des Bêtes* (Franju).

APPENDIX E

Extracts and study units

1. BRITISH FILM INSTITUTE DISTRIBUTION LIBRARY

Full details of the film study extracts and film study units available from this library are to be found in the Education Department's Study Extract Catalogue and Supplement to the Study Extract Catalogue, available from B.F.I. Publications, 81 Dean Street, London W1V 6AA at 25p each. For each extract the catalogues give credits, the story of the original film, summaries of the narrative covered in the excerpt and uses to which the extract may be put. The contents of each Film Study Unit are also detailed.

A checklist of the material available follows:

EXTRACTS

Accident
The Adventures of Huckleberry
    Finn
Ambitious Annie
An American in Paris
Anatomy of a Murder
Angel Face
Ashes and Diamonds
L'Atalante
The Atonement of Gosta
    Berling
L'Avventura

Baby-face Nelson
Back of Beyond
Bande à Part
Barrier
Battle of the Century
Battleship Potemkin
Bicycle Thieves

The Big Heat
The Big Sky
Billy Budd
The Birds
Birth of a Nation
Blackmail
The Blind Man
The Blue Angel
Le Bonheur
Born Yesterday
Boudu Sauvé des Eaux
Breathless
The Bridge on the River Kwai
Brief Encounter
Bringing Up Baby
Brute Force

The Cabinet of Dr Caligari
Carve Her Name with Pride
Catch Us if You Can

Cathy Come Home
Charlie Chaplin's Burlesque on
   Carmen
The Childhood of Maxim Gorky
Chronique d'un Eté
Citizen Kane
Comin' Thru' the Rye
Coronation Street
The Covered Wagon
Cowboy
Le Crime de M. Lange
The Criminal
Crossfire
Culloden

David Lean Openings
Day of Wrath
The Day the Earth Caught Fire
The Defiant Ones
Diamonds of the Night
Dr Strangelove
Dr Who
Dracula

Earth
Easy Street
The Eclipse
$8\frac{1}{2}$
El
Elstree Calling
The End of St Petersburg
The Entertainer
Eroica
Eve
Eyes without a Face

Face in the Crowd
Face to Face
Fallen Idol
Une Femme Mariée

Le Feu Follet
Film and Reality
Foolish Wives
A Fool There Was
Foreign Correspondent
The Forsyte Saga
Frankenstein
French Cancan
Freud
From Russia with Love

The General Line
A Generation
Gervaise
The Ghost That Never Returns
The Goddess
Goodbye Mr Chips
La Grande Illusion
The Great Man
The Gunfighter
Guns of Navarone

Hamlet (1913)
Hamlet (1948)
Hancock
A Hard Day's Night
The Harder They Fall
Hearts of the World
Henry V
Hiroshima Mon Amour

The Importance of Being Earnest
The Informer
Intolerance
In Two Minds
The Italian Straw Hat
Ivan the Terrible
I was a Fireman

Jeanne Eagels
Judex

Jules et Jim
Julius Caesar

Kameradschaft
The Killers
Kind Hearts and Coronets
A Kind of Loving
King Kong

The Ladykillers
The Lady of the Camellias
The Last Laugh
The Last Stage
Laura
Lavender Hill Mob
The League of Gentlemen
The Leather Boys
Little Caesar
Lonely Are The Brave
Lord of the Flies
The Lost World
Lotna
Louisiana Story
Love is My Profession

M
Macbeth
The Maggie
The Magnificent Ambersons
The Maltese Falcon
The Manchurian Candidate
A Man Escaped
The Man from Laramie
The Man in the White Suit
Man of Aran
Marty
Marx Brothers
Metropolis
Midsummer Night's Dream
The Miracle Worker

Mr and Mrs Smith
Mr Deeds Goes to Town
Monsieur Vincent
Morgan
Mother
Moulin Rouge
My Darling Clementine
My Sister Eileen

Nanook of the North
Nazarin
New Babylon
A Night to Remember
Nothing but the Best

October
Oh! Mr Porter
Oliver Twist
Los Olvidados
Orphée
Our Man in Havana

Paisa
Paths of Glory
The Pawnshop
La Peau Douce
Peeping Tom
The Pickwick Papers
Il Posto
The Prisoner
Proud Valley
Psycho
The Pumpkin Eater

Rashomon
Reach for the Sky
La Règle du Jeu
Richard III (1911)
Richard III (1955)
Rin Tin Tin

The Rival World
Romeo and Juliet
Room at the Top

Sailor Made Man
Sally in Our Alley
San Francisco
Sapphire
Saturday Night and Sunday
    Morning
Sawdust and Tinsel
The Scarlet Empress
Sergeant York
The Seventh Seal
Shadow of a Doubt
Shadows
She Wore a Yellow Ribbon
Siegfried
La Signora Senza Camelie
The Silence
Softly, Softly
The Soilers
Some Like It Hot
Song of Ceylon
Spare the Rod
Stagecoach
The Stars Look Down
Steptoe and Son
La Strada
Streetcar Named Desire
Sullivan's Travels

A Tale of Two Cities
A Taste of Honey
Television Material (Vox Pop,
    Dr I.Q., TV Commercials)
Tell England
La Terra Trema
Terror
They Live by Night

They Were Expendable
The Third Man
This Sporting Life
Till Death Us Do Part
The Tomb of Ligeia
Tom Brown's Schooldays
Top Hat
Touch of Evil
Treasure of Sierra Madre
The Trial of Joan of Arc
Twelve Angry Men
Two Daughters
Two Rode Together

Ugetsu Monogatari
Under Capricorn
Up the Junction

The Vagabond
The Vanishing Corporal
Very Important Person
Violent Playground
Viridiana
Vivere in Pace

Wages of Fear
Warning Shadows
What's New, Pussycat?
Whistle Down the Wind
Wild Strawberries
The Winslow Boy
The Wonderful Country
World of Apu

Yangtse Incident
The Young Chopin
The Young One

Z Cars
Zéro de Conduite

STUDY UNITS

Each Study Unit contains a full-length feature film, selected extracts from relevant films, detailed notes and other material.

Study Unit 1 Breakthrough in Britain
             2 War on the Screen
             3 Low-Budget Realism
             4 Young People on the Screen
             5 Silent Screen Comedy
             6 Imprisonment
             7 The Polish Cinema
             8 Jean Renoir
             9 Orson Welles
          10 Fritz Lang
          11 Humphrey Jennings
          12 The Western
          13 Satyajit Ray

2. RANK FILM LIBRARY

The Rank Film Library, P.O. Box 70, Great West Road, Brentford, Middlesex, has a series of study extracts which are described in the Study Extract Catalogue and Supplement, and which can be booked through the B.F.I. Distribution Library.

Extracts are available from the following films:

Brief Encounter	Man of Aran
Billy Budd	A Night to Remember
Carve Her Name With Pride	Oh! Mr Porter
David Lean Openings	Oliver Twist
The Fallen Idol	Reach for the Sky
Hamlet	Richard III
Henry V	Sapphire
The Importance of Being Earnest	The Third Man
Kind Hearts and Coronets	This Sporting Life
The Ladykillers	Very Important Person
The League of Gentlemen	Violent Playground
Macbeth	Whistle Down the Wind
The Maggie	The Winslow Boy

3. CONTEMPORARY FILMS LIBRARY

For details of the extracts in the Contemporary Library, write to:
Contemporary Films Ltd, 55 Greek Street, London W1. Extracts are
available from the following films:

Adieu Philippine
Alexander Nevsky
Aparajito
An Autumn Afternoon
A Blonde in Love
Bicycle Thieves
The Childhood of Maxim Gorky
Children of Hiroshima
The Cranes are Flying
Earth
Far from Vietnam
The First Teacher
Friends for Life
Hands Over the City
Ivan the Terrible
Kino Pravda
The Last Stage

Léon Morin, Priest
Lotna
Mahanagar
Miracle in Milan
Naked Hearts
New Gulliver
Nine Days of One Year
Once there was a War
Peter and Pavla
Prologue
She and He
Storm over Asia
Strike
World of Apu
The Young Chopin
Zéro de Conduite

4. OTHER LIBRARIES

John King (Bond Street, Brighton, Sussex), Watso Films (Film House,
Charles Street, Coventry), and Wallace Heaton (127 New Bond Street,
London W1) have a number of sections from feature films which could
be used as extracts.

APPENDIX F

Books and series

Only a few years ago, despite the international film bibliographies listing up to five thousand books, the teacher interested in film would perhaps have found it difficult to find a couple of dozen books in print and in English which would stimulate relevant thoughts or provide reliable information for film-teaching: now the situation is very different, and each month sees almost a flood of film-books in English. The list, therefore, makes no attempt at comprehensive coverage, but rather concentrates on two areas:

(1) books regarded as having immediate value to the English teacher seeking ideas about film and film-teaching; and

(2) sources of more specialised information for those wishing to pursue subjects in depth.

FILM HISTORY
Rotha, Paul and Richard Griffith. *The Film Till Now*. Vision Press.
  The standard film history in English, though the main section of the book was written some time ago.
Knight, Arthur. *The Liveliest Art*. Mentor Paperback.
  Described as a 'panoramic history', it compresses an amazing amount of (generally accurate) information into one slim volume.

CONTEMPORARY FILM
Houston, Penelope. *The Contemporary Cinema*. Penguin.
  Written in 1963, the book surveys major post-war developments from a not very well defined viewpoint.
Taylor, John Russell. *Cinema Eye, Cinema Ear*. Methuen.
  The film-critic of *The Times* collates various pronouncements of and on nine key film-makers of the Sixties.
Battcock, Gregory (Editor). *The New American Cinema*.
                                                    Dutton Paperback.
  A comprehensive anthology of views on the American Underground cinema.

FILM AESTHETICS AND CRITICISM

Balasz, Bela. *Theory of Film*. Denis Dobson.
One of the more interesting and readable film theorists.

Bazin, André. *What is Cinema?* University of California Press
(C.U.P. in England).
A collection of essays by perhaps the most brilliant, and certainly the
most admired, French critic and theorist.

Kracauer, Siegfried. *Theory of Film*. Oxford Galaxy Paperback.
Almost impossible to read, but everyone refers to Kracauer; it does
contain insights into aspects of silent cinema.

Montagu, Ivor. *Film World*. Penguin.
Sections on film as Science, as Art, as Commodity (the best section)
and as Vehicle: an interesting, if painstaking, introduction to many
aspects of film.

Stephenson, Ralph and Jean Debrix. *The Cinema as Art*. Penguin.
Detailed analysis of various screen techniques of handling time,
space, scale, sound – the 'wood' gets lost in the 'trees', but the
inspection of the trees is thorough.

Agee, James. *Agee on Film I*. Beacon Press.
An exhaustive collection of reviews during the 1940s by one of the
most perceptive film critics of any time.

Kael, Pauline. *I lost it at the Movies*. Jonathan Cape.
Another collection of American critical writing – 1950s and early
1960s – always lively, often infuriating.

USEFUL ANTHOLOGIES

MacCann, Richard Dyer. *Film: a montage of theories*. Dutton
Paperback.
A comprehensive collection of extracts from the major film theorists,
with some important periodical essays as well.

Jacobs, Lewis. *An Introduction to the Art of the Movies*. Noonday
Press.
Fewer 'standard' extracts, and some more unusual contributions
than MacCann's: they complement each other.

Geduld, Harry M. *Film Makers on Film Making*. Penguin.
More than thirty sections (articles, interviews, lectures, etc.) from
Lumière to Kenneth Anger.

Graham, Peter. *The New Wave*. Cinema One series.
A key collection of writings by and about French New Wave directors.

BY OR ON DIRECTORS

See particularly the Series checklist but note also

Wood, Robin. *Hitchcock's Films.* Zwemmer.
An original and perceptive critical approach, and a model of detailed analysis of films.

Truffaut, François. *Hitchcock.* Secker & Warburg.
Pages and pages of Truffaut/Hitchcock interview: at times more illuminating of Truffaut than Hitchcock.

Sternberg, Joseph von. *Fun in a Chinese Laundry.* Secker & Warburg.
The idiosyncratic autobiography of a genuine and self-aware *auteur*.

Budgen, Suzanne. *Fellini.* B.F.I.
Some consistently intelligent writing about a director of often evasive talent.

FOR REFERENCE

Halliwell, Leslie. *The Filmgoer's Companion.* MacGibbon & Kee.
A mine of information, but more valuable for stars and topics than exhaustive treatment of directors.

Graham, Peter. *A Dictionary of the Cinema.* Zwemmer.
An invaluable pocket checklist of reasonable reliability.

Enser, A. G. S. *Filmed Books and Plays 1928–1967.* André Deutsch.
An exhaustive checklist of the interrelationship of films and literature.

Eyles, Allen. *The Western.* Zwemmer.
A quite incredible reference work to actors, directors and themes in Western films.

FILM TEACHING

Hall, Stuart and Paddy Whannel. *The Popular Arts.* Hutchinson.
Despite abuse from some critical circles, far and away the most valuable book for teachers of a whole range of media studies.

Kitses, Jim. *Talking about the Cinema.* B.F.I.
Detailed descriptive studies of thematic approaches in one particular course.

Perkins, W. H. *Learning the Liveliest Art.* Angus and Robertson.
A comprehensive survey of film courses recommended for Australian teachers: the new edition comprises more varied material than the first edition.

Sullivan, Sister Bede. *Movies: Universal Language.* Fides, Indiana.
Some lively ideas used in High School teaching in the U.S.A.

Hodgkinson, A. W.   *Screen Education.*   UNESCO Mass Communication Paper No. 42 (H.M.S.O.)
An introductory survey to a variety of courses and approaches to film and television.
Hall, Stuart, Roy Knight, Albert Hunt and Alan Lovell.
Film teaching.   B.F.I.
Accounts of work in four courses in further and higher education, with appendices on other courses.

The above list makes no reference to film sociology, censorship, film-making, techniques, genres, national cinemas, stars or screen acting, origins of film, silent cinema, perception, film scripts, illustrated reference – one could carry on the list indefinitely. Many famous and favourite books will have been omitted – all selections are inadequate. All the compiler would assert is that any teacher exploring film would find something of value, something of interest, something to provoke or to reassure in every one of the above volumes: they may not be the 'best buys', but they would provide value for money.

The list of paperback series below fills some of the gaps above, and indicates further sources to be explored (via the specialist bibliographies that may be found in most of them). Additionally,
The British Film Institute Education Department
will provide book-lists on the cinema, television and mass-media research.
The National Film Archive Book Library (available to full members)
will provide a Catalogue of the Lending Library (about 2,000 titles) and specialist bibliographies on the following topics:
Eisenstein, Bergman, American musicals, History of the Cinema, Film Music, Marilyn Monroe, Amateur film-making, Renoir, Editing, Script-writing, Film and TV production, Film-teaching, Animation, American serials, Horror films, British Cinema, Westerns, Godard, Penn, Pasolini, Garbo, Keaton, American Underground, Resnais, Ford, Kazan, etc.

Cinema One
A series of critical and historical texts with reference material. Published by Secker and Warburg, in association with the British Film Institute.

Richard Roud *Jean-Luc Godard*
Tom Milne *Losey on Losey*
Geoffrey Nowell-Smith *Luchino Visconti* (revised edition 1973)
Kevin Brownlow *How it Happened Here*
Peter Graham *The New Wave: Critical Landmarks*
John Ward *Alan Resnais or The Theme of Time*
Robin Wood *Howard Hawks*
Axel Madsen *Billy Wilder*
Peter Wollen *Signs and Meaning in the Cinema* (revised edition 1972)
David Robinson *Buster Keaton*
Oswald Stack *Pasolini on Pasolini*
Jim Kitses *Horizons West: Studies in Authorship in the Western*
Tom Milne *Rouben Mamoulian*
Carlos Clarens *George Cukor*
Charles Higham *Hollywood Cameramen*
Nicholas Garnham *Samuel Fuller*
Rui Nogueira *Melville on Melville*
Richard Roud *Jean-Marie Straub*
Jon Halliday *Sirk on Sirk*
Joseph McBride *Orson Welles*
Colin McArthur *Underworld U.S.A.*
Alan Lovell and Jim Hillier *Studies in Documentary*

International Film Guide Series
A general handy-size series which includes books on directors, genres, periods, films of a single country, and reference books. Published by Zwemmer. After January 1972, published by Tantivy Press. Price range 65–80p unless stated otherwise.

Peter Graham *A Dictionary of the Cinema* (h/b only – £1·25)
Peter Cowie *The Cinema of Orson Welles* (out of print)
Robin Wood *Hitchcock's Films*
Alan Eyles *The Marx Brothers*
Roy Armes *French Cinema Since 1946* (two volumes)
Peter Cowie *Swedish Cinema* (out of print)

H

Douglas McVay *The Musical Film* (out of print)
J. P. Lebel *Buster Keaton* (out of print)
Ralph Stephenson *Animation in the Cinema*
James Leahy *The Cinema of Joseph Losey*
Allan Eyles *The Western* (out of print)
Gordon Gow *Suspense in the Cinema*
Roy Armes *The Cinema of Alan Resnais*
Donald W. McCaffrey *Four Great Comedians:
   Chaplin, Lloyd, Keaton and Langdon*
David Robinson *Hollywood in the Twenties*
John Baxter *Hollywood in the Thirties*
Charles Higham and Joel Greenberg *Hollywood in the Forties*
Denis Gifford *British Cinema* (out of print)
Ivan Butler *Religion in the Cinema*
Gerald Pratley *The Cinema of John Frankenheimer*
John Baxter *Science Fiction in the Cinema*
Paul M. Jenson *The Cinema of Fritz Lang*
Tom Milne *The Cinema of Carl Dreyer*
Ivan Butler *Horror in the Cinema*
Anthony Slide *Early American Cinema*
Paul O'Dell *Griffith and the Rise of Hollywood*
Ivan Butler *The Cinema of Roman Polanski*
Graham Petrie *The Cinema of François Truffaut*

Modern and Classic Film Scripts
A series of film scripts containing the dialogue in English with details
of the action and camera shots, stills, a critical introduction, and the
credits. Published by Lorrimer. Price range – paperback, 63p–£1·26;
hardback, £1·25–£2·25 unless stated otherwise.

Jean-Luc Godard *Alphaville*
Jean-Luc Godard *Made in U.S.A.*
Jean-Luc Godard *Le Petit Soldat*
Jean Renoir *La Grande Illusion*
Sergei Eisenstein *The Battleship Potemkin*
Josef von Sternberg *The Blue Angel*
Fritz Lang *M*
François Truffaut *Jules et Jim*
Ingmar Bergman *The Seventh Seal*

Marcel Carné *Les Enfants du Paradis*
Akira Kurosawa *Ikiru*
Luis Buñuel *L'Age d'Or* and *Un Chien Andalou*
Graham Greene and Carol Reed *The Third Man*
Vittorio de Sica *Bicycle Thieves*
Jean-Luc Godard *Pierrot le Fou*
Lindsay Anderson and David Sherwin *If*
Jean Renoir *The Rules of the Game*
Ingmar Bergman *Wild Strawberries*
Sergei Eisenstein *Ivan the Terrible*
Robert Wiene *The Cabinet of Dr. Caligari*
Marcel Carné *Le Jour se Lève*
Akira Kurosawa *The Seven Samurai*
Erich von Stroheim *Greed* (p/b £1·95; h/b £4·95)
Orson Welles *The Trial*
G. W. Pabst *Pandora's Box*
René Clair *A Nous la Liberté* and *Entr'acte*
Luis Buñuel *The Exterminating Angel* (out of print)
Luis Buñuel *La Voie Lactée* (out of print)
Michelangelo Antonioni *L'Avventura* (out of print)
Federico Fellini *Satyricon* (out of print)
Claude Lelouch *A Man and a Woman*
Luis Buñuel *Tristana*
Luis Buñuel *Belle de Jour*
John Ford *Stagecoach*
Jiri Menzel *Closely Observed Trains*
Pier Paolo Pasolini *Oedipus Rex*
Michelangelo Antonioni *Blow-Up*
Robert Wiene *The Cabinet of Dr. Caligari*
Fritz Lang *Metropolis*
Arthur Penn *Bonnie and Clyde* (h/b only)
Jean-Luc Godard *Weekend* and *Vent d'Est*
Luis Buñuel *Exterminating Angel; Nazarin; Los Olvidados*
Joseph von Sternberg *Shanghai Express* and *Morocco*
(Marx Brothers) *Monkey Business* and *Duck Soup*
Andrzej Wajda *Ashes and Diamonds; Kanal; A Generation*
Andrew Sinclair *Under Milk Wood* (p/b only)
Michelangelo Antonioni *Zabriskie Point* and *The Red Desert*
Milos Forman *The Firemen's Ball* and *A Blonde in Love*
Eric Rohmer *Claire's Knee; My Night with Maud; La Collectionneuse*

Movie Paperbacks
A series of monographs on directors, books of interviews and essays, and reference works. Published by Studio Vista. Price range 50–90p.

Joel Finler *Stroheim*
Raymond Durgnat *Franju*
Charles Barr *Laurel and Hardy*
Ian and Elisabeth Cameron *The Heavies*
Raymond Durgnat *Buñuel*
Ian Cameron and Robin Wood *Antonioni*
Ian and Elisabeth Cameron *Broads*
Robin Wood *Arthur Penn*
Peter Bogdanovich *Fritz Lang in America*
Ian Cameron *The Films of Robert Bresson* (h/b £1·05)
Robin Wood *Ingmar Bergman*
Ian Cameron *Second Wave* (h/b £1·25)
Ian Cameron *The Films of Jean-Luc Godard*
Elizabeth Sussex *Lindsay Anderson* (h/b £1·05)
Jose Luis Guarner *Rossellini* (h/b £1·40)
Albert Johnson *William Wellman* (out of print)
Robin Wood *The Apu Trilogy* (out of print)
Peter Bogdanovich *Atlan Dwan: The Last Pioneer* (h/b £1·75)
Billy Wilder and I. A. L. Diamond *The Apartment* and
    The Fortune Cookie: two screenplays by Billy Wilder (h/b £1·75)
Robin Wood and Michael Walker *Claude Chabrol* (h/b £1·50)
Peter Bogdanovich *Interviews with John Ford*
Phil Hardy *Samuel Fuller* (h/b £1·50)

Picturebacks
A series of pictorial surveys on art and design which includes a number of books on the cinema. Published by Studio Vista. Price range 65–80p.

Roger Manvell *New Cinema in Europe*
Liam O'Leary *The Silent Cinema*
Raymond Durgnat and John Kobal *Greta Garbo*
George Perry *The Films of Alfred Hitchcock*
Isabel Quigly *Charlie Chaplin*
John Kobal *Marlene Dietrich*
Roger Manvell *New Cinema in the U.S.A.*
Roger Manvell *New Cinema in Britain*

David Robinson *The Great Funnies*
Dennis Gifford *Movie Monsters*
Peter Gidal *Andy Warhol: Films and Paintings* (h/b £1·80)
Roy Armes *French Film* (h/b £1·50)
Alistair Whyte *New Cinema in Eastern Europe* (h/b £1·80)
Denis Gifford *Science Fiction Film* (h/b £1·80)

Screen Series
A new series of reference books devoted to the films of a single country
and genres. Published by Zwemmer. After January 1972, published by
Tantivy Press. Price range 90p–£1·25.

Nina Hibbin *Eastern Europe*
Peter Cowie *Sweden* (two volumes)
Tom Vallance *The American Musical*
Peter Cowie *A Concise History of the Cinema* (two volumes)
John Baxter *The Gangster Film*
Felix Bucher *Germany*
Arne Svensson *Japan*
Marcel Martin *France*

H*

APPENDIX G

Periodicals

This list is mainly confined to British periodicals but a select number of overseas publications is included as they contain material which is not systematically covered by British periodicals. Also included are some technical publications, and some periodicals which are concerned with film as an aid to teaching, and not as a medium for study. They are included here for completeness and because they often contain useful information.

A.B.C. Film Review 5 Chesterfield Gardens, London W1Y 8AH
    Monthly 5p, £1·20 annually
Film Artiste 61 Marloes Road, London W8
    Quarterly 10p, 50p annually
Showguide 8 Welbeck Way, London W1
    Monthly. Free
The magazines of Associated British Cinemas, the Film Artistes' Association and Rank Theatres respectively. They are all 'fan' magazines but invariably contain pictorial matter which is most useful for classroom display or for illustration of projects or other written work. *Showguide* is available free from any Rank cinema; surplus copies of *A.B.C. Film Review* may often be obtained free from A.B.C. cinemas.
L'Avant-Scène du Cinéma Tantivy Press, 108 New Bond Street, London W1Y 0QX
    Monthly. £3·80 annually
A magazine published in Paris but available from the British agents, Tantivy Press. It reprints film scripts with stills, credits, biographies and critical data in an attractive format.
British Kinematography, Sound and Television 110–112 Victoria House, Vernon Place, London WC1B 4DJ
    Monthly 50p, £6 annually
The journal of the British Kinematography, Sound and Television Society which contains technical (some highly technical) articles and

news of the society and, therefore, mainly of professional interest.

British National Film Catalogue 193–197 Regent Street, London W1
  Bi-monthly and annual cumulated volume £7 annually
  Records all films, fiction and non-fiction produced in Britain with details of distributors, producers, sponsors, technicians and artists; and a factual note on content. The major reference work on British films published since 1963. Is obviously too expensive for school purchase but copies are kept in major libraries and may be consulted for reference and for information about new films.

Cahiers du Cinéma 39 rue Coquillière, Paris 1er
  Monthly. £6·50 annually
  An attractive magazine which gives priority to long, critical interviews with individual directors. Has lost some of its former authority but is still one of the world's best film periodicals.

Cinema 10 Greek Street, London W1
  Quarterly 30p, £1·20 annually
  A magazine in its second year of publication which has improved consistently since the first number. Has a most attractive format and contains a variety of features, including series of articles and interviews.

Continental Film Review 71 Oldhill Street, London N16
  Monthly 10p, £1·50 annually
  An unusual mixture of glamour photographs and excellent notes and articles. A source of information on European films which is always up-to-the-minute but with a tendency towards the lurid.

8 mm Magazine Craven House, 34 Fouberts Place, London W1
  Monthly 17½p, £2·75 annually
  An amateur cine magazine which contains general articles on film-making with specialised articles on 8 mm in all its varieties. Useful for information about new equipment and for ideas on film-making.

Film 21 Larchwood Road, St John's, Woking, Surrey
  Quarterly 15p, 60p annually
  The magazine of the British Federation of Film Societies.

Film Culture G.P.O. Box 1499, New York, N.Y.10001
  Quarterly. £2 annually
  A magazine with erratic publishing habits, but the best source of information on the *avant-garde* cinema in the U.S.A.

Film News 81 Dean Street, London W1V 6AA
  Quarterly. 70p annually

Another publication of the Federation which is obtainable only on subscription. Contains short reviews of a variety of documentary and feature films; useful as a source of information on films for school film society and classroom bookings.

Film Quarterly University of California Press, Berkeley, California 94720

Quarterly. £3 annually

Another American magazine which tends to be irregular but is particularly good for its long articles on a variety of film topics.

Film and Television Technician 2 Soho Square, London W1

Monthly 7½p, 80p annually

The journal of the Association of Cinematograph, Television and Allied Technicians. A mixture of general, technical and industrial relations articles with up-to-date information on new film productions. Of particular use to schools where film study or film making has a technical bias.

Film User Davis House, 69–77 High Street, Croydon, Surrey

Monthly 15p, £1·80 annually

A publication with a variety of articles on films, equipment and kindred topics with the emphasis on documentary and industrial films. Has a monthly guide to newly issued films, including new releases from the 16 mm film renters, which is the only means of keeping film catalogues up-to-date. The July issue each year is essential for reference as it contains the only published comprehensive list of 16 mm film libraries.

Films and Filming Hansom Books, Artillery Mansions, 75 Victoria Street, London SW1

Monthly 30p, £3·90 annually

A general film magazine intended for both enthusiasts and casual film-goers alike which contains reviews, articles, picture previews and regular features. The latter include film music record reviews, book reviews, film society notes and lists of films which are due to appear on television. Has fluctuated widely in quality since it was first published in 1954 but has improved again recently under new editorship.

Focus on Film 108 New Bond Street, London W1Y 0QX

Bi-monthly 25p, £1·20 four issues

A new magazine which has had some excellent early issues. Particularly strong on research material and film-stills which are included on almost every page.

I.A.C. News 63 Woodfield Lane, Ashtead, Surrey
  Bi-monthly. Members only. £2·10 annually
The journal of the Institute of Amateur Cinematographers which contains Institute and cine-club news and general articles on film-making.
Journal of the Society of Film and Television Arts 80 Great Portland Street, London W1N 6JJ
  Quarterly 25p, £1 annually
An authoritative journal which takes a particular topic for each issue, e.g. 'Series and Serials for Television', 'Economics of British Film Production'. Excellent collections of specialised articles by some of the leaders in the film and television world which are most useful as sources of information for reference or for written work.
Kinematograph Weekly 161 Fleet Street, London EC4P 4AA
  Weekly 17½p, £8·50 annually
Today's Cinema 142 Wardour Street, London W1
  Twice weekly 9p, £8·50 annually (including supplements)
These trade papers provide accurate and up-to-date information about the film and cinema industry. Apart from their expense, their value in the classroom is marginal but they are useful for reference material on the industry.
Monogram 63 Old Compton Street, London W1
  Bi-monthly 25p, 5 issues £1
A new magazine from the editors of the *Brighton Film Review*, committed to a detailed study of the cinema, especially American cinema. Contains auteur analyses, general articles, reviews of films shown on TV and on the circuits, and book reviews.
Monthly Film Bulletin 81 Dean Street, London W1
  Monthly 15p, £1·80 annually
A publication of the British Film Institute which is free to B.F.I. Educational Corporate Members. Reviews all feature films released in Britain with full credits and notes which are a mixture of fact and comment. Invaluable for reference.
Movie 23–29 Emerald Street, London WC1N 3QL
  Quarterly 25p, £1·05 annually
A magazine of the highest quality which now appears rather infrequently. Influential in shaping serious film criticism in the early-and mid-1960s.
Movie Maker 46 Chancery Lane, London WC2
  Monthly 20p, £2·90 annually
An amateur cine magazine with a variety of articles and regular

features on film making in all gauges. Invariably has something of interest in its articles and the regular features form a useful source of reference material.

Photoplay 12–18 Paul Street, London EC2A 4JS
        Monthly 20p, £2·40 annually
A 'fan' magazine which occasionally has useful articles; of particular value for some good pictorial material.

Screen and *Screen Education Notes* 63 Old Compton Street, London W1
        Quarterly 50p, £1·80 annually
The journals of the Society for Education in Film and Television; free to members of the Society. *Screen* is a journal of theory and criticism; the *Education Notes* provide thought on and accounts of classroom practice. The only British periodicals which are wholly concerned with screen education; should be regarded as essential reading for all who use film and television in education and youth work.

Sight and Sound 81 Dean Street, London W1
        Quarterly 30p, £1·40 annually
An independent critical magazine sponsored and published by the British Film Institute; free to members of the Institute. A general magazine consisting of notes on feature films, varied articles, film reviews and book reviews.

Silent Picture 613 Harrow Road, London W10
        Quarterly 15p, 60p annually
A new periodical which is 'the only serious quarterly devoted entirely to the art and history of the silent motion picture'. A magazine for the enthusiast of silent films but a model of its kind.

University Vision Royalty House, 72 Dean Street, London W1V 5HB
        Bi-annually 42½p
The journal of the British Universities Film Council; it is not available on subscription but copies may be bought individually or on a standing order basis. Contains articles on various aspects of the use of film and other audio-visual media at university level.

Visual Education 33 Queen Anne Street, London W1M 0AL
        Monthly 20p, £2·40 annually
The magazine of the National Committee for Audio-Visual Aids in Education. Concerned with film as a teaching aid but often includes useful information on films, film-making and equipment and, therefore, is useful for reference.   **Eric Martin**

Checklist of availability of films mentioned

Information given below indicates the directors, dates of making and distributors. It was as accurate as possible at the time of printing, but it is advisable to check with the distributors before booking films since availability is not always permanent. Those films which are shown to be unavailable at the present time have been included because they have particular relevance – either to the text or to syllabuses in the appendices; films listed in Appendix E have not been specifically included in this index unless they are mentioned elsewhere in the book.

(*Note:* Additional information on suitable films not mentioned in this book can be obtained from two B.F.I. Education Department documents entitled 'A Short Film List' and 'Some Suggested Themes and Materials'.)

List of abbreviations:

B.B.C. TV Enterprises	B.B.C. TV Enterprises Film Hire, 25 The Burroughs, Hendon, London NW4
B.F.I.	British Film Institute Distribution Library, 42/43 Lower Marsh, London SE1
B.T.	British Transport Films, Melbury House, Melbury Terrace, London NW1 6JJ
Can. F.L.	Canada House Film Library, Canada House, London SW1
C.B.A.	Central Booking Agency, British Film Institute, 81 Dean Street, London W1V 6AA
C.F.L.	Central Film Library, Government Buildings, Bromyard Avenue, Acton, London W3 7JB
Col.	Columbia Pictures Ltd, Film House, Wardour Street, London W1V 4AH
Conc.	Concord Films Council, Nacton, Ipswich, Suffolk
Concordia	Concordia Films, 117/123 Golden Lane, London EC1Y OTL
Conn.	Connoisseur Films Ltd, 167 Oxford Street, London W1R 2DX

Cont.	Contemporary Films Ltd, 55 Greek Street, London W1V 6DB
Curz. Pub.	Curzon Publicity, 31 St James's Place, London SW1
Darvill	Darvill Associates, 280 Chartridge Lane, Chesham, Bucks.
Embassy	Embassy Films, 1/2 Berners Street, London W1P 3HG
E.T.V.	Educational and Television Films, 2 Doughty Street, London WC1N 2PJ
F.D.A.	Film Distributors Associated (16 mm) Ltd, P.O. Box 2JL, Mortimer House, 37/41 Mortimer Street, London W1A 2JL
Films of Poland	16 Devonshire Street, London, W1
Films of Scotland	Film House, 3 Randolph Crescent, Edinburgh EH3 7TH
Fr. Inst.	Institut Français, Queensbury Place, London SW7
Gala	Gala Film Distributors Ltd, Gala House, 15–17 Old Compton Street, London W1
Golden	Golden Films Ltd, Stewart House, 23 Frances Road, Windsor, Berks.
G.S.V.	Guild Sound and Vision Ltd, Wilton Crescent, Merton Park, London SW19
Hunter	Hunter Films Ltd, 182 Wardour Street, London W1V 4BH
I.B.M.	Film Library, I.B.M. (UK) Ltd, 101 Wigmore Street, London W1
I.C.I.	I.C.I. Film Library, Imperial Chemical House, Millbank, London SW1
Kingston	Robert Kingston Films Ltd, 645/7 Uxbridge Road, Hayes End, Middlesex
N.A.V.A.	National Audio Visual Aids Library, 2 Paxton Place, Gypsy Road, London SE27
N.C.B.	National Coal Board, 70 Wardour Street, London W1
Oxfam	1 Mitre Court Buildings, Fleet Street, London EC4
P.F.B.	Petroleum Films Bureau, 4 Brook Street, Hanover Square, London W1Y 2AY

Rank	Rank Film Library, P.O. Box 70, Great West Road, Brentford, Middlesex
R.H.	Ron Harris Cinema Services Ltd, Glenbuck House, Glenbuck Road, Surbiton, Surrey
U.A.	United Artists Corp. Ltd, Mortimer House, 37/41 Mortimer Street, London W1A 2JL
Unilever	Unilever Film Library, Unilever Ltd, Unilever House, Blackfriars, London EC4
Watso	Watso Films Ltd, Film House, Charles Street, Coventry, Warwickshire
Walt Disney	Walt Disney Productions Ltd, 68 Pall Mall, London SW1
W.H.	Wallace Heaton Ltd, 127 New Bond Street, London W1Y 0AB
W/D	Withdrawn

A Bout de Souffle – Jean-Luc Godard – 1959 – (Conn.; Extract – B.F.I.)

An Actor's Revenge – Kon Ichikawa – 1963 – (Cont.)

The Adventurer – Charlie Chaplin – 1917 – (B.F.I.)

The African Queen – John Huston – 1951 – (Kingston)

A L'Assaut de la Tour Eiffel – Jacqueline Jacoupy and Alain Pol – 1948 – (Fr. Inst.)

All Quiet on the Western Front – Lewis Milestone – 1930 – (Col.)

All the King's Men – Robert Rossen – 1949 – (Col.)

Alone with the Monsters – Nazli Nour – 1958 – (B.F.I.)

Ambulance – Janusz Morgenstern – 1961 – (Conc.)

Amelia and the Angel – Ken Russell – 1958 – (Cont.)

Analysis by Mass – Brian Kaufman – 1962 – (C.F.L.)

Animal Farm – Halas and Batchelor – 1951/4 – (Col.)

Antarctic Crossing – James Carr – 1958 – (P.F.B.)

The Apple – George Dunning – 1962 – (Conn.)

A Propos de Nice – Jean Vigo – 1930 – (Cont.)

Araby – Zbigniew Raplewski – 1964 – (Cont.)

Armand and Michaela Denis on Safari – A. and M. Denis – 1960 – (G.S.V.)

L'Arroseur Arrosé – (*Watering the Gardener*) – see *The Lumière Programme*

An Artist Looks at Churches – John Taylor – 1960 – (B.T.)

Ashes and Diamonds – Andrez Wajda – 1958 – (Cont.; Extract – B.F.I.)

L'Atalante – Jean Vigo – 1934 – (Cont.; Extract – B.F.I.)

A to Zoo Countries – Derek Twist – 1963 – (B.F.I.)

Attention – Jiri Brdecka – 1959 – (Conc.)

An Autumn Afternoon – Yashujiro Ozu – 1962 – (Cont.; Feature and Extract – Cont.)

Bachelor Party – Delbert Mann – 1957 – (W/D)

Bandits at Orgosolo – Vittorio de Sica – 1961 – (W/D)

Barabbas – Richard Fleischer – 1961 – (Col.)

Battleship Potemkin – Sergei Eisenstein – 1925 – (Cont.; Extract – B.F.I.)

Bear Country – James Algar – 1952 – (Walt Disney)

Between the Tides – Ralph Keene – 1958 – (B.T.)

Beyond the Missouri – (see *West is West*)

Bicycle Thieves – Vittorio de Sica – 1948 – (Cont.; Extract – B.F.I.)

The Big Heat – Fritz Lang – 1953 – (Col.; Extract – B.F.I.)

The Big Mill – Lawrence Henson – 1963 – (Films of Scotland)

Billy Budd – Peter Ustinov – 1961/2 – (Rank; Extract – B.F.I.)

Billy Liar – John Schlesinger – 1963 – (Rank)

Bird Hunt – Richard Hawkins – 1950 – (B.F.I.)

Blackboard Jungle – Richard Brooks – 1955 – (W/D)

Blackmail – Alfred Hitchcock – 1929 – (B.F.I.; Feature and Extract)

Blacktop – Charles and Ray Eames – 1952 – (B.F.I.)

The Blood Donor – (see *Hancock Extract*)

The Boat People – Jesse Ramos – 1961 – (P.F.B.)

Boomerang – Elia Kazan – (1946) – (W/D)

Boudu Sauvé des Eaux – Jean Renoir – 1932 – (Cont.; Extract – B.F.I.)

The Boy with Green Hair – Joseph Losey – 1948 – (Kingston)

Bread and Circuses – Paula Neurisse and Max Sautet – 1962 – (Conn.)

Bridge on the River Kwai – David Lean – 1957 – (W/D; Extract – B.F.I.)

The Builders – 1960 – (Cont.)

The Burmese Harp – Kon Ichikawa – 1956 – (Conc.)

The Cabinet of Dr Caligari – Robert Wiene – 1919 – (W/D; Extract – B.F.I.)

The Caine Mutiny – Edward Dmytryk – 1954 – (Col.)

Capital Visit – Sid Sharples – 1954 – (B.T.)

Le Caporal Epinglé – Jean Renoir – 1961 – (Cont.; Extract – B.F.I.)

The Captive River – Blake Dalrymple – 1960 – (P.F.B.)

Les Carabiniers – Jean-Luc Godard – 1963 – (Conn.)

Castle and Country – Shirley Cobham – 1964 – (P.F.B.)

Cathy Come Home – Ken Loach – 1966 – (Extract – B.F.I.)

The Caucasian Chalk Circle – (B.B.C. Schools TV – not available)
The Chair – Robert Drew and Richard Leacock – 1962 – (Conc.)
Challenge – Neville Thomas – 1967 – (Conc.)
The Champion – Mark Robson – 1949 – (Embassy)
The Childhood of Maxim Gorki – Mark Donskoi – 1940 – (Cont.;
   Extract – B.F.I.)
A Child's Guide to Blowing Up a Motor Car – Ronald Spencer – (G.S.V.)
Chinese Theatre – Marc Maurette and Victoria Mercanton – 1960 –
   (B.F.I.)
Christmas in Germany – Gunther Schnabel – 1960 – (Curz. Pub.)
Chuk and Gek – I. Lubinsky – 1952 – (Cont.)
Citizen Kane – Orson Welles – 1940 – (B.F.I.; Extract – B.F.I.)
City of Gold – Colin Low and Wolf Koenig – 1957 – (B.F.I.)
Coalface – Alberto Cavalcanti – 1935 – (B.F.I.)
Colour – Jack Cardiff – 1947 – (I.C.I.)
The Colourful Marsh – Gerhard Klammet – 1957 – (Curz. Pub.)
Colour of Life – V. Durden – 1955 – (Can. F.L.; G.S.V.)
Corral – Colin Low – 1954 – (B.F.I.)
Coventry Cathedral – 1962 – (G.S.V.)
Crin Blanc – Albert Lamorisse – 1953 – (Conn.)
Crossfire – Edward Dmytryk – 1947 – (Kingston; Extract – B.F.I.)
The Cruel Sea – Charles Frend – 1952 – (Rank)
Culloden – Peter Watkins – 1964 – (B.F.I.; Conc.)
The Cure – Charlie Chaplin – 1917 – (B.F.I.)
The Day – Peter Finch – 1960 – (Cont.)
The Day Manolete Died – David Butler and B. Conrad – 1958 –
   (C.B.A.)
The Days of Whiskey Gap – Colin Low – 1961 – (B.F.I.)
Death of a Salesman – Laslo Benedek – 1952 – (W/D)
Deckie Learner – Michael Grigsby – 1965 – (B.F.I.)
The Decorator – (also called *Work*) – Charlie Chaplin – 1915 – (B.F.I.)
Desist Film – Stan Brakhage – 1959 – (B.F.I.)
The Devil Came to Drink – Jack Smith – 1958 – (B.F.I.)
Dial Double One – James Hill – 1965 – (P.F.B.)
A Diary for Timothy – Humphrey Jennings – 1945 – (B.F.I.)
The Diary of Anne Frank – George Stevens – 1959 – (R.H.)
Dieppe 1942 – (German newsreel) – 1942 – (B.F.I.)
The Digboi Story – Brian Salt – 1953 – (P.F.B.)
Distant Drums – Raoul Walsh – 1951 – (W.H.; Watso)
Dots and Loops – Norman McLaren – 1948 – (B.F.I.)

Double Whooppee – Lewis R. Foster and James Parrott – 1929 – (B.F.I.; Watso)

Drawings that Walk and Talk – Marie Seton and K. H. Frank – 1938 – (B.F.I.)

Dreamland in the Sky – Bretislav Pojar – 1964 – (W.H.; G.S.V.)

Dream of Wild Horses – Denys Colomb de Daunant – 1960 – (Conn.)

Early Actualities – (Compilation – 1899–1905) – (B.F.I.)

East of Eden – Elia Kazan – 1954 – (Rank)

L'Eclisse – Michelangelo Antonioni – 1962 – (Conn.; Feature and Extract – B.F.I.)

8½ – Federico Fellini – 1962/3 – (B.F.I.; Extract – B.F.I.)

Eléna et les Hommes – Jean Renoir – 1956 – (W/D)

The Empty Quarter – Richard Taylor and Mostafa Hammuri – 1967 – (Darvill)

End of a Street – Norman Swallow – 1964 – (B.F.I.)

The Energy Picture – John Halas and Gerald Potterton – 1959 – (P.F.B.)

En Passant par la Lorraine – Georges Franju – 1951 – (Fr. Inst.)

The Entertainer – Tony Richardson – 1960 – (Rank; Extract – B.F.I.)

Every Valley – Michael Clarke – 1957 – (B.T.)

Exterminating Angel – Luis Buñuel – 1962 – (Conn.)

Eyes Without a Face – See *Les Yeux Sans Visage*

The Fallen Idol – Carol Reed – 1948 – (W/D; Extract – B.F.I.)

Fan Fever – Peter Morley – 1958 – (B.F.I.)

Father – Istvan Szabo – 1966 – (Cont.)

Le Feu Follet – Louis Malle – 1963 – (Conn.; Extract – B.F.I.)

A Few Days – Howard Blake – 1963 – (B.F.I.)

Film-making in School: Planning a Film Script – 1963 – (B.F.I.)

Film-making in School: Shooting the Film – 1963 – (B.F.I.)

Fire at Dukhan – Martyn Wilson – 1954 – (P.F.B.)

Fire Below – Geoff Busby – 1962 – (P.F.B.)

Firefight at Ahwaz – 1959 – (P.F.B.)

Fires Were Started – Humphrey Jennings – 1943 – (B.F.I.)

The First Americans – (see *West is West*)

Five Boys from Barska Street – Aleksander Ford – 1953 – (Cont.)

Flight into Life – Ulrich Schultz – 1954 – (Curz. Pub.)

The Flying Deuces – A. Edward Sutherland – 1939 – (Watso; W.H.)

The Flying Man – George Dunning – 1962 – (Conn.)

Floating Around – (also called *The Balloonatic*) – Buster Keaton and Eddie Cline – 1922 – (Watso)

Forth Road Bridge – Gordon Lang – 1964 – (P.F.B.)

40 Minutes at the Zoo – Ratcliffe Holmes – 1949 – (Kingston)
French Cancan – Jean Renoir – 1955 – (Cont.; Extract – B.F.I.)
Game of Cards – (see *The Lumière Programme*)
The General – Buster Keaton and C. Bruckman – 1927 – (W/D)
A Generation – Andzej Wajda – 1954 – (Cont.; Extract – B.F.I.)
The Gentleman in Room 6 – Alexander Hammid – 1951 – (B.F.I.)
Gentleman's Agreement – Elia Kazan – 1947 – (R.H.)
Getting Warmer – Henk Kabos – 1961 – (P.F.B.)
Giant – George Stevens – 1956 – (W/D)
Giuseppina – James Hill – 1960 – (P.F.B.)
Glass – Bert Haanstra – 1958 – (Cont.)
La Grande Illusion – Jean Renoir – 1937 – (W/D; Extract – B.F.I.)
Le Grand Méliès – Georges Franju – 1952 – (Fr. Inst.)
The Great Adventure – Arne Sucksdorff – 1953 – (Conn.)
The Greater Community Animal – Derek Phillips – 1966 – (Conc.;
  Darvill)
Great Expectations – David Lean – 1946 – (Rank)
The Great Synthesis – Horst G. Koch – 1964 – (P.F.B.)
The Great Train Robbery – Edwin S. Porter – 1903 – (B.F.I.)
The Gunfighter – Henry King – 1950 – (R.H.; Extract – B.F.I.)
Guns in the Afternoon – Sam Peckinpah – 1961 – (R.H.)
The Guns of Navarone – J. Lee Thompson – 1959/61 – (W/D; Extract –
  B.F.I.)
Hancock Extract – (B.B.C. TV) – 1965 – (B.F.I.)
The Hand – Jiri Trnka – 1965 – (Cont.)
The Hangman – Les Goldman and Paul Julian – 1964 – (Cont.)
Happy Anniversary – Pierre Etaix and Jean-Claude Carrière – 1962 –
  (Conn.)
Harry's Half-Crown – Roy Knight – 1963 – (B.F.I.)
Haunted Spooks – 1920 – (B.F.I.)
The Haunting – Robert Wise – 1963 – (R.H.)
Henry V – Laurence Olivier – 1944 – (Rank; Extracts – B.F.I.)
Herrings for Sale – Guy Blanchard – 1956 – (Unilever)
Hiroshima Mon Amour – Alain Resnais – 1958/9 – (Cont.; Extract –
  B.F.I.)
History of the Cinema – John Halas – 1956 – (G.S.V.)
Holiday – John Taylor – 1957 – (B.T.)
The Home-made Car – James Hill – 1962 – (P.F.B.)
Home of the Brave – Mark Robson – 1949 – (Watso; W.H.)
Hook Line and Sinker – Roy Layzell – 1959 – (P.F.B.; C.F.L.)

Hôtel des Invalides – Georges Franju – 1951 – (B.F.I.)
House-Warming – Lionel Griffith – 1964 – (Nat. Coal Bd)
Hull Now – Bob Privett – 1967 – (B.T.)
Los Hurdes – (*Terre Sans Pain*; *Land Without Bread*) – Luis Buñuel – 1932 – (B.F.I.)
The Immigrant – Charlie Chaplin – 1917 – (B.F.I.; Kingston)
Incident at Owl Creek – Robert Enrico – 1961 – (Conn.)
The Inconvenience – Geoff Busby – 1961 – (G.S.V.)
Inheritance – John Irwin – 1963 – (Conc.; Oxfam)
Intruder in the Dust – Clarence Brown – 1949 – (R.H.)
In Two Minds – Ken Loach – 1966 – (B.B.C.: Extract – B.F.I.)
The Ipcress File – Sidney J. Furie – 1965 – (Rank)
Iron Helmet – Josef Kabrt – 1964 – (Conc.; E.T.V.)
I Think They Call Him John – John Krish – 1964 – (Cont.; Conc.)
Un Jardin Public – Paul Paviot – 1955 – (Fr. Inst.)
La Jetée – Chris Marker – 1962 – (Cont.)
Les Jeux Interdits – René Clément – 1952 – (W/D)
Journey into Spring – Ralph Keene – 1957 – (B.T.)
Julius Caesar – Joseph Mankiewicz – 1953 – (Rank: Extract – B.F.I.)
Kameradschaft – G. W. Pabst – 1931 – (W/D; Extracts – B.F.I.)
La Kermesse Fantastique – J. Mizik – 1950 – (G.S.V.)
Key Largo – John Huston – 1948 – (W/D)
A Kind of Loving – John Schlesinger – 1962 – (Rank; Extract – B.F.I.)
King and Country – Joseph Losey – 1964 – (Col.)
King Rat – Bryan Forbes – 1965 – (Col.)
Kodak Films on Film-making (1, 2 and 3) – Brian Coe – 1963 – (B.F.I.)
Die Kreuzpine – E. Schumacher – 1960 – (Curz. Pub.)
Labyrinth – Jan Lenica – 1962 – (Cont.)
The Lady Killers – Alexander Mackendrick – 1955 – (Rank; Extract – B.F.I.)
The Lake District – Alex Strasser – 1954 – (B.T.)
The Last Laugh – F. W. Murnau – 1924 – (W/D; Extract – B.F.I.)
Let's Go to Birmingham – Jack Strauss – 1962 – (B.T.)
Let's Have a Party – Paul Verhoeven – 1963 – (Cont.)
Lifeboat Coming – Dr Guild – 1961 – (G.S.V.)
Listen to Britain – Humphrey Jennings – 1941 – (B.F.I.; C.F..L)
Listen to Steel – Daniel Ingram – 1963 – (G.S.V.; C.F.L.)
The Living Pattern – John Taylor – 1962 – (Rank; P.F.B.)
Lonely Are The Brave – David Miller – 1962 – (Rank; Extract – B.F.I.)
Lonely Boy – Roman Kroitor and Wolf Koenig – 1962 – (B.F.I.; Cont.)

Look Back in Anger – Tony Richardson – 1959 – (Col.)
Lord of the Flies – Peter Brook – 1961/3 – (Rank; Extract – B.F.I.)
Louisiana Story – Robert Flaherty – 1948 – (B.F.I.; P.F.B.)
L. S. Lowry – John Read – 1957 – (B.F.I.)
Lumière Programme – 1895 – (B.F.I.)
La Lutte – M. Fournier, M. Carrière and Claude Jutra – 1961 – (B.F.I.)
M – Fritz Lang – 1931 – (B.F.I.; Gala; Extract – B.F.I.)
Macbeth – Orson Welles – 1948 – (Darvill)
Major Dundee – Sam Peckinpah – 1964 – (Col.)
Mammals – Roman Polanski – 1962 – (C.B.A.)
Man in Flight – 1965 – (G.S.V.)
A Man is Ten Feet Tall – Martin Ritt – 1956 – (W/D)
Man of Aran – Robert Flaherty – 1932/3 – (Rank; Extract – B.F.I.)
Manouane River Lumberjacks – Arthur Lamothe – 1963 – (Cont.)
The March of the Movies – 1939 – (Golden; Watso)
Marty – Delbert Mann – 1955 – (W/D)
Master of the House – Carl Dreyer – 1925 – (B.F.I.)
Match Girl – Andrew Meyer – 1965 – (B.F.I.)
Mekong – John Armstrong – 1964 – (P.F.B.)
The Men – Fred Zinnemann – 1950 – (Hunter)
The Messengers – (Granada Schools TV – not available)
Metropolis – Fritz Lang – 1926 – (W/D; Extracts – B.F.I.)
The Miracle Worker – Arthur Penn – 1962 – (F.D.A.; Extract – B.F.I.)
Mirror of Holland – Bert Haanstra – 1950 – (N.A.V.A.)
Les Mistons – François Truffaut – 1957 – (B.F.I.; Gala)
Money Talks – Robert Brownjohn – 1965 – (G.S.V.)
Monsieur et Madame Curie – Georges Franju – 1954 – (Fr. Inst.)
Monsieur Vincent – Maurice Cloche – 1947 – (Conn.)
The Most – Gordon Sheppard – 1962 – (Conn.)
Mouchette – Robert Bresson – 1966 – (Cont.; Conn.)
Mountains and Fjords – Ronald Craigen – 1955 – (B.T.)
The Moving Spirit – Bob Privett – 1953 – (P.F.B.)
The Music Box – James Parrott – 1932 – (B.F.I.; Watso)
My Darling Clementine – John Ford – 1946 – (W/D; Extract – B.F.I.)
Nahanni – Nicholas Ballas – 1962 – (Can. F. L.)
Nanook of the North – Robert Flaherty – 1922 – (B.F.I.)
The Nature of Fire – Cedric Maggs – 1965 – (G.S.V.; C.F.L.)
Neighbours – Norman McLaren – 1953 – (B.F.I.; Conc.)
Nice Time – Claude Goretta and Alain Tanner – 1957 – (C.B.A.)
Night – Tadeusz Makarczynski – 1961 – (Films of Poland)

Night Mail – Basil Wright and Harry Watt – 1936 – (C.F.L.)

A Night on the Bare Mountain – Alexandre Alexeieff – 1934 – (B.F.I.)

Nobody Waved Goodbye – Don Owen and Roman Kroitor – 1964 – (Cont.)

No Limit – Neville Thomas – 1963 – (Conc.)

North by Northwest – Alfred Hitchcock – 1959 – (R.H.)

North Slope Alaska – Derek Williams – 1965 – (P.F.B.)

Nothing But the Best – Clive Donner – 1964 – (Col.; Extract – B.F.I.)

Nuit et Brouillard (*Night and Fog*) – Alain Resnais – 1955 – (Cont.)

Off the Beaten Track – Sid Sharples – 1960 – (B.T.)

The Oil Rivers – Sydney Latter – 1957 – (Unilever)

Oliver Twist – David Lean – 1948 – (Rank; Extract – B.F.I.)

One of Them is Brett – Roger Graef – 1965 – (Conc.)

On the Twelfth Day – Wendy Toye – 1955 – (Cont.)

On the Waterfront – Elia Kazan – 1954 – (Col.)

Openings (David Lean) – 1946 – (B.F.I.)

Ordet – Carl Dreyer – 1955 – (B.F.I.)

Our Daily Bread – (Conc.; Oxfam)

Pacific 231 – Jean Mitry – 1949 – (B.F.I.)

Painting a Chinese Landscape – 1948 – (B.F.I.)

Une Partie de Campagne – Jean Renoir – 1937/8 – (Conn.)

Pas de Deux – Norman McLaren – 1968 – (Conn.)

La Passion de Jeanne d'Arc – Carl Dreyer – 1928 – (Cont.)

Paths of Glory – Stanley Kubrick – 1957 – (W/D; Extract – B.F.I.)

Paul Tomkowicz – Roman Kroitor – 1954 – (B.F.I.; G.S.V.)

La Peau Douce – François Truffaut – 1964 – (W/D; Extract – B.F.I.)

Pembrokeshire, My County – Ronald Stark – 1960 – (P.F.B.; C.F.L.)

Phoebe – George Kaczender – 1964 – (B.F.I.; Conc.)

Physics and Chemistry of Water – Sarah Erulkar – 1965 – (Unilever)

Le Pilier de la Solitude – Hélène Dassonville – (Fr. Inst.)

Pinky – Elia Kazan – 1949 – (W/D)

Pour un Maillot Jaune – Claude Lelouch – 1966 – (Conn.)

The Power to Fly – Halas and Batchelor – 1954 – (P.F.B.)

Praise the Sea – Herman van der Horst – 1958 – (N.A.V.A.)

La Première Nuit – Georges Franju – 1957 – (Cont.)

Prince Electron – Joop Geesinks – 1957 – (G.S.V.)

The Prize – Mark Robson – 1963 – (R.H.)

Psycho – Alfred Hitchcock – 1960 – (Col.; Extract – B.F.I.)

The Pumpkin Eater – Jack Clayton – 1964 – (Col.; Extract – B.F.I.)

Les Quatre Cents Coups – François Truffaut – 1958 – (W/D)

The Question Tree – 1961 – (I.B.M.)
The Quiet One – Sidney Meyer – 1948 – (Conc.)
The Radio Sky – Michael Crosfield – 1966 – (G.S.V.)
Rail – Geoffrey Jones – 1967 – (B.T.)
Rain – Joris Ivens – 1929 – (B.F.I.)
Raisin in the Sun – Daniel Petrie – 1961 – (Col.)
Rashomon – Akira Kurosawa – 1951 – (Conn.; Extract – B.F.I.)
The Real Thing – Gordon Begg – 1962 – (I.C.I.)
Rebel Without a Cause – Nicholas Ray – 1955 – (W/D)
The Red Balloon – Albert Lamorisse – 1956 – (Conn.)
Red Stain – Zdenek Miler – 1963 – (Cont.; Conc.)
La Règle du Jeu – Jean Renoir – 1938 – (Cont.; Extracts – B.F.I.)
Renaissance – Walerian Borowczyk – 1963 – (Conn.)
Rescued by Rover – Cecil Hepworth – 1905 – (B.F.I.)
Rescued from an Eagle's Nest – Edwin S. Porter – 1907 – (B.F.I.)
The Revealing Eye – Walter Storey – 1960 – (P.F.B.)
Rhythmetic – Norman McLaren – 1955 – (B.F.I.)
Rhythm of a City – Arne Sucksdorff – 1947 – (B.F.I.; W.H.)
The Rink – Gilles Carle – 1962 – (B.F.I.)
The Rival World – Bert Haanstra – 1955 – (B.F.I.)
The River Must Live – Alan Pendry – 1966 – (W/D)
River of Wood – Raymond Garceau – 1962 – (Can. F.L.)
Robinson Crusoe – Luis Buñuel – 1953 – (Conn.)
Room at the Top – Jack Clayton – 1958 – (Conn.; Extract – B.F.I.)
Le Sang des Bêtes – Georges Franju – 1949 – (B.F.I.)
Saturday Night and Sunday Morning – Karel Reisz – 1960 – (Rank; Extract – B.F.I.)
Sausalito – Frank Staffacher – 1951 – (B.F.I.)
Sawdust and Tinsel – Ingmar Bergman – 1953 – (B.F.I.; Extract - B.F.I.)
Seal Island – James Algar – 1949 – (Walt Disney; W.H.)
Secrets of the Marshland – Eugen Schumacher – 1951 – (Curz. Pub.)
September Spring – John Haggarty – 1964 – (P.F.B.)
The Set-Up – Robert Wise – 1949 – (Kingston; Watso)
The Seven Samurai – Akira Kurosawa – 1956 – (Conn.; Extract – B.F.I.)
The Seventh Seal – Ingmar Bergman – 1957 – (B.F.I.; Gala; Extract – B.F.I.)
Seven Up – Paul Almond – 1964 – (B.F.I.)
Sewermen – Michael Ingrams – 1956 – (B.F.I.)

She Wore a Yellow Ribbon – John Ford – 1949 – (Extract – B.F.I.; Kingston)

A Short Vision – Joan and Peter Foldes – 1956 – (B.F.I.; Conc.)

Simon – Peter Zadek – 1957 – (Cont.)

The Singing Fool – Lloyd Bacon – 1928 – (W/D)

Sing of the Border – Tony Thompson – 1964 – (B.T.)

Ski on Water – Michael Syson – 1965 – (P.F.B.)

The Smoking Machine – Sarah Erulkar – 1964 – (C.F.L.)

The Sniper – Edward Dmytryk – 1952 – (W/D)

Snow – Geoffrey Jones – 1963 – (B.T.)

Snowdrift at Bleath Gill – Kenneth Fairbairn – 1955 (B.T.)

S.O.S. Notlandung – Erhard Kohler – 1957 – (Curz. Pub.)

Speed the Plough – Halas and Batchelor – 1956 – (P.F.B.)

Sport in Germany – Erich Kobler – 1954 – (Curz. Pub.)

Spring in the Mountains – Edmund Geer and Karl Aulitzky – 1958 – (Curz. Pub.)

Stable Door – Pat Jackson – 1966 – (C.F.L.; G.S.V.; Rank)

Stagecoach – John Ford – 1939 – (B.F.I.; Feature and Extract)

Stampede – Claude Fournier – 1963 – (Can. F.L.)

The Star of Bethlehem – Wilhelm Doderlein – 1953 — (Concordia; Curz. Pub.)

Steptoe and Son (TV extract) – Duncan Wood – 1964 – (B.F.I.)

Stockholm Story – Arne Sucksdorff – 1951 – (N.A.V.A.)

Strangers on a Train – Alfred Hitchcock – 1951 – (Rank)

Strike Action – David Barker – 1962 – (B.F.I.)

The Substitute – Dusan Vukotic – 1961 – (Cont.)

Sunday – Dan Drasin – 1961 – (Cont.)

Surf Boats of Accra – Sydney Latter – 1958 – (Unilever)

A Taste of Honey – Tony Richardson – 1961 – (Rank)

Telling a Story in Pictures – S. G. P. Alexander – 1953 – (B.F.I.)

Terminus – John Schlesinger – 1961 – (B.T.)

They Caught the Ferry – Carl Dreyer – 1945 – (Golden)

They Were Expendable – John Ford – 1945 – (W/D; Extract – B.F.I.)

Third Avenue El – Carson Davidson – 1956 – (B.F.I.)

Thomas L'Imposteur – Georges Franju – 1964 – (Darvill)

Three Lives and a Rope – Henri Storck – 1937 – (B.F.I.)

The Threepenny Opera – G. W. Pabst – 1931 – (B.F.I.)

Throne of Blood – Akira Kurosawa – 1957 – (Conn.; Extract – B.F.I.)

Thursday's Children – Lindsay Anderson and Guy Brenton – 1954 – (B.F.I.)

Time Is – Don Levy – 1964 – (B.F.I.)

A Time out of War – Denis Sanders – 1954 – (B.F.I.)

Together – Lorenza Mazzetti – 1955 – (B.F.I.)

Tom Brown's Schooldays – Gordon Parry – 1951 – (Conn.; Extract – B.F.I.)

Tomorrow's Saturday – Michael Grigsby – 1962 – (B.F.I.)

Tora-no-o – Akira Kurosawa – 1951 – (Conn.)

Tous les Garçons s'appellent Patrick – Jean-Luc Godard – 1957 – (Conn.)

Towed in a Hole – George Marshall – 1932 – (B.F.I.; Golden; W.H.; Kingston)

Traders in Leather – Sydney Latter – 1958 – (Unilever)

Tramps – Michael Ingrams – 1958 – (B.F.I.)

The Trial – Orson Welles – 1962 – (Conn.)

Twelve Angry Men – Sidney Lumet – 1957 – (F.D.A.; Extract – B.F.I.)

23 Skidoo – Julian Biggs – 1964 – (Cont.; Conc.)

Twilight Forest – Sydney Latter – 1957 – (Unilever; C.F.L.)

Two Men and a Wardrobe – Roman Polanski – 1957 – (Conn.)

Ugetsu Monogatari – Kenji Mizoguchi – 1953 – (Cont.; Extract – B.F.I.)

Umberto D – Vittorio de Sica – 1952 – (Conn.)

Under Night Streets – Ralph Keene – 1958 – (B.T.; Embassy)

Up the Junction (TV Extract) – Ken Loach – 1965 – (B.F.I.)

The Vanishing Corporal – (see *Le Caporal Epinglé*)

Vanishing Prairie – James Algar – 1954 – (Rank)

The Vanishing Street – Robert Vas – 1962 – (B.F.I.)

Very Nice, Very Nice – Arthur Lipsett – 1961 – (Cont.; Conc.)

Vox Pop – Donald Baverstock – 1958 – (B.F.I.)

The Wages of Fear – H. G. Clouzot – 1953 – (Conn.; Extracts – B.F.I.)

The War Game – Peter Watkins – 1966 – (B.F.I.)

War on the Screen – B.F.I. Study Unit – (B.F.I.)

Water Birds – Patrick Carey – 1968 – (B.T.)

Water in Biology – David Morphet – 1965 – (Unilever)

Way Out West – James W. Horne – 1937 – (Watso; Hunter)

We Are the Lambeth Boys – Karel Reisz – 1959 – (B.F.I.)

We Shall Never Die – Alim and Yoran Gross – 1959 – (B.F.I.)

West is West (TV series) – Tim Slessor – 1964 – (B.B.C. TV Enterprises)

Whistle Down the Wind – Bryan Forbes – 1961 – (Rank; Extract – B.F.I.)

Why Bother? – 1963 – (Unilever)

Wiesensommer – Heinz Sielmann – 1956 – (Curz. Pub.)

Wild Highlands – Ian Ferguson – 1961 – (B.T.; Embassy)
The Wild One – Laslo Benedek – 1953 – (Col.)
Winchester '73 – Anthony Mann – 1951 – (Col.)
The Wind on the Heath – Leon Bijou and Peter Jessop – 1963 – (G.S.V.; P.F.B.)
Window on Europe – T. Dewit – 1959 – (G.S.V.)
The World of Apu – Satyajit Ray – 1958 – (Cont.)
World of Sport (Series) – 1968 – (Col.)
Les Yeux Sans Visage – Georges Franju – 1959 – (Darvill; Extract – B.F.I.)
The Young Chopin – Aleksander Ford – 1951 – (B.F.I.)
The Young Törless – Volker Schloendorff – 1966 – (Darvill)
Yo-yo – Pierre Etaix – 1965 – (Conn.)
Z Cars (TV extract) – David E. Rose – 1962 – (B.F.I.)
Zéro de Conduite – Jean Vigo – 1933 – (Cont.; Extract – B.F.I.)
Zoo – Bert Haanstra – 1962 – (Cont.)